Speed Tribes:

Days

and

Nights

with

Japan's

Next

Generation

ALSO BY
KARL TARO GREENFELD

STANDARD

DEVIATIONS

VILLARD
NEW YORK

STANDARD

DEVIATIONS

Growing

Up

and

Coming

Down

in

the

New

Asia

**KARL TARO
GREENFELD**

Portions of this book have appeared in various forms and at various times in
Condé Nast Traveler, Salon.com, and *Time.* Certain identifying characteristics
and chronologies have been altered for legal reasons and narrative coherence.
Names have been changed to protect the guilty.

LIBRARY OF CONGRESS CATALOGING-IN-PUBLICATION DATA

Greenfeld, Karl Taro
Standard deviations: growing up and coming down in the new Asia/
Karl Taro Greenfeld.
p.   cm.
ISBN 0-375-50276-9
1. Asia—Description and travel. 2. Greenfeld, Karl Taro—Journeys—
Asia. I. Title.

DS10.G69 2002
950.4'3'092—dc21   2001057511

Villard Books website address: www.villard.com
Printed in the United States of America on acid-free paper
2   4   6   8   9   7   5   3
First Edition

BOOK DESIGN BY DEBORAH KERNER/DANCING BEARS DESIGN

For Silke

CONTENTS

INTRODUCTION

The winter is hot and damp but not as hot and damp as the rest of the year, and that is why hundreds of us are here on this island, in the Gulf of Siam, sweating in tiny bungalows waiting for the sun to go down and the moon to come up. There is a rumor of a party in honor of the full moon, and this is before all around the world the idea of parties in honor of the full moon become a tourist cliché—the e-generation's narcotic equivalent to visiting the Louvre or spending an afternoon at Epcot. But even though I have never before heard of full-moon parties, I am skeptical. A Canadian magazine writer is here, and he is chasing down the story of these parties, supposedly the Asian manifestation of the acid-house dance-music movement that is just now blowing over from Belgium and Holland to Manchester and New York. Alistair has long blond hair and is older than me, and he is working for a real magazine, albeit a Canadian one. He seems assured, and when he asks about what kind of music they will be playing, the *farangs* who have been here longer than us answer him and don't condescend to him the way they do when I try to talk to them.

It is already a bit of a disappointment to me that I've come thousands of miles and put up with unsafe and questionable forms of transport only to find that these cool kids seem as cliquish as the popular kids in my high school cafeteria. They wear batik, sport these sorts of swirly tattoos, and whenever I try to find out what they are doing or where they are going they pointedly say that I ask too many questions. But I sincerely want to know: Who are they?

Where are they going? Which of these little shacks sells the best fresh fish? How do you wipe your ass without toilet paper? Can the guy who sells the mushroom omelets also get good E's, as he promises? I need these answers, and so I loiter on the fringes of these little bands of travelers, pestering them and making them progressively more annoyed.

Most of them are British, with a few Germans and Aussies and Canadians thrown in, and they are all of those things I want to be: confident, self-sustaining, knowledgeable, trendy, good-looking. My connection is this Canadian magazine writer; it is by his sufferance that I am allowed to stay on the outskirts of the grooviness, to find some trendy shadow. And it is from him that I learn you don't ask questions, you simply wait until the answers are manifest.

But I do probe Alistair for tips and secrets. To me, he seems vastly successful. He's written for cool magazines in England, the U.S. and Canada.

He's underwriting the cost of this trip with the story he will produce. How does one go about getting these sorts of assignments? Who do you have to know? Can I do it too?

I think I'm a good writer, I tell him. I'm not sure what it is I want to write: books, magazine articles, screenplays. I want to write, and try, everything. That is, after all, why I came out here.

I was twenty-three and I had set off for Asia to become a writer, intrigued by lurid tales of booms, busts, drugs, sex, violence, magic. There was a wicked sorcery in Asia, in the economic profligacy of the early nineties, in the way financiers and businessmen took a rapidly wiring and developing continent and looted billions, like a titanic parlor trick converting all that wealth into abandoned office complexes and half-completed shopping malls. There was sexual magic, the licentious cousin of that fiscal corruption, in the fleshpots where girls and boys stood behind glass partitions with numbers pinned to their G-strings; in the way you could pick up a fellow traveler in Bangkok or Manila and spend a few nights together before parting, maybe forever or maybe to run into each other again at a different guest house, on another island, in a strange new nightclub. Whatever defenses these girls may have carefully fostered in their native Stuttgarts or Vancouvers were easily breached by salvos of tropical heat and dope. And there was narcotic alchemy, in the illicit drugs so easily grown and refined in the arid highlands and fecund jungles and in the licit pills and powders dispensed by chemists in the squalorous coastal cities. I wanted it all—the money, the sex, the drugs. And to this day I believe that if I am honest with myself, despite all I have learned the hard way over the past decade, I would still want it all again, the fucking and the getting loaded and the scheming to get enough money to pay for that life.

A word about myself: I was born in Asia—in Kobe, Japan—of a Japanese mother and Jewish American father. As an Asian American brought up in California, I still looked to the Far East. It was the continent of my ancestors and the source of so many of the images that haunted me as I grew up: that naked girl running from napalm smoke and flame down a Vietnamese road; Indian yogis hanging stones from their penises; heads propped on stakes outside a raped and pillaged Nanking. But the fascination was with more than just the macabre and atrocious; I was transfixed by the continent of my birth for other, obvious reasons. Wasn't I lumped in census forms and demographic breakdowns with Indians, Thais and Chinese as Asian? Wouldn't my Amerasian features, my jet-black hair, my half-Asian eyes blend in with the majorities in such great, burgeoning nations? Never quite at home in America because of my mixed racial heritage, I liked to think that I would be more at home in Asia, that perhaps my mother's Japanese blood would allow me to pass as one of the masses as I had never really managed to in the West. (Or am I now just deluding myself, and it was always about fucking and getting loaded and scheming a way to make more money?)

I don't think so. Visiting the Far East as a child, I was always amazed at how well I fit in. This was during the seventies, when the Asia of economic boomtowns and upward spiraling stock markets was still a decade away. But already in Bangkok, Tokyo and Hong Kong, there was a creeping, gaudy neon decadence on display. I caught glimpses of it in Yakuza movies and smelled it in tear gas fumes in the aftermath of a Seoul riot. Among my first and clearest memories are Asia's supercities: Tokyo, like a neon-lit beating heart; Kobe, a giant transistor radio split open and set by the sea; zirconia-bright Hong Kong crawling up the sides of Victoria Peak, matching precisely a child's concept of what a big city should look like. And everywhere there was an energy, a vibe that bespoke the fantastic human and intellectual resources that would soon be unleashed.

When I went back in the late eighties, I joined thousands of Westerners who were then discovering the Asian travel circuit. We were all living a little, partying a lot, earning a bit of money in Tokyo or Hong Kong and then blowing it raving in Koh Phangang or Goa. Getting lost in Thai jungles. Getting lucky in Cambodian discotheques. You would see a bangled, tattooed girl in Bangkok, and then see her a week later in Koh Samui and then a month later in Tokyo. We rode the Far East east with the casual ease borne of months and years on this modern-day, brocaded, silk road. We became a common sight. In the economy check-in line at Bangkok's Don Muang airport or Hong Kong's Kai-Tak you could spot us, wearing Discman headphones, knockoff Gucci shades, fake gold Rolex watches, our hair cut in a jaunty buzz, stubble, earrings, tattoos, piercings, camouflage T-shirts, orange peg-legged trousers, bright Nike trainers. As moneyed as we may have looked, that backpack was the dead giveaway of our dubious finances and questionable provenance. Our stacks of traveler's checks or the money deposited in some giro accounts might as well have been ticking clocks because when the money ran out it was back to work, slinging drinks to salarymen in Tokyo or explaining the past perfect to a fab engineer in Taipei.

We're sitting around the bonfire on the beach, the full moon coming up, but either the turntables or the DJs haven't arrived yet, so the music, instead of mad acid house and Summer of Love Manchester proto-happy hardcore, is, of all things, Deep Purple's "Smoke on the Water." This party in honor of the moon, for which all sorts of psychotropic narcotics were procured and consumed, which was supposed to have hundreds of us up on our feet, doing our little trancey two-steps to nowhere, has the crowd seated and numbed to the dirgey guitar work of Ritchie Blackmore. There's nothing to do but talk and pass along the joints that circulate with tedious regularity. I feel like I've come thousands of miles to rediscover the banality of a high school party, and a dull high school party at that.

Alistair says the music will get sorted, that some bangin' DJs from Goa or Amsterdam are here and that it's still early. In the meantime, I insist, Tell me how it works; tell me what I need to do to start writing for cool magazines and have them pay my way to Asian hot spots.

He mumbles something about writing queries, about how it's all a sales job, about how you almost feel like you are harassing an editor when you keep calling him and reminding him of your existence and your great ideas. Editors don't give a fuck about Asia, Alistair explains to me. They care about movie stars, pop singers, and Super-Bowl-winning quarterbacks. At a glossy monthly, they run one story a year about Asia. So it'll be you and a dozen other guys competing for that slot. Wire service reporters, newspaper correspondents, scholars, hacks, all of them would rather be writing for a New York glossy that pays five thousand dollars for a story and that their family back home can actually read rather than their little local outlet or daily broadsheet. Alistair exhales as if the thought of it all fatigues him. He's been living in Bangkok for five years, selling stories around the world, and what does he have to show for it? Nothing, mate, but the slim chance he'll get to do it again.

This isn't what I want to hear. This isn't why I followed him here from another island, clambering over the rigging and upper deck of a sunken trawler to reach the ferry boat and then walking a few paces behind him as he made his way across the island, down a trail where Thai kids called out to sell us mushroom smoothies. He eventually took a bungalow for about a buck a day and I rented the one right alongside him, paying two dollars a day, and waited while he went out to find a telephone.

Now, as we sit side by side on the sand as the bonfire crackles before us and a hundred stoned foreigners wait for something, anything, to happen—their drugs to kick in, the Deep Purple to subside—Alistair tells me to fuck off. He needs to talk to some people, and they've arrived. A few tall, skinny British lads in sarongs and Thai fisherman's pants have shown up and are skulking outside the circle, smoking cigarettes and looking forbiddingly bitchin'. Alistair joins them, and there is some mutual nodding and off they go, down a trail, behind some palm trees.

The music does change, the Deep Purple ends with an abrupt click, and then a woman's voice with an English accent singsongs, "Here we go, here we go, here we go," and then bleaty, breathy house music comes on and a recorded voice says "We're gonna go back, way back" and slowly, in groups of twos and threes, the circle around the bonfire is transformed into a seething mass of boogiers and I'm left sitting there, feeling once again like an outcast, a loner, the uncoolest of kids. Trying to talk to some of these dangerously sullen girls with the tattoos and piercings takes all the courage and bravado of asking a popular cheerleader to the prom. I have tried it several times, plopped myself down into a little conversational circle on the beach, withstood the glares and stares of the guys in the groups who are naturally territorial about their little crew of girls, and then attempted to make small talk. But, again, I always break some sort of etiquette, ask too many questions, want to know names, last names, home-towns, colleges, professions. Heads shake. I just don't get it. Out here, on these beaches along these techno islands, you're not supposed to say too much about yourself, to divulge those sorts of details.

We're all trying to forge a new identity, Alistair told me, we're all seeing what we can get away with.

If I had never gone to Asia, I probably would have stayed in New York, starting as a fact checker at some magazine, working my way up, trying to catch a break or two. But by saying good-bye to home, country and family and taking off for Tokyo, Hong Kong, Bangkok, Jakarta and points west I strived to become that person I always wanted to be: carefree, extemporaneous, dangerously free, perpetually living in the perpetual now. A postindustrial godless yogi drifting aimlessly, replacing pecuniary gain with pleasure, success with satiation. It was in Asia, during this giddy decade, that I began to imagine that anything was possible, that just as an economic miracle could be forged out of little more than an admixture of greed and energy, so too could a life be forged out of nothing more than a zest for journalism and a little bit of hard work. For a few stoned moments in a Thai jungle or on an Indian beach, it really seemed like it was all possible, that this life—the money, drugs, girls—would go on forever, and that it all added up to more than just the sum of its parts. I told myself I wasn't just escaping, I was exploring. I wasn't just taking drugs, I was experimenting. Somehow, at the end of all this, I would end up a better, stronger, smarter person. Right?

I never saw Alistair again, and I never read his story.

STANDARD
DEVIATIONS

THE BIG LIFE

As an English teacher in a Japanese high school, I stand before stuffy rooms crammed with kids who desultorily practice English on me three classes a day, five days a week. I went to college, I graduated, I came here to Kugenuma, to a little Japanese beach town at the end of a two-car commuter line that snakes through other tiny towns. My apartment is a pair of six-tatami-mat rooms next to a pebbled, weed-strewn parking lot. The narrow-gauge train clangs by on the other side of the lot. I live exactly at the midpoint between two stops. In the mornings I tune the radio to the Armed Forces Network. Disc jockeys from the American base at Yokosuka give public-service announcements between Bon Jovi songs, reminding servicemen that even though they live overseas, they still have the right to vote and that it is important to keep firearms properly cleaned. I am lonely. I have never been so lonely.

One weekend I take the bullet train down to Kyoto to see my grandmother. When I get there, I call a girl I know, an American named Kirstin who has brown hair and green eyes the color of mold on a penny. We meet for dinner. She talks about all the friends she's making and how much fun she's having in Japan. She takes me to a bar where everyone—American, Japanese, Australian—knows her. She is beautiful and the center of attention. During the train ride down, I had fantasized about kissing her, about making some sort of connection with her and finding a soul mate, and then, I don't know, I would take this train down every weekend to see her. We would fall in love.

Instead I go back to my grandmother's house and spend the rest of the weekend eating sweet bean cakes and watching Japanese baseball.

Stuck is how I'd describe myself. But I am just becoming sufficiently aware of my own condition to put words to it. My friend Drew, he's living a similar life, and like most people living shitty lives, he's unwilling to analyze exactly why it's so awful because that would be a tacit admission that something is going wrong. On weekends we drink in bars or guzzle bottles of cough syrup. The best cough syrup, a brand called Sariam, makes your scalp tingle for about forty-five minutes, then you feel like you're floating, and then you sleep like roadkill for fifteen hours, which suits me just fine. (I once met an American ex-sailor who was cashiered out of the service and stayed on in Japan to ensure his access to Sariam.) One night, after drinking some cough syrup, Drew and I go to a hostess bar where I steal a two-and-a-half-foot-tall bronze statue of the Buddha copulating in the lotus position with a maiden. I hide the statue behind me, bow to the mama-san and back out of the bar. As soon as the door closes behind us, Drew and I run down to the street and catch a cab. I sleep at Drew's house, and when we wake up, he gets so freaked out about the stolen statue that he makes me take it home. I stick it in my closet. I look at it every morning when I'm pulling a shirt off a hanger, and I think, Huh, there's that Buddha statue.

Do I have greater expectations than Drew? I don't think so. Yes, I am keenly aware that life should be more than this, more than pretending to teach English a couple hours a day and reading comic books and masturbating and drinking cough syrup. Drew smokes a lot of pot and listens to alternative rock, so he has that. Drew was also molested by his dad or something, so that's why he's happy to be living anywhere this forty-five-year-old bald guy isn't jumping into bed with him every morning. And me, why am I so dissatisfied? I can't even say. Except that I know there's more. I've read about it in books. I've even caught glimpses of it when I've been with a girl and I realize that she likes me and we're going to get together, or, well, I guess that's really the only time.

What my life suffers from is smallness. It is the tiniest life I could imagine. I live in this little apartment. I ride this HO-scale commuter train. I teach in this pathetic high school. I have this paltry circle of friends. Nothing new or big or wild ever happens. And that sameness just reinforces the narrow borders of my life. The confines of my puny world are so clearly demarcated; even the topography of my small days and nights is marked and unchangeable. I don't know how this happened to me, but it has, and it is all predictable and repetitious, down to the flavors of the soba noodles I eat and the canned coffee I drink every morning.

A few crucial points: I know that Tokyo is just a dozen or so miles from here. But psychologically, the city is as far from Kugenuma as it is from Galveston, Texas. I know that in Tokyo are nightclubs, models, drugs, rock bands, all those cool things that in my mind are the components of a big life. I want to get loaded, go to nightclubs and fuck models. I am so far from that right now that even thinking of it makes me sad. But it's there, and I know it's there, and I feel that if I just get a boost, like if someone would put their hands together and give me a leg up, then maybe I could clamber over this psychological and sociological fence that is keeping me in this pathetic life. But Drew? He's not going to give me a boost. In fact, he acts like there's nowhere else but here.

On Friday, Drew and I take the train down to Hakone. We're going to a hot-springs resort where a bunch of foreign English teachers from around Kanagawa prefecture are gathering for a re-treat. It's the one perk of being a government-sponsored English teacher: every few months they send us on these weekend-long parties that are kind of like grown-up versions of the field trips we used to take in elementary school. The schedule calls for vari-ous confabs about teaching English and then discussions about adjusting to life in Japan. I'm not adjusting, I want to say, but I won't. Drew has brought a small bong, and as soon as we get there he retires into a bathroom, turns on the fan and rips a few hits. He comes out with his eyes glazed and this big grin on his face, and for a moment I regret that I don't smoke pot. But I have a bottle of Sariam that I chug down, burping up a little of the syrupy potion that tastes almost like Kahlúa. Fortified by the codeine, I look forward to a weekend of lolling around in natural baths and saunas.

I've never met English teachers in other countries, but I think the ones in Japan are the lamest people on earth. They're not teachers, or at least they weren't before they came here. Their only skill, their defining attribute as far as their employers are concerned, is that they speak their native tongue. How hard is that? And they don't even speak it particularly well. (Drew, when he's stoned—which is much of the time—barely speaks it at all.) But so many of them still act as if what they're doing is highly skilled labor, like they're lab technicians working on Martian probes or something. They exchange notes, they prepare flash cards and cassettes and CD-ROMs, they talk about which videos their classes enjoyed. All for Japanese high school classes full of kids who are usually asleep. It's pointless, really, and once in a while I mention this to Drew, but he just shakes his head like, whatever, what does that have to do with anything? We're getting paid, right? Like that's enough.

And when I raise these sorts of existential questions at these conferences—like, what are we really doing here? I mean, no stu-dent in the history of Japanese high schools has ever really learned English—all the eager-eyed English teachers look at me like I'm insane, but that's because I told the truth and nobody is ever supposed to tell the truth when it's this depressing. Or at least that's my take.

After dropping off our stuff and getting sufficiently medicated, Drew and I head downstairs to the main tatami room, where we assume they're going to serve lunch. On the way down we see a few English teachers from Yokohama. They're coming up from the baths and are wearing white cotton robes. I've seen these hags before. They're all about lending and borrowing TOEFL cassettes and preparing lesson plans. But with them is this foxy new girl I haven't seen before, a bobbed brunette with freckles and pouting lips. How did I miss her?

We exchange glances. And she does this half shrug when she sees me smiling. Her robe hangs a little loose on her shoulders so that I see a V of freckled cleavage between the blue lapels. I feel like my blood is jumping. I'm warm. I don't know what to say.

Drew, nodding his head, speechless, freezes when he sees her like he's just seen a six-foot bong. "Whassup?" he says.

And he sounds so lame that I yank him by the *obi*. I don't want to contaminate my chances with her by having to make up for the terrible impression of a stoned Drew. But she's made my weekend. Just the sight of her. There's hope.

In the basketball-court-size baths, I sit against the tile floor in near-boiling water, the steam getting to my sedated head so that I feel light and airy like an inflated balloon. Drifting, drifting, for a moment up and out and away from this burnt life, from the English classes and the lame commuter train. I'm imagining bigger things, better places, where there are, like, strippers and models and the guys from Guns N' Roses and everybody likes me and I'm not an English teacher.

Then Drew burps this really stinky, fishy-smelling burp and I'm back here.

"Let's get some beer," he says.

I shake my head. I don't like drinking when I'm on the Sariam. Something about the combination gives me the urge to urinate. "Go ahead."

He climbs out of the tub, towels down and slides into his

robe. Maybe it's the cough syrup, but I doze off for a while, and when I finally wake up, I'm all pruned and haggard, and another English teacher, Nathan Applesworth, is shaking me, telling me I've been in too long.

Nathan Applesworth is one of those Americans who come to Japan and get super into everything Japanese. Sake, sumo, flower arranging, tea ceremony, Kabuki, No, karate, Bunraku, regional wasabis and exotic sweet bean pastes. This guy has become a Japanophile to the point of getting uncomfortable whenever the Rape of Nanking comes up. No one really knows the exact numbers of rape victims, he says hurriedly.

Nathan Applesworth spends every minute he isn't teaching English or practicing flower arranging or sampling a delightful batch of radish paste from Odawara studying Japanese, which he has now become proficient enough at to suck up to Japanese principals and teachers and, I don't know, traffic cops. He has a peculiar, earnest Nathan Applesworthesque quality that repels me. He's like the human version of one of those birds that pick detritus out of a crocodile's mouth. He flits around, so eager to please with his polite Japanese words, and he is perfectly happy to subsist on the scraps the Japanese will throw him.

I, of course, with my aspirations to a monstrously grand life, will kowtow to no one, Japanese or not. I am, after all, half Japanese, but I grew up in California and went to college in New York and I've seen how big life can get. I swear, even in high school my life was bigger than it is now. I was banging girls Nathan Applesworth could never even dream of. I was smoking some of the best pot in the world—although I never really liked the stuff—eating the freshest magic mushrooms, swallowing the best pills and snorting the greatest coke while Nathan Applesworth was studiously preparing for his SATs or thinking about asking out that cute girl from French class. Clearly, I am made for bigger experiences. This is all just a detour, some cosmic punch line for which my life has unwittingly become the windup.

But it is Nathan Applesworth who saves me from being steamed to death. It has already turned dark outside, and the *onsen* bath is empty. I can watch the vapors rise from the spring-water in ribbony sheets that intertwine like double helixes up near the skylights. I climb from the tub and almost lose my footing on the tiles. My legs have become wobbly.

Nathan Applesworth is smiling. He says something in Japanese. I recognize the word, it means "be careful" or "dangerous" or something. I remember my mother saying it to me when I was little. I nod. I need to find my towel and that girl I saw on the steps. Nathan Applesworth standing before me naked, with his disturbingly pink body and little tuft of brown pubic hair and those annoyingly stout thighs, is like an anatomical chart of a small man living a minuscule life. The smallness is coming off him in waves as palpable as the steam rising from the tub. It's all a trick. The interest in all things Japanese, the fascination with bean paste and sake—he has fooled himself into looking at his pint-size life through a magnifying glass so that it doesn't look so pathetically microscopic. I pity him for his inability to understand that he is trapped, that his world is a little bubble in which he putters around oblivious to the Godzillas and Mothras (like me!) tromping around right outside.

"Have you tried the wasabi?" Nathan Applesworth asks. "It's so much spicier than you would think it would be from this part of Japan. You should bring some back for the other teachers in your schools."

Right. In my whole time in Japan I have never once brought back *omiyages*, the little gifts Japanese foist upon one another on returning from wherever it is they've gone, whether it's down to Hakone for the weekend or Rwanda for a decade. That's one of the reasons all the other teachers at the high school hate me. That and the fact that when I'm not teaching a class, I sit in the teachers' room listening to Guns N' Roses on my Discman or playing Donkey Kong on my GameBoy. (So what if my students aren't allowed to bring their GameBoys to school. I'm not a student.)

"We're playing charades at dinner," Nathan Applesworth tells me. This doesn't concern me. I'm thirsty. I have to pee. I stumble out to the dressing room and find my cotton robe, slipping into it as I check myself in the mirror. I'm not in bad shape. Drew and I have been playing soccer a couple times a week with a few Iranians in Yokohama. I'm not thin and waifish like a young David Bowie, but I've got a six-pack, okay, call it a two-pack. I've lost some weight and I'm definitely looking a little better. My black hair has grown long, and when it's down, I actually have some kind of a look going, not like some randomly arrived-at series of features and affectations that don't add up to anything. You know what I'm talking about: those guys who have, like, a goatee, a mullet with one long braid and maybe a clip-on earring—a lot of affect that doesn't cohere. Well, I've got a look. It veers a little too much toward the *Dances with Wolves* kind of Native American thing, but I can't help that, because I'm half Japanese. But with the long hair, and when I keep the weight off, it's not a bad image. It's just rock-and-roll enough to get me by. I mean, compared to Nathan Applesworth or even Drew, I'm practically ready for my toothpaste commercial.

But as I walk up the stairs, I begin wondering: why haven't I been having any luck with the ladies? This nine-month dry spell has been the longest of my adult life. Something's changing, though, I can feel it. I'm finally so fed up with the tiny life that I'm ready to take drastic measures. I'll do whatever it takes.

Drew is sitting in our tatami room, drinking from a tall Sapporo and picking at his toenails. "Dude, where have you been?"

I tell him I've been pruning in the tub but that I've been cleansed, purified and am now a new man, ready for new challenges. Aren't you tired of this little world, of this puny plot, don't you need to break out? I want to give him a pep talk, to let him know that enormous changes can be made, must be made, lest we descend with the Nathan Applesworths of the world to a planet of wasabi sampling and tea tasting. We are bigger than that, or at least I am.

It is my version of Lombardi in the locker room, right before he sent the Packers out to storm Omaha Beach or whatever they did. Getting big isn't everything, it's the only thing.

But Drew just looks at me. "Whatever."

I get dressed, throwing on this very cool Stussy mock turtleneck that I got from Shawn Stussy himself. (You see, evidence of my previous bigness.) And these stylin' black trousers and a fresh pair of socks. I'm looking stupendously huge. I must have lost like fifteen pounds in that tub.

We head down to the big tatami room to join the rest of the teachers. They are seated on flat cushions around two low, rectangular tables. Before the two dozen teachers, all of them rosy-faced and red-cheeked after their baths, are place settings featuring various lacquered bowls, boxes, little dishes of pickles, soy sauce, tonkatsu sauce. I scan the room, looking for the girl with the freckled cleavage I saw on the steps. She's there, on the far side of the room, seated next to . . . Nathan Applesworth. This will not do. I slide off my slippers, pass under the lintel and stalk across the tatami. She looks at me. There are open seats around the room. But I am determined to take my place next to the girl, who is now smiling at me. She knows it. She must be in awe of me. She can tell that I have been reborn. That this sleeping giant has at last awakened, a little pruned but ready to assume his rightful place in the cosmic order. I feel bad about leaving Drew behind. But he has to make his own way in this new world. I work around the tables, my knee brushing aside the shoulders of seated teachers. They bend forward, parting for me as I slide down the tatami. I stop behind the girl and Nathan Applesworth.

Everyone is watching me. They too, I am sure, can sense the change. Can sense that the Karl of a few hours ago, a few days ago, is gone and in his place is this new man who reaches out and takes whatever he wants.

"Excuse me," I say. "Can everyone slide down one place? I'd like to sit here."

"But—" Before Nathan Applesworth can object, the coterie has already slid down. And Nathan Applesworth realizes that it would be more awkward to stay than to move. He shifts one cushion.

And I take my place.

It all feels very natural. For the rest of the dinner, as we go through our grilled fish and tempura and chicken and sashimi all washed down with beer and sake, I am charming, witty, gallant. (I don't drink. I've gotta stay frosty.) On closer inspection, Karen exudes a carefree pulchritude. I guess if I had to pick a celebrity she resembles, it would be the mature Tatum O'Neal. Karen has a light dusting of freckles on her cheeks that dissipate just over the high cheekbones. Her bored eyes are smoky, sleepy brown— she looks like she really doesn't give a fuck, about me or anything else. In fact, that's her image: vaguely condescending, imperious; she has one of those pert noses that she always seems to be looking down. Just to glance at her, you might take her to be a bit posh. But she's Australian, from Melbourne, South Yarra or somewhere, and despite her sleepy eyes, I can tell by the way she laughs at my jokes, answers my questions and then poses her own that she is interested.

After some intricately sliced melons and then these little bean cakes, a game of charades begins in earnest. The topic, of course, is movie titles. *Top Gun. The Godfather. Rain Man.* Eager English teachers silently go through the motions as—who cares? Let me tell you about Karen's body. When she excuses herself to go to the bathroom, I do an official once-over. Nice feet, medium-size but not overly large. She looks like she can hold her ground. She's wearing a pair of faded jeans, her calves are thin, her thighs nicely proportioned and her ass full and muscular and shaped like half of an overripe peach. It is this sight, I am sure, that encourages lascivious yearning in the minds of every man in the room. There is such a thing as collective consciousness, I believe, and it occurs whenever a woman walks from the room. All male eyes turn to appraise the retreating posterior and formulate one simple conclusion: is she doable or not? In this case, I am quite sure there is unanimous agreement: Karen is very doable.

And then there are her tits. Generous, reassuringly mammalian, I can think of a hundred more adjectives but instead let me describe them like this: Karen is twenty-three. That's a great age for breasts—they are finally more readily accessible to the rest of the world, but gravity has not yet won its inevitable victory.

I don't know how it happened or why. But for some reason I am confident and make conversation with aplomb. Nathan Applesworth, who ventures forth several times to make repartee about the pickled plums or this special type of first-growth sake he's got a cask of, is dispatched by my cutting comments like the small-worlder that he is. I'm not quite sure why this is happening, but I am sure I seem much bigger than I really am. Is it just a matter of thinking big? I am impressing myself, and I keep rolling it out. Karen can't help but be taken with me. It's not fair, really. She's practically defenseless.

After dinner, instead of retiring with Drew to smoke pot and drink cough syrup, I stay downstairs with Karen and a group of other Australian and American English teachers who gather in the *onsen's* deserted front room. They are such a good-natured lot it's almost sickening. Even Karen's friend Cheryl is so glibly talkative about, well, nothing. She goes on about how much she misses Oz and her boyfriend, Samuel, who's coming up for a visit, and Karen just sits there, arching her back, bending once to stretch her legs like a dancer. It is an impressive silence. She stays quiet without seeming to pass judgment.

I, on the other hand, can't seem to shut up. I interrupt Cheryl to promulgate my views in favor of American colonization of Australia, of Australia's unworthiness to host an Olympics, of Australia's hopelessly remote location and, most important in my view, Australia's interchangeability with Canada. In my opinion, the two countries are virtually identical. Former British colonies spun off to develop bizarre accents in inhospitable conditions. Both have perverted sporting cultures and, in their favor, attractive women. I assure all the Australians and Canadians present that as an American, I don't mind one bit keeping these quasi-colonies safe under our nuclear umbrella.

The various Commonwealth attendees rage against me in their curious accents. I deflect their criticisms with a peremptory wave of my hand. And I notice that Karen, for her part, is laughing quietly.

"You never shut up, do you?" she says, smiling.

This is really the beginning of my life in Asia. I came to Japan because my luck ran out, because after graduating from college and moving to Manhattan, where I spent a year aspiring to be a writer, playing rummy 500 with a few similarly employment-challenged cronies and losing a good deal of my parents' money betting on college football, I had no choice. During an angry telephone conversation, my father told me he would no longer support me, and then my mother picked up the phone and mentioned the possibility of a job teaching English in Japan. Considering the circumstances, I was interested. The place remained for me exotic and foreign—a wealthy island empire at the edge of the world where an indigent young man could start over. I decided I would try my luck there.

And that's when I got stuck in this apartment, in this podunk town. As soon as I am back from the weekend retreat and walk into my apartment, I am struck by a wave of loneliness. It is palpable in this place, the dust on the chest of drawers and along the top of the TV, the little kettle on the gas stove, the table with its mess of unpaid NTT and Nippon Gas bills. I can't believe I live here. I call Karen. I have to get out of here. I want to tell her I'm going to take her out, that she is powerless to resist me. But when I hear her voice, I waver for a moment and lose all my momentum. I simply ask her out. It is surprisingly appropriate for the moment, full of humility rather than hubris, and endearingly traditional.

We meet at Yokohama Station and take a taxi to this French-Japanese fusion place in Motomachi, across the street from Tower Records. While we drink wine at a green Lucite table, Karen tells me about her Japanese boyfriend: some singer in a band that plays Tokyo live houses, he also did a turn as the Shinkansen, in *Starlight Express*. For a moment my hopes are dashed. But then I vow to redouble my efforts. This is my chance to get out of my squalid little life. I can't be deterred this easily.

After dinner we walk along the canals beneath the elevated expressways between Motomachi and Chinatown. It is damp and warm, with a misty shroud creeping down the sides of the concrete buildings. The streets are narrow, but cars swing their yellow high beams down them in groups of two and three, as if cruising for a party in this quiet district. Karen wears black pumps, a tight black skirt, a black cashmere sweater and pearls. You can see for moments in the streetlights the woman she will one day become. The chin will drop, the cheeks will settle. She will always be pretty, but at some point her handsomeness will seem matronly rather than maidenly. For now, however, she remains a girl, redolent with promise and potential and possibility. Tonight. This city. The future. What do you want to do with your life? These are all open-ended questions. And at our age, you frankly feel you can lose a week or a month or a decade, just blow it, I don't know, masturbating or playing Ping-Pong or drinking cough syrup and so what? I've got nothing but time. As we walk, she talks about jazz, about Billie Holiday and Sarah Vaughan and Ella and Lena and I don't know who. She cares about music, and she cares about sex. She's let me know that in little bits of conversation during dinner. She has a sly sexuality that is omnipresent, but it's not the first thing you notice. On some girls: bam, there it is. They're all about sex. With Karen, yes, she is all about sex, but you don't know at first, that's why you find her so attractive. It's a neat trick, and it lures me and drives me crazy, so that as we're walking, I let my hair down and shake it out and then pull her by the shoulders to a streetlamp and turn her around and stand with my face buried in her hair, kissing her neck.

She finds it strange. "What are you doing?" But her voice softens as she says this, so that it comes out do-*ing* and trails off, and then she takes a deep breath and we stand there in silence. She can feel me through her skirt and she grinds herself back into me. The friction is almost too much for me, so I push her away. Then we kiss, with a lot of tongue, and I'm pressing her again and she feels down the front of my pants to where I'm stiff. "Oh my God, baby, you're so hard."

Every thirty feet or so we stop and make out again. Feeling

each other all over and rubbing against each other and she reaches into my pants and I stick my hand up under her skirt and pull aside her underwear and rub against her cunt. It's sort of embarrassing, cars are still driving by and every once in a while one of them honks because we're so obviously going at it, and Karen, I am quickly realizing, likes doing it in public, enjoys showing herself off and being felt up in front of a crowd.

We finally make it to a bar, some little place with an Old West motif where most of the customers are regulars who keep bottles of bourbon up on the high shelves that go all the way around the place. We settle down in a booth and order Wild Turkey and then it's like we're on a date again, as if all that groping outside never happened. We earnestly chat about our nonsexual desires and wants. I tell her about my plans for a big life. I will write books, novels—and if that doesn't work, then I will make films or perhaps paint great canvases. I also have a knack for illustration, and though I've never actually done it, I'm sure I could be a DJ. Oh, and there's fashion, I know a thing or two about fashion. I am abundantly talented, just terribly miscast as an English teacher here on the outskirts of Tokyo.

Karen is less overtly ambitious. She studied Japanese at the University of Melbourne, and she also was a theater and music major. She sang in school plays, college productions of *Pajama Game* and *Grease* and *Runaway*. For a while she sang with a little quintet that played in a few Melbourne clubs. Nothing serious, but she does have this voice, it's sonorous and full and sometimes it sounds like she's talking in two tones at once, like she's her own echo.

She's never lived anywhere but Melbourne and Japan. She's never been to the U.S., never been to Europe. Her family has a farm up in Toorak where they keep sheep. I've never known anyone who owned a sheep before. What does she want? She really can't tell me, because she hasn't given it any thought. Men? Drugs? Sex? She guesses: all those things. But she doesn't share my view that life must be this ruthless mission of self-definition. I am passionate about this. If you don't create something, you will never know yourself; then what is the point of the whole trip? These are ideas that have been kicking around in my head for months and gone unexpressed, or maybe I told some of them to Drew but didn't get any kind of response. I explain to her that it is a zero-sum game, there is only a certain amount of pleasure and success out there in the world, and if someone else uses some of it up, that means there will be less for me. It is a brutal picture I am painting for her, and I don't know if I really believe it myself, but it feels macho and powerful to be posturing this way. Yes the world is cruel and mean and selfish, I am telling her, but I am man enough to handle it. I fear nothing. I have been preparing for this deadly race all my life.

Karen and I drink three bourbons each. I believe I have talked her into submission. The last Tokaido-line trains from Yokohama Station left hours ago. There is no way for me to get home, so when we walk out of the bar, I tell her I will need to sleep at her apartment.

"On the first date? What would my mum say?" She giggles.

We fall into each other. That night we don't have intercourse, but I go down on her, and she is well groomed with a pleasant smell. She urges me to turn around and takes my cock in her mouth. She turns out to be one of those women with an obsession for penises. She loves to have my dick in her hand, in her mouth, to run her tongue up along the shaft. She loves the taste of sperm. Later in our relationship, if we meet in the early evening at a train station or restaurant, she'll tug me close to her and pull the front of my pants away from my waist and peek down at me, reaching her hand in for a quick feel. She's also the first woman I've ever had who can actually deep-throat the whole of my penis at one time. It's usually after she's had a few drinks. She relaxes her throat and takes a breath first. It's a strange feeling, pleasurable certainly, but also a little awkward because she's concentrating so hard that I feel almost like I'm watching a scientific experiment. It is interesting, watching every inch go into her mouth. At first you don't see how it will fit, it doesn't seem geometrically possible, but that's where the relaxed glottis and the breathing exercises come in. I can actually feel the back of her mouth giving way with the head of my penis. That's a good feeling.

Karen is part of a wholesale upgrading that begins in my life. Suddenly I'm a player again, and the ripples of her impact into my life spread outward. One afternoon I take the train up to Tokyo to the Yohji Yamamoto boutique in Harajuku. I buy a black wool three-button suit. It sets me back about a hundred thousand yen ($800), but I need a good suit. The next week I put on my good suit to meet a contact of my mother's who is an editor at an English-language newspaper in Tokyo. With my new girlfriend and new suit, I am very confident and make a good impression. I am hired as a reporter. The same day I tell Karen about my new job, she tells me she has dumped her Japanese boyfriend, the musician. He came over last night, she explains. He was drunk and wondered why Karen hadn't gone to see him at Club Niman Volto. She'd honestly forgotten. Then he got mad and called her a foreign whore and then he asked her if she had any more whiskey and then he took out his penis and tried to get her to suck him off. She tells me it was horrible. This drunk Japanese heavy-metal singer waving his little dick around and begging her for one last blow job.

I don't ask her if she acquiesced.

I quit my teaching job. I call the principal of the school and tell him that I'm leaving.

"No, not next month, now. Today. Yesterday."

My Japanese is barely good enough to give him a false reason why it all has to happen so quickly. The newspaper doesn't need me to start for a few months. But I can't stand the idea of another day of English teaching. Those high school kids in their grubby dark uniforms, the boys with their crew cuts or wavy pompadours and the girls with their long, straight black hair. In their moody silences they all intimidate me a little. I'm just a few years out of high school myself, and I know how high school students think. Their thought process goes something like this: That guy, standing up there in front of the chalkboard, he's a dick.

I can't tell the principal all this. But in my halting Japanese, I make up something about a sick father. Ailing. Heart. Bad. Must go now.

The principal doesn't believe me. But he's probably glad to be rid of me. I was a terrible teacher, and he must have known that. This has been the worst nine months of my life. But they're over, finally over. The change has happened—new suit, new job, new girl.

My performance at my weekly soccer game at Yokohama University also improves. We play on pavement next to a gravel track, under the lights, with a mixture of Japanese college students and Iranian immigrants. It's a surprisingly good run, better than exclusively Japanese games, in which everyone seems to cluster around the ball like children. The Japanese simply don't pass. It's as if in a country this crowded, they're afraid if you give up the ball you'll never get it back. But this game, with its mix of foreigners and Japanese, tends to feature more team play. Besides the Iranians, there's Drew and me and a British fellow who seems to work for the college in some capacity. My skills seem to have evolved to a higher level. My first touches are better. My passes crisper. I have a great feel for what to do with the ball. Every fucking touch results in something good: a pass, a dribble, a smart back heel, a good strike. I've never had so much fun on the pitch. The other guys all notice, complimenting me after the game. "*Tsugoi!*" the Japanese guys tell me as we're resting on a narrow stretch of grass next to the pitch.

When we're walking back along the track, Drew asks me if I want to score some cough syrup. That had been our ritual after Thursday-night soccer: cough syrup, maybe Drew would take a bong hit or two and we'd either play video games or listen to CDs or read comic books. Plus, Drew had brought over Signet pro-basketball handbooks going back to the mid-sixties. I loved getting all loaded on cough syrup and flipping through those old paperbacks and reading Warren Jabali's or Lucius Allen's career numbers.

But I tell Drew I can't. I actually have something to do. This is shocking. Neither of us has *ever* had anything to do. In all our months stuck in Kanagawa, the one thing you could count on is that Drew and Karl are doing nothing. Right now. As sure as the emperor of Japan lives in a rock house. It does seem a bit unfair. Drew must be wondering what's happened.

He takes my explanation that I'm going to see Karen like it doesn't bother him. But it must, it has to. It would kill me. Drew nods his head. We part at the station, he's taking the Tokaido south, I'm on the Toyoko west.

Karen takes me to Tokyo nightclubs. Every club has a theme. There's one with a sort of Aztec setting, another with a tropical reggae vibe, another with cracked floors and broken windows that I guess is going for an earthquake theme. I don't know. They all serve crappy liquor. Karen sneaks in small bottles of vodka that she mixes with orange soda. I stick with my Sariam cough syrup. Buzz, Zipang, Java Jive, Cleo, the places are packed with Western models and tall, skinny Japanese guys with expensive clothes and long hair. I guess I'm trying to fit into the latter category. Dancing comes easily to Karen, she can mimic almost anyone: John Travolta, Paula Abdul, Axl Rose. When she's drunk she loses herself on the dance floor, and after a few numbers, when we're hot and sweaty, she'll pull me into some dark corner and grab my hand and stick it down her skirt. Or she'll guide us to a table where she'll sit us down, reach under and unzip my fly and start stroking my erection right there, all the while looking me in the eye and carrying on a serious conversation. Her exhibitionist streak adds a little extra edge to an otherwise typical night at a club.

One afternoon Karen and I are taking the train back from Tokyo. My mother transferred a few thousand dollars into my bank account, and I've just put down all the money as deposit on this brand-new six-mat apartment up in Kagurazaka. The place is tiny, but it's freshly built, smelling of pristine tatamis, with fresh black and white linoleum in the kitchen, and there's a little veranda where I can hang out my shirts to dry.

And it's in Tokyo. It's all part of my plan to supersize my life. I show it to Karen and she shrugs. She's not totally on board the big life plan, just yet. She thinks Yokohama is fine. It's not, I assure her, you might as well live in fucking Philadelphia, but that doesn't make any sense to her. So I'll lead by example.

The train rolls past the shopping-mall ventilation ducts and pulls into Fujisawa Station. We step off. We're walking with our hands clasped. Karen looks hot in this white one-piece denim dress with a wide brown belt. We hand over our tickets and walk past the stand-up soba stands and the fare machines and into the crowds of salarymen in their black loafers and gray and blue suits carrying their satchels and briefcases. There are thousands of them, all dark-haired and hurrying, like statistics on the move. We slide into the current, riding it to the staircase, where we almost bump right into Drew and Nathan Applesworth on their way up.

It's shocking at first. What's Drew doing with Nathan Applesworth?

I reintroduce Karen. They've both met her. Karen asks, in her little Australian toot, "How's it going?"

It's going fine, they both claim. But I detect jealousy and lingering unhappiness. Fuck Nathan Applesworth and his tanka paintings and haiku and sweet bean cakes, I really don't give a shit about him. But Drew, man, Drew shouldn't be hanging out with Nathan Applesworth.

We talk about my suddenly quitting teaching. It has taken the whole Kanagawa community of government-sponsored English teachers by surprise. Nathan Applesworth frankly doesn't approve. It was very un-Japanese. Better that I had stuck it out and *gamaned* through the hardship rather than lose face by bailing out. Screw that, I tell them, it was either quit or throw myself under a train.

Nathan Applesworth takes a deep breath and nods, because *that* would have been the Japanese thing to do.

I'm moving, I explain, to Tokyo. I've taken an apartment. I'm gonna rent a van and load my stuff and drive it up to Kagurazaka and start my new life. Drew looks a little saddened by this. I know how that feels. I've had friends go on to do exciting things while I stagnated, it's like everyone going to Disneyland while you're doing your math homework.

What was Drew to me? Maybe he was actually like Billy Mackleby. I remember the summer after fifth grade, when all my good friends went to Europe or sailing to Hawaii or wherever they went. Erich, John, Warren, they all went off to do exotic family things that took up the whole summer. And my family didn't go anywhere. We stayed in Pacific Palisades, and I had no one to play with. Except Billy Mackleby up the street. I didn't like him. I actually hated him. His family were devoutly Christian, and his mother once scolded me because I claimed man had descended from monkeys. But this one summer there was no one else. So I ended up riding dirt bikes and skateboarding and playing army men with Billy Mackleby all summer. And the whole time, even when we built this really cool bike jump out of bricks and plywood, I was still thinking, This isn't really fun because Billy Mackleby is a dork. As soon as Erich came back from Europe and John from this sailing trip to Hawaii, I never played with Billy Mackleby again.

Now, as I see Drew's hangdog expression, the way his glazed eyes sag behind his wire-frame glasses and his cheeks bristle with flecked acne, I get that Billy Mackleby feeling. There was really no one else to hang out with for all these months. Drew was fine for that. But does he have any place in my new life? I kind of doubt it.

So now maybe Nathan Applesworth is his Billy Mackleby? That sort of makes sense. Or am I Drew's Billy Mackleby? You never know who's the Billy Mackleby in any relationship.

I look over at Karen. That light dusting of freckles, that highlighted russet-colored hair, the pouting lips set in their vaguely disdainful cast. She's all mine, every inch and part of her, and that's a powerful idea that can make a man confident and optimistic about his prospects. If this delicious creature has chosen me, then I must be doing something right.

I tell Drew I'll call him. I'll let him know my new number as soon as I have it. He tells me he has some of my stuff, a few books, a couple CDs. I'll get it all back, I explain, it's not like I'm leaving the country.

But we both know I'll never pick that stuff up.

Karen knows some nice restaurants, a few smoky, bourbony bars where Japanese with spiky hair and shiny trousers and platform sneakers dance around to trance music and swallow tranquilizers. But we're really exploring the city together, the famously expensive boutiques, the funny little yakitori places, the three-stool shot bars. All the crawling around Tokyo, however, is really just prelude and elaborate foreplay for the most vigorous and healthy sex I have ever had. We talk about this sometimes, when we're lying on my new tatami floor. I live upstairs from a printer, and during the day you can hear the roll of the press. Karen is terribly loud when we fuck. She likes to talk about exactly what I'm doing to her and how it feels. "Oh God, fuck me, baby, do you know how good that feels? Oh God, don't you fucking stop." She's so noisy that I worry at night about Mrs. Tango next door hearing us. The landlady, a seventy-ish woman who dyes her hair a preposterous shade of purple, likes to have me over for lunch and dinner and seems to think, because I work at a newspaper, that I am some sort of intellectual.

In the mornings I climb out of the futon, leaving Karen sleeping there in the damp room, and throw on a button-down shirt, trousers, loafers, then head down to the subway toward Tsukiji, where the newspaper's shabby office building hunkers on a narrow lot like a smashed stack of shoe boxes. At the paper, there are about a dozen Americans and Brits who do the reporting and rewriting and a dozen Japanese journalists who have screwed up so badly in their careers they've been consigned to this forsaken division of their company. They are a tired, disgruntled lot, stoically translating stories from the Japanese parent newspaper or writing their incomprehensible English headlines that we will have to rewrite. They are also vigorous drinkers, prone to popping open Ozeki one-cups or canned Scotch-and-sodas at nine A.M. Their briefcases clang with the sound of empty bottles and cans when they leave in the afternoon. It is hard to imagine any of these men having once been ambitious: editors of their college newspapers, cub reporters, foreign correspondents. But that's what they all were. They covered assassinations, wars, bombings, and now they are writing captions that will be nixed by some fresh-out-of-college punk.

I always wonder what they make of my ambition. Most of the foreigners on the staff are on the same career trajectory as our Japanese counterparts. They are happy to have work. And journalism beats English teaching. So they make sure that the Jumble answers run every day and that we pick up the correct "This Day in History" from the wires. I struggle to reconcile this little rag with the greater girth of my aspirations. Yet there are tremendous advantages to starting small. Within a few weeks I am writing 25 percent of the newspaper on some days. I become the film reviewer, the book reviewer, I start up a weekly column and I assign myself most of the page-one stories. The newspaper will publish anything I write, vast book reviews—why not try to wrap up Saul Bellow's entire career?—that sprawl over entire broadsheet pages, film reviews in which I discuss every Vietnam War movie ever made, columns that are reminiscences about first dates, an old Volkswagen I once owned, slot-car racing or—my favorite subject—how much I hate English teaching. It pours out of me. As much as I write, the only thing I can be sure of is that no one is reading a word. The circulation of our newspaper, officially fifty thousand, is somewhere under ten thousand. I ask Ozawa, my boss, how many subscribers we have.

"Twenty-three," he tells me.

"Twenty-three thousand?" I ask.

"No. Twenty-three subscribers."

But he assures me we kill them on the newsstand.

After work there's Karen. She tells me she believes the most important factor in two people getting along is sexual compatability. She believes that if the sex works, you can fudge all the rest. I don't disagree. Because when you're our age and having great sex regularly and getting drunk and exploring this exotic new city and feeling like you're getting someplace in your career and as a person, you can't pull the strands that make up the web apart. It all coalesces into this flow of life that is complicated and intoxicating. She jokes that we live on iced oolong tea and sperm. I refine my existential theories about life and art. We must stay in the moment, I tell her, and if staying in the moment means having great sex, then we must have more sex.

Standing there, drinking cheap red wine in my kitchen while wearing a green skirt, gray blouse and green-striped jacket, she looks very pulled together. She doesn't mind English teaching—that makes her a little suspect in my mind—but she's got a good job instructing at a girls' junior college where everyone dotes on Karen-san and gives her little gifts and confesses to her all their dreams and crushes. She's found out more about Japan in an afternoon eating tiramisus and drinking iced coffee with the Keikos and Reikos from her college than most of us will pick up in a decade. Who would have guessed that Keiko had picked up two African guys on Guam and had sex with both of them? Or that Rei prefers other women and has a regular girlfriend, a bank teller, and that the two of them go on vacations together? Karen's telling me all this while she drinks her wine. I've seen pictures of Keiko, and I can't get that image of her and the two Africans out of my mind.

"Can you believe that?" Karen asks. "She used the Japanese word *nama,* like 'They dicked me.' "

Karen laughs and shakes her head. It is one of her gifts, perhaps, that she uninhibits people, makes guys and girls alike confess their secrets and pursue their desires. If she were prettier, truly beautiful, then no one would tell her a thing. But instead she is subtly, powerfully sexual without being intimidating. Those freckles help. As does the mousy hair color. She's just Karen, and somehow in her quiet, steady, drunken way, she gets you to let loose.

A few nights a week she goes back to Yokohama and I'm left on my own. When she's gone, I go over to Mrs. Tango's for dinner. She has two daughters, one of whom reads English and translates some of my stories for Mrs. Tango. I have no idea what she makes of those long ruminations on soccer in cinema or discursive columns on the state of soccer in North America. But Mrs. Tango is suitably impressed.

I sit on the floor, my legs crossed beneath me, as Mrs. Tango lays out chicken, fish, pork, tofu, raw fish, spinach, cabbage, pickles, and it just keeps on coming until I am stuffed. Mr. Tango, whom I will never hear utter a word, eats about two bites of some fish and then returns to smoking Caster cigarettes. And in the corner, resting on a futon with her head propped up on a wooden cushion like what geisha used to sleep on, is Obasan Tango. Too weak to sit up, she lies in the corner and subsists on rice gruel poured from a glass bottle. She's 103, and the second-oldest person in Shinjuku ward. The only lady who's older lives in Yotsuya. But she's sick. And if she dies, then Obasan Tango becomes the oldest person in Shinjuku.

"*Ganbatte,* Obasan," says Mrs. Tango, "keep it up."

Obasan Tango moans. Mrs. Tango pours some more rice gruel down her throat. That's all she can digest.

At work, there is a tall, thin, bespectacled girl named Toshimi who, amazingly enough, works for a dummied-up version of our newspaper that is printed for children. As if our paper wasn't juvenile enough. Anyway, her job of late has been to abridge my stories for the young readers. As remarkable as it is that anyone feels the need to distribute a youth version of our paper, even more astounding is the fact that they pay me extra each time they pick up one of my stories, and since I'm writing a huge proportion of the paper, they pick up four or five of my pieces a week. Toshimi comes over and talks to me about my stories, asking me about some of my idiosyncratic usages—" 'Dan Quayle is so stupid, he could have been an English teacher in Kanagawa,' what does this mean?" Then she writes down my explanation.

She is always impeccably dressed. Black Comme des Garçons trousers. Distressed cotton Issey Miyake tops. Polished Susan Bennis Warren Edwards pumps. Since she has a figure like a runway model's, all this stuff hangs on her exactly as the designers intended. She has a studious face, but beneath those wire-frame glasses, she's very pretty. Fine, delicate, almost feline features make me sneak second and third glances when she walks by. And her body is lean and graceful, where Karen's is voluptuous and full. We are always curious about a new body. What do her breasts feel like? How does her cunt look up close? For a moment or two whenever she is around, I slip into that inquisitive reverie. It takes me ten seconds to wrench myself back to writing my book review.

I still have that statue. I stuck it in the corner of my kitchen. The patinaed brass looks gray in the shadows. The Buddha sits in the lotus position, his face beatifically sagging and his eyes delphically blank. The maiden he has entered straddles his lap and has thrown her head back in open ecstasy. She is lithe-limbed and small-breasted. Her hair is done up in an elaborate, almost Khmer-style headdress. It is the most frankly sexual Buddhist sculpture I have ever seen. I wonder if it is modeled on some famed Khmer or Tibetan statue I've never seen. And despite its erotic content, when I look at it I see one thing: English teaching. It is a reminder of that lost season. Of Drew. Of Matsuoka High School. Of the Enoden train line and Fujisawa. Of reading those old NBA handbooks. When I look at it, I shake my head and turn away quickly, as if that tantric statue will somehow revolve me back into that boring old life.

One evening after work, just before I'm leaving to catch the train to Shin-Sugita to meet Karen, I grab the statue and drag it out into the street, setting it beside me on the asphalt as I hail a taxi to the station. On the train, other passengers stare at the statue. It really is mesmerizing. The way the Buddha sits there at rest but also seems to be simultaneously thrusting into the maiden. The sculptor did an exquisite job of rendering the taut thigh muscles and the arching of the back to get across the concurrence of carnality and repose. My fellow commuters recognize the quality of the work yet find suspect anyone who would port this by public transport. It is as if I am reading a hard-core porno mag; no one wants to be too near the pervert. This should be secreted away in some darkened closet or the front room of a hostess bar or brothel—the kind of place I stole it from.

Karen has admired the statue before. And when I present it to her, lugging it into her apartment, she is genuinely surprised. I want her to have it, I tell her. She *should* have it. The statue being some sort of small monument to sex, it really does suit her better than anyone else I know. I don't tell Karen this, but her greatest attribute, I have concluded, is her sexuality. It's what makes her go. So it's only natural that she should keep the statue. She's the one person I can think of who's deserving of it, actually.

"You do care for it, right?" I ask.

"Of course," Karen says, smiling. She has her hair tied up in a ponytail and wears a pair of old Levi's. "I also know how much you like it. Karl, it's too much."

I tell her it reminds me of my boring past. I tell her I don't want it anymore. I tell her there is no way I'm taking that thing back on the train. We find a place for it in the main room, in a wooden alcove beneath a window and next to the futon. She wants it to look over us when we are fucking. Sometimes, from the strangest angles—between Karen's ass cheeks or just over her nipples or down the inside of her freckled thighs—I see the Buddha and his smile, and it is as though he is blessing us.

If I sleep in Kibogaoka, I have to get up at six A.M. to get to the office and do my part putting out the newspaper. I am late most mornings, and so the headlines, subheads, captions and translations have been piling up on my desk by the time I get there carrying my Dutour coffee and muffin. Printed from an ATEX machine onto rolls of paper with green fringe at the margins, the stories are torn from the printers so the tops and bottoms are jagged and frayed. It is my job to retext and edit the front page of the newspaper, including writing the heds, deks and caps. The work is simple, and after the five or six page-one stories have cleared, I am free to write my own columns and reviews and to daydream about Toshimi.

Is this really a big life? I ask myself this one afternoon when I am riding the subway to Tokyo Station to interview a baseball player. I'm certainly making more money. I'm at least being paid to write. But this newspaper is the journalistic equivalent of T-ball; from here you dream of the minor leagues. And all the stories I'm doing don't add up to anything. Any progress I've made toward my leviathan aspirations has been incremental. I am at least employed in a field that is vaguely related to something I might want to do. Although at this point, being a rock star, painter, actor, movie director or, I don't know, graffiti artist would all be more appealing than being a writer. And most mornings I'm rewriting the copy of washed-up alcoholic Japanese journalists. And in the evenings, I either see Karen and we get drunk somewhere or I slurp down a cheap meal of some soba or ramen noodles and then chug some cough syrup back at my little apartment. Some nights I eat at Mrs. Tango's and watch the old granny gallantly fight through another day and root with the family for another old granny somewhere else in Tokyo to die so that Obasan Tango will become the oldest in the ward.

I still see Drew once in a while, when I head down to Yokohama University for soccer games. He tells me what some of the other teachers are doing. They've been reading my stories in the newspaper. My columns decrying the profession of English teaching have been getting a chilly reception. Drew explains that my former coworkers feel it is bad form for me to slag the hand that fed me. And besides, Drew says, they don't think I'm very funny. Drew looks about the same. His brown hair is still wavy and parted down the middle. The cheeks full of zits and those cheap wire-frame glasses give him the appearance of a supergenius computer hacker. Only he doesn't even own a computer.

He's a good soccer player, however. I have to admit he has that on me. I admire his game. He's so weedy and bowlegged you'd never guess it, but he was one of those kids who went to soccer camps and played tricounty youth soccer and then played in high school and Division III college ball. As we play, you almost forget for a second that he's Drew, this stoner English teacher who hasn't gotten laid in like a decade and who spends his nights hunched over a bong listening to, like, Tracy Chapman records.

After soccer we walk along the red rubberized track for a while to cool down.

"Nathan Applesworth is thinking of quitting too," he tells me.

"No way. I thought he'd never quit."

"Yeah, you know what?"

"What?"

Drew trots a few steps ahead of me and then turns around so that he is jogging backward. Behind him I can see a university building and beyond that an office tower with a blue NEC lit up on its brim. "He's getting another job."

"Where?" I ask.

"At a newspaper."

I stop. How has Nathan Applesworth managed to land a job at a paper? "Which one?"

He mentions the name. It's another of the local English-language rags, but it's arguably a better place than the one that hired me. Suddenly I feel a great shrinking of my world, unseen walls closing in on me and an invisible ceiling crashing down, all while the air is being vacuumed from what little space I have left.

Nathan Applesworth. He'll be moving to Tokyo soon. I thought I might never have to see him again. In Karen's bed that night, after I've showered and she's in the middle of performing the trick where she takes my cock all the way down her throat, I still can't get over the idea of Nathan Applesworth having a life that is as big, or perhaps bigger, than mine. What does my life comprise, really? The job at the paper, Karen here sucking me off every night. Is that really a huge life? I look around the room, the calendar with its erotic Ukiyoe prints, a few of Karen's outfits on hangers suspended from nails, her little CD/cassette player, the empty wine bottle, her soiled cotton panties in a pile by the futon and my old statue, staring at us.

I try to remember what it was about Karen that had intoxicated me. She had seemed so urbane when we first met. Her stories about going to Melbourne nightclubs and doing coke with the daughters of Australian tycoons and hanging out with Mick Jagger when he was in town on his solo tour, it all made her sound vaguely glamorous. And she had sung in clubs and was vowing to do that again. Even her being from Australia seemed exotic compared to New York or Tokyo. Can I still see the promise that she represented to me those months ago? Well, yes and no. She drinks too much and she sings along with her Billie Holiday CDs in a way that kind of bothers me, like she's trying to show me how well she sings. It's embarrassing. If you want to sing along with CDs, I feel like telling her, then go to a fucking karaoke bar. Doesn't she want more than this? How can she be satisfied with this shabby little apartment on the outskirts of Yokohama and her lunches with her students and having a few drinks in the evening and cutting loose on the dance floor on Friday and Saturday nights? It's like some kind of coal miner's life. Where's the ambition, hunger and aspiration, the raging dissatisfaction? Is she just happy? What's wrong with her?

I look down at her. She is working on my dick, slurping it up. Even this athletic interest in the male organ strikes me as a little annoying. She's too needy when it comes to sex. Why can't there be more mystery about her? Let me want it more.

Afterward, we lie on the futon, Karen curling up with her head on my chest. She's making these little murmuring noises like she wants me to do something to her. Her hair smells like my crotch.

Toshimi smells like a mixture of roses and talcum powder. The next afternoon at work, we are talking about fashion—that is Toshimi's favorite subject—and she mentions she is going to a club that night, a venue in Ebisu where an African guitarist is playing. She'll be with a few friends from college. As she says this, she just leaves it out there, like I can come if I want, but she doesn't make it seem like she's asking.

But when I show up at the club by myself, wearing a Gaultier hooded jacket and these expensive Belgian boots I picked up at Isetan, Toshimi smiles and then asks me if she can get me a drink. She introduces me to the bartenders and the manager. Handsome Japanese guys in expensive black suits grin broadly as they greet me. Leading me to a table in the back, Toshimi introduces me to a couple of her friends: Ayumi and Rie. They are slender and dressed in designer black, like Toshimi. These girls are a different breed than Karen. Forget about race. This is a matter of sophistication and class. They reek of elitism and easily secured prestige. There is something sexy about women who haven't had to work for a thing.

Toshimi shows me to a plush burgundy bench and takes the seat next to me. On the table they have a bottle of Chivas that they are mixing with oolong tea and ice. Toshimi smiles as she pours me a drink in a tall glass and sets it down on a coaster.

The attentions of a beautiful woman uplift and inspire and make me feel at my absolute best. Suddenly, with Toshimi doting on me, I am the coolest guy in the joint, in this whole frickin' town. This girl, this club, my job, I am right where I should be. Don't you see? The rest of you here in this club have been reduced to bit players in my story. Perhaps this tale is predictable in its narrative arc—you can tell by my mischievous grin, suave demeanor and killer looks that I am the hero. There will be a few moments of peril, dire circumstances and surprising twists, but you know from my Roger Moore-esque sangfroid as I entered the club that I will emerge triumphant. I get the girl, the drugs, the money, the fame. On a night like this, I am sure I will run the table.

The Nigerian guitarist plucks quiet, complicated songs that are vaguely reggae-influenced. He wears sunglasses in the smoky club, and while he plays, he leans back and smiles, as if to admire his own finger work. The music is sedate yet sensual: my soundtrack. Toshimi turns out to be a fan of African music—so much more sophisticated than Karen and her jazz torch songs. Toshimi's musical tastes seem to say that she goes to the source of things. Hope cigarettes and Scotch and oolong tea make me drunk and a little dizzy. Toshimi tells me about a trip to Africa. She was in Zanzibar. There was a British guy. He came to Tokyo. He's gone.

I struggle to envision Toshimi in Africa. While the music plays, the only images that flicker to my mind are great herds of wildebeests migrating along the Zambesi. And those parasites some Africans have. These worms that get into your bloodstream and then poke their heads out your legs. The only way to remove them is to wrap a stick around the head and then wait for the worm to crawl out on its own. The process can take years and feels like a drill boring into you. What a courageous girl this Toshimi must be. Despite her gentility and docile feminine sexuality, she is unfrightened by thundering wildebeest herds and deadly parasites. She puts other women to shame.

After the guitarist finishes his set, Toshimi and I stroll toward Ebisu Station to the Magenta Overhigh, an expensive, rectangular bar with stainless-steel counters along both sides, each of them charging $20 a drink. Her friends tag along. By now their only function is to witness our mating ritual. That's what we are doing. It is pleasantly reassuring, like being lost in a car and suddenly turning and realizing you're on a familiar road. Everything is proceeding just as it should. She likes me. I like her. And we are winding our way, like a sailboat tacking against a gentle breeze, toward our destination. We all know it, even Ayumi and Rie, and now it is a matter of patience and banalities. Little conversations. Witty jokes. I relate childhood stories that show me in a rascally positive light. Toshimi tells me about how she grew up near here and attended International School in Meguro.

At some point, while we are sitting there, I take her hand in mine. We lock eyes for a moment. She quickly turns away.

It will be a slow, pleasing seduction. We finally kiss a few nights later. We haven't made love yet. But in my heart, I know what I have done to Karen is worse than betray her. I am moving on.

At dusk a few days later I am walking down the narrow street from Kagurazaka Station to my apartment. The fluorescent light spilling from windows and shopfronts casts a silvery pall over the sidewalk. A weak, misty drizzle has left pinprick beads of water on the hoods of parked cars. The pavement is dark with moisture. The air smells like wet concrete.

When I turn the corner to my street, I see a ghost. A white, sagging skeleton hung with degenerating, dangling flesh staggers toward me. There are more wrinkles than skin on this naked woman—she must be a woman, for there is no male organ in sight. And those white sacks of what seem like cottage cheese swaying in front of this ghost's belly would have to be breasts. This must be a demon, I'm thinking. This is like some peculiar Lafcadio Hearn story where the spirit appears naked and grotesque. But why now? Has my infidelity to Karen earned me this sort of condemnation?

I look behind me. There is no one. Just the cars rushing by on Sotobori Dori. I am alone with my demon lurching toward me, her skin sickly white in the mist, the flesh from her arms jiggling with her uneven steps as she limps up the street. She has no teeth. Her eyes seem wild and unfocused. I shiver once because I never expected any spirits to be this run-down. This is one rotten and decayed zombie, but she seems unthreatening and, in fact, a little bit confused. As she gets closer, I stand back to let her pass.

It's Obasan Tango, the granny next door who is making a run at being the oldest person in Shinjuku Ward. She must have gotten out somehow. I'm not sure what I should do. She's so old and . . . naked. You really don't want to touch old naked people. But if I don't stop her, she might make it all the way to Sotobori Dori and get hit by a car. She would probably explode on impact.

Forget about the oldest-person prize. I hold my breath and grab Obasan Tango by the wrist. It feels like raw chicken. She stops and turns to me.

"Osamu-kun," she says in Japanese, mistaking me for someone else. "Can you tell me where the toilet is? I've forgotten my slippers."

She looks down at her feet. Slippers are the only thing she *is* wearing.

Finally, Mr. and Mrs. Tango come running up the street, panting. "Obasan, Obasan," they are saying. When she sees that I have Obasan Tango safely by the wrist, Mrs. Tango begins patting her chest. *"Yokata, yokata."*

They both bow deeply with gratitude when they reach me. I have saved Obasan Tango. In fact, as Mrs. Tango hurriedly explains to me, the woman in Yotsuya has just died. I have saved the oldest person in Shinjuku Ward. I am a hero.

A ceremony has been scheduled. The ward boss will come by with a medal, a plaque and an envelope stuffed with cash to give to the Tango clan as they proudly stand around a propped-up Obasan Tango. Mrs. Tango had been making a bath for Obasan Tango, and while they had managed to stand her upright, she was seeing if she still fit into any of her old kimonos. When Mrs. Tango went to the closet, Obasan Tango saw the opportunity and bolted, miraculously bounding down a flight of stairs to run naked up the street.

"We are so lucky you live here, Karl," Mrs. Tango says later, when Obasan Tango is safely tucked away in her futon, sucking on rice gruel through her glass tube. "You have saved her life. *Ganbatte* Obasan."

Yet my heroism, recounted in my weekly column, is the subject of intense discussion around the office. In the past my editors have let me write endlessly about soccer, the horrors of English teaching, even a service piece rating various brands of cough syrup; yet for some reason, they object to my story of saving Obasan Tango. What they find so distasteful is her nudity. Did she have to be naked?

If you put her in clothes, I explain, you kind of take the edge off it. Naked, and the story becomes a little creepy.

"But it's so disrespectful," says Mr. Tsugui.

"And she's the oldest person in Shinjuku," echoes Mr. Ogawa. "We can't say she was naked."

I don't see why not. This is supposed to be journalism. I was there, and believe me, she was naked. And old.

Then the editors decide to refer the matter to the president of the newspaper. For an afternoon I struggle to understand what is happening here. Suddenly my story has to be vetted by the president? Last week I did an entire column about the virtues of slot-car racing versus newer, slotless track racing, and nobody said a word. My book reviews, my movie reviews, all of them were arguably more controversial than this, yet none of them roused the ire of anyone in the company. None, as far as I could tell, were even read by anyone in the company.

Then Toshimi comes over and stands docilely by my chair, smiling awkwardly, her hands fluttering for a moment before she folds them behind her back. "Hi."

Behind her I can see them all. Ogawa. Watanabe. Kyodo. All the editors. All the washed-up ex-journalists. They see Toshimi flirting with me. Something in our body language must give away that we are together. And that drives them crazy. It was one thing for this punk to come in and start writing half the newspaper; it's quite another when he starts banging the cutest Japanese girl in the office. I have transgressed some unspoken barrier. They will not forgive me for this. I don't know if it is jealousy or old-fashioned racism, more likely a combination of both. If a piece of ass like Toshimi is out of their reach now, they still don't want it in the paws of a mongrel like me.

That night Toshimi and I have sex for the first time. She is quietly powerful in bed, her moans coming from deep in her lungs and her panting heavy and steady like the chugging of a train. She likes to talk about sex in her broken English. She says "hold me" when she means "fuck me."

"Don't shoot in me," she pleads as I'm about to come.

I pull out, ejaculating all over her tightly cropped black pubic hair.

The next day, the editors reject a book review I've written on the grounds that I haven't sufficiently quoted the book in question.

It is a bright, sunny day and Toshimi and I go up onto the roof, where I fuck her standing up against the stairwell.

The day after that, Ogawa tells me they are going to try someone else out as a movie reviewer.

I convince Toshimi to suck me off in the third-floor bathroom after the production staff has gone home.

My job is reduced to checking the business-page heads and subheads.

One morning I open a competing newspaper and find that Nathan Applesworth is now writing a twice-weekly column entitled "All Things Japanese."

By the time the Shinjuku ward chief comes to present Obasan Tango with her medal, the paper tells me I cannot cover the story myself. They send another reporter.

As a neighbor and the hero who saved Obasan Tango, I have to attend and am given a place of honor with the Tango family, standing next to Obasan Tango, who looks more alert than she's ever looked. There are bright lamps on black poles set up in the Tangos' tatami room, cloying the whole scene with too much light. A television crew stands by. For the special occasion, Obasan Tango has been forced into a blue, gray and silver kimono with a crane and water pattern on it. It strikes me as a bit inappropriate for this type of ceremony. Shouldn't she be in something gray or black?

They have propped her up and strapped her into a board like paramedics use to move a spinal injury victim. If you nailed her arms up so they were horizontal, this would look like a crucifixion. Obasan Tango eyes me once. No, she's looking past me. She must be planning her next break.

The ward chief is a stocky man with gray-streaked black hair greased back into a pompadour. He has bushy eyebrows and a wide, flat nose that is uneven and long like the thumb of a baseball mitt. He is accompanied by lesser civil servants and what seems like a public relations man who is flitting about the place, making sure everyone is standing in the right place for the official photograph, which he will also be taking. Oblivious to the fact that she is the cause of all this hubbub, Obasan Tango catches my glance at one point. I can tell by her look that she wants an explanation. What is going on here? I don't know how to tell her that it's all for her.

"What did I do?" her eyes seem to be asking.

"You stayed alive."

Mrs. Tango combs her purple hair and smiles. Mr. Tango snuffs his cigarette in a green ceramic ashtray. The two daughters fold their hands at their waists. I try to smile. The ward chief presents the medal, the cash, a box of mikans and a honeydew melon in a small wooden crate. There are hearty banzais all around and then a toast of first-growth sake. Obasan is given a cup and a straw. She drinks greedily. Then moans. Then falls asleep, strapped upright in place.

The rest of us keep drinking cold sake and eating skewered chicken and raw fish until we are bloated. Mr. Tango keeps opening these Asahi tallboys and making me drink glasses of beer and we all shout hearty *kampais* for Obasan Tango, who, horizontal on her futon, may as well be dead.

At midnight I stagger back to my futon. I plop myself down. What is my next move in the office? I don't know. How am I going to get back my reviews and columns? My life seems to be shrinking. From my own column to editing heds and deks. I can't stand this diminution. Even with Toshimi, with Karen, with all the sex in my life and this apartment in Tokyo—and don't forget, I am a neighborhood hero—I relentlessly yearn for more. That's why this is happening. It must be time for me to move on. Even if they give back my column, beg me to write two broadsheet-page reviews summing up the career of Junichiro Tanizaki, I will refuse. I must refuse. Wouldn't that be regression? Like going back to Kugenuma and becoming an English teacher. I will miss the paycheck, but I can always borrow some more money from my mother. I have a closet with three good suits hanging in it. I'm dating two ladies. By all external appearances, I am still living very large.

There is a knocking at my door. Karen stands there, wearing a brown skirt and a fringed leather jacket. She looks like fucking Annie Oakley with her wet hair and those cowboy boots. She's drunk, her makeup streaking a little bit around the eyes.

"Can I stay?" she's slurring. She needs words with hard consonants. I shrug. She tromps in and sits down on the entryway steps, struggling to kick off her cowboy boots. The entryway fills up with the smell of wet leather, cigarettes and damp feet.

"Where have you been?" I ask.

"I had a few at Rolling Stone," she says.

I've been to Rolling Stone with her before. It's an embarrassing scene: Karen all hopped up, dancing around and singing to "Can't You Hear Me Knocking" with a few drunk Japanese guys.

Standing unsteadily, she shuffles through the kitchen to my bedroom—it's the only room in the apartment. I follow her, crawling back into the futon, pulling the thick *kagebuton* over me. Rolling over, I see Karen wrestling her blouse over her head, and for a few moments I see her stomach, pallorous, white, and then her tits encased in their black wire-frame bra. Karen needs heavy bras with elaborate support systems. The Occidental opposite of Toshimi's delicate, budding, almost adolescent breasts. Finally she is naked and climbs into bed with me. Immediately she begins groping for my penis, running her hand down my leg, and then she starts kissing and licking my chest and my stomach, and then she's back to work on my dick, aggressively jamming it into her mouth. She's smoked too many cigarettes and had too many drinks and her mouth feels dry and scratchy. There is something mechanical about the way she goes down on me, as if whenever she gets near a penis she just wants it in her mouth. And when her mouth is this chafing, that's not where you want to put your penis. We're both drunk and forget to turn off the fluorescent light.

I push her away. Not now. I don't want this now.

She sighs. The room is bright, and I feel as if I'm looking

down on the two of us lying on this cheap futon in this tiny room. This girl with her mousy brown hair and her freckled shoulders and her small back. What a bad perspective.

Karen starts whimpering. Now she's crying.

"What?" I ask.

"I thought sex would work," she says. "But no, I'm losing you."

She's right. I am past her.

The next morning, we are both asleep when the doorbell rings. I fumble for the clock. Seven A.M., too early for Mrs. Tango to be bringing me breakfast. Climbing unsteadily onto my knees, I take my robe from the back of a folding chair. Sliding into it, I step over Karen, who sleeps making quick, short gulping noises. The sound is cute, almost canine in its rhythm. Morning half-light is disorienting; I almost bash my knee into a bookcase before I stumble into the kitchen and reach for the front door. Who else could it be but the Tangos? No one ever visits me.

"Hi." Toshimi's wearing jeans and a black mock turtleneck. Her hair is tied back carefully into a tight chignon, and her glasses are slid into the pulled-back strands, the tortoise earpieces disappearing into her black hair. In the chilly morning, she looks beautiful, her skin unblemished and her lips pink as a cat's tongue.

"I wanted to see you. I missed you," she says, smiling.

I can tell she is waiting for me to reach out to her, to pull her in and tear into her. What's called for here is a carnal session right on the floor of the kitchen. I know that. She knows that.

How do I keep her out? "It's awfully early."

"We can sleep."

I can hear Karen rustling in the futon behind me. If Toshimi peered over my shoulder, she could see Karen's prostrate form in the futon. I loom large to block the doorway. "N-now's not a great time," I stutter. "Maybe later."

Of course she knows something's wrong. I was so eager just

the day before in the third-floor bathroom, and now I won't even let her into my apartment. There's someone here, I tell her, a friend, he's asleep.

Just then, Karen moans and turns over, sitting up to see what's going on. Toshimi can see over my shoulder: Karen's freckled back, the long hair.

I don't even bother telling Toshimi it's not what she thinks. Because I don't even know what I think.

Toshimi leaves without saying a word. I call after her a couple times, but she keeps on going. I slide into some flip-flops and chase after her, down the open hallway, the stairs, out into the windy streets. After following her for a block, I feel stupid in my bathrobe. I stop. What a mistake, I think, as I watch her go. She's really great. I really like the ones who dump me.

By the time I make it back to bed, Karen is getting dressed. She's in her bra and panties and turning her skirt right side out. Before she can get dressed, I grab her shoulders from behind and start kissing her neck. She pauses, takes a few deep breaths and then sighs as if to say why not. We fuck violently for the rest of the morning. In between my orgasms, I go down on her wet pussy and she sucks me off and I rub my cock on her tits and in her face. She keeps saying in her nastiest, nasaliest Australian accent, "Come on, you can fuck me harder than that." We both have sour breath and taste of come and sweat. She comes a half-dozen times. When we are finally done, she says, "God, I feel like I've had a pole shoved up me," and then she cries. When she leaves, a few tears dropping onto her fringed jacket, the metal door closing behind her, we're both sad, because we know this is the last time we're going to do it.

I don't have any more girls. And I am going to quit my job.

I buy some Sariam cough syrup and guzzle it on the sidewalk. My scalp tingles. I cap the bottle, tossing it in a metal waste basket. It is late afternoon, and a few other pedestrians share the narrow street with me. I am wearing my black Yamamoto suit. A beautiful woman walks toward me. Short, with pale skin, wearing a thigh-length beige raincoat, she quickly turns away when I smile at her. We pass each other. We keep going our separate ways.

Where is my big life?

NIPPLES AND VODKA EXPRESS

The only mistake they made was not killing him.

None of the bouncers working at SuperPussy that Tuesday night could have guessed that the *farang*—foreigner—who showed up at midnight would change their lives forever. A big man, immense by Thai standards, he bounded up four steps through the curtained doorway and eased himself into an upholstered booth in the back so that he was level with the stage and the dancers who had plastic numbers safety-pinned to their bathing-suit tops. His six-foot-two-inch, two-hundred-and-ten-pound frame was clad in a silk Versace print top, embroidered MCM tracksuit pants, a fat, diamond-encrusted Rolex Daytona and a distinctive platinum pinky ring thick as a plumbing fixture, featuring an onyx cobra-head setting with emerald eyes. The bouncers and doormen guessed he was drunk when he came in; he had that glazed, haughty leer they had come to associate with drunken *farangs* on Patpong. But being drunk had never gotten anyone barred from a Patpong strip joint, and the guy looked ready to part with a few thousand baht on liquor and women. Drunk foreigners are what Patpong is all about.

And even when the guy became belligerent, calling out for vodka and spitting the first sip of the first bottle onto the magenta carpet, the Thai bouncers—most of them retired kickboxers and prizefighters—didn't move to oust the burly foreigner. No harm in letting him play the big man, allowing him to think he was impressing the ladies with his discerning taste in vodka. The one thing they were having trouble figuring out was where the swarthy *farang* was from. The girls he had called over to his table found it difficult conversing with him—his heavily accented English was hard for them to understand. He could have been German, maybe Finnish.

He had already downed half a bottle of Stolichnaya and had been throwing five-hundred-baht notes around generously and, despite his churlish manner and arrogant demeanor—he flicked the remnants at the bottom of each shot glass onto the carpet— the manager told the boys to leave him alone. The manager, a thin, nervous man wearing a knockoff Armani suit and sitting near the door, wringing his hands and fending off complaints from the bar girls, told his staff to keep a close eye on the foreigner. But be discreet, the manager insisted, don't let him know he is being watched.

The big foreigner had gathered three of the girls around him at the table and was snuggling up with one of them, #35, while another, #60, sat on his lap, kissing his neck. The girls were doing their usual best to get this well-heeled foreigner to cash them out for the night—to pay the bar in order to take them home—so they could go with him back to his hotel or take him back to their apartments where the real fun, i.e., moneymaking, could begin. They could tell by the clothes, the watch, that weird ring with the cobra, that this was a fat cat, the sort of *farang* who could turn a good week into a great month. But he just kept drinking, and the more he drank, the worse his mood became. As he grew despondent, his thick slabs of cheek muscle sagged into a frown and his bulbous, red-as-raw-steak lips clamped shut. He seemed to be thinking, his cleft chin bobbing as he pensively drank his vodka. The celebratory mode of earlier in the evening was gone, and now, as he gazed at the girls onstage, the cashiers, the Thai bouncers, the glistening mirror ball, he began to seem angry.

But that didn't dissuade the girls. "You horny me," said #35, a tall, dusky beauty whose boob-job perfect breasts broke in fleshy waves over her too tiny bikini top. "You super horny me."

She rubbed against his MCM tracksuit bottoms.

But the big foreigner only shook his head, as if weary of advances from ladies of the night. Smirking at the gaudy, carnal spectacle before him, he lashed out and viciously grabbed #35 by the bikini bottom, ripping the Day-Glo orange poly-rayon blend off her, exposing a white Kotex pad that glowed purple in the club's black light. And while Lynyrd Skynyrd's "What's Your Name" blasted on the club's sound system, the foreigner swiped at the Kotex and revealed that #35 was actually what is known on Patpong as a *katoey,* or lady-boy. She was a transsexual, one of many who work in Patpong's bars.

The foreigner laughed, tossing the Kotex aside while the humiliated #35 hissed a stream of Thai profanities, vowing his/her revenge and stomping through the bar to the girls' dressing area.

"Your women are faggots," the foreigner said in English. He spat in the face of the two other "girls" seated next to him, turned over the low table he had been sitting at and threw a glass against the mirror across the bar. Now standing, he seemed immense, like a professional wrestler, and while he leered, the Thai bouncers who had gathered around the table backed away. They parted and let the foreigner pass between them.

After he was out the door, the posse of bouncers took off after him, joined by #35, now dressed in a black T-shirt, jeans and high-heeled shoes, her makeup precisely reapplied.

The burly *farang* was admitted a little before dawn to Samitivej Hospital, suffering from multiple stab wounds, severe contusions and lacerations indicative of being slashed with a straight razor. His wristwatch and wallet were gone, but whoever had worked him over had been unable to pull the pinky ring from his swollen, broken finger. The flesh of his face had actually been peeled back in several places, exposing the off-white bones of the skull, a few remaining teeth and a bloated, mangled tongue. When he was admitted, his scalp was so thickly matted with blood that his hair appeared black, causing the admitting nurse to believe he was an abnormally large Thai. It was only upon cleaning him up that attending nurses and physicians realized this man was a foreigner.

What they did not know was that this man was Gennady M., a Russian "businessman" living in Bangkok. The staff of Super-Pussy had beaten up and left for dead Naddy the Pimp.

The only mistake they made was not killing him.

Trey had arrived in Bangkok two weeks before me. And he had already availed himself of some of the most lax pharmaceutical laws in Asia to get so loaded on Sosegon and Valium and ethyl-amphetamine that by the time I flew into Don Muang and made my way to the King's Corner and found him there, bending over a badly scarred pool felt and a freshly racked diamond of chipped nine-balls while a Filipino band caterwauled through "Livin' Lovin' Maid," he was genuinely surprised to see me. Not because he didn't know I would be arriving today or what flight I would be taking or that we were supposed to meet later, tomorrow or next week. But because he had totally forgotten I was coming.

Which was surprising, considering Trey had originally been disappointed that we wouldn't be flying together to Bangkok. He had to go for visa reasons: he lived in Tokyo on ninety-day tourist visas, so had no choice but to leave the country every three months. I had a better deal in terms of resident status: as a child of a Japanese national, I had a *nikkeijin,* or "Japanese descendant," stamp in my passport, which allowed me to stay as long as I liked or to come and go as I pleased. So when Trey's ninety days had once again expired, he asked me to join him on a foray to

Bangkok. He said the world was hungry for stories about Thailand. Japan was all played out, he reasoned, it was time to discover a new territory. There were enough stories for both of us. In fact, he'd already convinced an American men's magazine to assign him a piece on a Harvard MBA who had become a champion kickboxer in Thailand.

At that point, writing for an American men's magazine sounded sumptuously cool, like Trey had been transformed into Hunter Thompson or Gay Talese while I was still writing stories for Inflight magazines about shoes and cameras and these special kind of cold noodles that were a delicacy up in Sendai. Essentially I was writing glorified press releases that were published in ridiculously glossy magazines perused by passengers who, strapped to their seats in metallic tubes hurtling through the stratosphere at seven hundred miles per hour, were literally captive audiences. And I still doubt they read those stories.

The work paid well enough, about $1,500 for the longer pieces—like the story about the single-lens reflex camera—and $750 for the shorts: the regional cold-noodle piece was typical of this length. And Trey and I did eke out a living producing stories for most of Asia's Inflight magazines. Think of an Asian carrier and I could tell you not only the name of their magazine but also the editor's name and fax number, the pay rates, pay schedules, even their formats and any redesign plans that were in the works. The stories were easy, requiring that I didn't write anything controversial, vaguely profane and/or salacious. And the same story could usually be turned around and sold to Cathay Pacific's *Discovery*, All Nippon Airways' *Wingspan* and Korean Air's *Morning Calm*—as long as I had good pictures.

And while I made my living writing for these complimentary magazines, I also had some occasional success getting assignments from American and English magazines, but none as storied and prestigious as the one for which Trey was now writing. I was jealous. Just a week before, we were both sitting in Trey's tiny Azabu Juban apartment cooking up Inflight-magazine ideas: flower arranging? He'd done it, for *Discovery*. Kimonos? I'd done it, for *Wingspan*. Japanese jazz music? He'd done it. Car design? I'd done it. It was hard thinking of ideas that were boring enough for an Inflight magazine but also lent themselves to the glossy, four-color, full-page photos that were the mainstay of Inflight editorial. It was then that I thought of cameras. Japanese loved cameras. They practically invented them. Okay, they didn't, not even close. But they did come up with the single-lens reflex mechanism that all modern cameras employed. That story sold immediately. Then I thought of shoes, and I read about noodles somewhere, and I was on a roll. Trey came up with tea ceremony, which I had to admit was a natural. And it had just been sitting there.

But the next day, after faxing to this men's magazine in New York a proposal that I told him was a nonstarter—who in America cares about kickboxing, even if the subject is an American?—the famous editor himself calls Trey, wakes him up at four A.M. Tokyo time, and tells him yes, we want to do this for our sports issue. He tells Trey they'll pay him $5,000 for the story and they'll cut him an expense check that will be DHL'd to Tokyo or Thailand or wherever Trey wants it sent. Would $4,000 in expenses suffice? Suddenly Trey doesn't care about Inflight magazines or the tea ceremony anymore.

He still wanted me to join him in Bangkok. It would be fun, he assured me. And I knew it would be. The last time we were there, we'd had a blast doing all the usual things guys in their early twenties do when they're in a country where hookers and drugs are plentiful and cheap. So I told him I would go, but after I had finished my stories about cameras and shoes. I needed the money, I explained. Actually, I had a few hundred thousand yen in the bank, and the passengers of All Nippon Airways and Cathay Pacific would have been no more uncomfortable for the duration of their flights without my contributions. What I really wanted to do was land a juicy assignment of my own, to fly into Bangkok powered by another big American glossy that would pick up my bills and smooth the path to high-octane Asian hedonism. In other words, I wanted to arrive as Trey's equal.

Yet despite all my midnight faxing of sexy story ideas to New York, no one was interested in sponsoring my visit to Bangkok. And so my arrival, rather than signaling the convening of two similarly statured magazine pros, was almost an admission on my part that for now, Trey was ahead—as a writer and, in our world, as a person. But he would at least be glad to see me, I reasoned.

The middle-aged Thai woman working behind the desk at the Federal Hotel handed me a note when I asked for Trey's room. It said simply:

"Please deliver all faxes and payments to the King's Corner."

I slung my Adidas duffel bag back over my shoulder and took a taxi down to Patpong to find Trey.

He looked up from his fresh rack, and his blue eyes widened with surprise. "Karl, what are you doing here?" His long dirty-blond hair was loose and hung around his slightly freckled face. If you caught just a quick glimpse of him here, you might guess he was a surfer from California, temporarily stopping off on his way to Bali or Irian Jaya. He had that broad-toothed smile, the prominent, aquiline nose and those enthusiastic, appraising eyes. But Trey wasn't from California, not even close. He grew up in Westchester, New York, attended college in Virginia and had lived in Manhattan for a few years before taking off for Asia. As far as I know, he has never even stood up on a surfboard.

And now, with that openmouthed gape, the beginnings of a smile on his face, the way he jerked upright, sending the pool cue skittering on the wet concrete floor—he was really surprised, not that I had arrived this evening instead of the morning, or today instead of tomorrow, or this week instead of next, but that I was here at all. It was as if he had completely forgotten I even existed. Which was odd, considering how much he had wanted me to come along on this adventure.

But now that I was here, he seemed eager to make the best of it, ordering Cokes for us, introducing me to Song and Bin, two beautiful Thai hookers who, having grown impatient with Trey, had started the game of nine-ball without him. They stalked the table after the break, as if probing the left balls for weaknesses. And they turned out to be robotically efficient pool players, cracking and sinking masses, combinations and banks with almost mechanical precision. I'd never seen women do anything with that sort of athletic exactitude. Even the report of the cue ball striking its target was crisp and almost martial-sounding.

But as soon as the nine-ball was sunk, they reverted to giggling and flirting and pushing a finger between Trey's lips when he yawned. We had taken rattan seats atop the three steep steps from the street. The bar was really just a covered concrete platform on which stood four independent rectangular galleys with two Thai girls in each of them, opening Klosters and Singhas to serve the *farangs* and Thais who sat on tall, rickety bamboo and red-cushioned stools.

Trey shook his head and looked over at me, his eyelids lowered and wavering over irises shot through with spidery veins. His pupils, however, were dilated and shining. A result, I knew, of the Ampo-Dentinil Ethylamph capsules that Trey emptied out and chewed like M&M's. The result of heavy ingestion of this low-grade speed was euphoric wakefulness that verged on a mild psychosis. On one occasion when I'd chewed a half dozen of these tablets, I'd spent fourteen straight hours in a paranoid delusion at a Roppongi newsstand, flipping through Japanese magazines, suspecting that somewhere in the swirling kanji was my name and some scandalous details about me. As I said, a mild psychosis.

Trey had obviously been crunching away on the stuff. In fact, he'd been awake so many straight nights that Song and Bin had taken to calling him Robocop, in tribute, apparently to his tirelessness.

How was his story going?

He'd been out to the gym. Gone to see the Harvard guy. Even gone to Ratchadamnoen Stadium to see him fight. That story was a no-brainer. What he was on to now, he told me, was this thing about a Russian pimp who was missing.

The first time I ever truly felt that I could have anything I wanted was two years prior to this current trip, when I was twenty-three and Trey and I were in Bangkok for the first time. The night we arrived, we stumbled down Patpong and gazed in wide-eyed, slack-jawed, postadolescent wonder at the array of beautiful women displayed and proffered. Patpong, that gaudy, fecund strip of Bangkok's Banrak district, is the center of the city's notorious sex-tourism industry, a dense cluster of bars, strip shows and bordellos where any salacious desire and carnal perversion may be sated. Bangkok was the first place I ever saw women shooting darts from their vaginas to pop balloons, ring bells and hit bull's-eyes; watched them remove live snakes from themselves, open beer bottles, douse flames, light cigarettes and hatch ducklings. I have witnessed every possible coupling of every possible gender on Bangkok's adult-theater stages, and have seen women lowered from the ceiling on fake Harley-Davidsons, in giant champagne glasses and, in one memorable show, on a tranquilized donkey painted as a zebra which the woman proceeded to—well, you get the idea: anything goes.

Despite prostitution being officially illegal in Thailand, there are an estimated three hundred thousand Thai citizens directly involved in offering sex services. Indeed, a visit to Patpong or any other Thai brothel district leads one to believe that not only is prostitution legal but authorities actively encourage it. Thailand actually has a long-standing concubinary tradition that makes it socially permissible for a man to keep several mistresses or carry on extramarital relations. Even Thai kings until recently kept *mia noi* (minor wives), and wealthy businessmen, *jaopor* (gangsters) and politicians still indulge in socially sanctioned extramarital dalliances. While most of the customers at the tony brothel districts appear to be foreigners, the vast majority of the Thai sex industry caters to Thai citizens.

The Patpong girl and similar "gold badge" (gold for the color of their plastic tags) escorts are at the top of an intricate hierarchy of call girls, bar girls, strippers, masseuses and streetwalkers, ranging in cost from fifty baht ($1.25) to ten thousand baht ($250). Traditionally, the girls who dance on the bars at Patpong have been the sex industry's elite, those who have a chance to latch on to visiting Americans, Australians and Europeans and parlay a night in the sack into big money. But for the past few years, the Patpong high rollers have been wealthy Asian businessmen in town to buy in to Bangkok's now burst real estate bubble or purchase equity on Thailand's now collapsed stock market. "Ten years ago Americans were number one," a brothel keeper in Pattaya told me, "now, Hong Kong Chinese, Singapore Chinese, Koreans and Japanese are number one. When they want a girl, they can pay top prices."

Yet sometimes girls will not be girls. Many foreigners are dismayed when they discover that the Patpong heartbreaker whom they've set their sights on is actually a *katoey* or lady-boy, that curious transsexual admixture who, with the help of Adam's-apple reductions, breast implants, collagen injections, skull planings and intense hormonal infusions, often are the most fetching creatures in the bar. If you've never been to Thailand, then you may have trouble believing this, but the best-looking ladies in Patpong bars are too often men, and that, as Naddy the Pimp well knew, is a Bangkok fact. Naddy, on his first night in Bangkok, had actually been humiliated when he unknowingly picked up a lady-boy and was orally serviced by him/her before he pulled down her jeans and up jumped the truth. The experience had left him confused and angry—and bearer of a grudge against lady-boys that festered until that night at SuperPussy.

These gender surprises notwithstanding, a visiting Japanese or Chinese businessman could have found whatever he fancied in Bangkok's notorious brothels until recently. Anything, that is, except for a white woman. It was the demise of the Soviet Union that ultimately provided the only missing ingredient in Bangkok's sexual stew. Caucasian Russian women flooded into Bangkok by the thousands to ply the world's oldest profession. (Russian prostitutes are also back in large numbers in Shanghai, Macao, Saigon and Tokyo.) One American law-enforcement official in the Far East once told me, "The Russians have retaken their rightful place as the white trash of Asia."

The number of Russian visitors to Thailand has increased from a few hundred in the late eighties to seventy thousand a year today. Though Thai law-enforcement officials have constantly denied there being Russian mafia presence in Thailand, a quick visit to Pattaya, to any of the bedroom motels along Sukhumvit Soi III or to Spazo, a Bangkok nightclub, suggests the contrary. Bangkok police estimate that there are now at least five thousand Russian prostitutes in Thailand.

Gennady Malevich, the man a crew of Thai bouncers and one angry transsexual left bleeding in a Bangkok hospital, was a *bandity,* a gangster, a bad boy sporting jailhouse tattoos who flew to Thailand on the "Nipples and Vodka Express," the eight-and-a-half-hour-long, no-meal, no-movie, no-frills flight from Vladivostok to Pattaya. As a fifteen-year-old, Naddy had done his first "sit," or jail sentence, at a Soviet juvenile facility in Khabarovsk. After a subsequent sit at Osurisk Atna Hotka Labor Camp No. 3, where he received his green, black and red tattoos, Naddy heard about a Vladivostok "team," or gang, that intended to provide Caucasian women for visiting Japanese, Korean and Chinese businessmen lured by Siberia's abundant natural resources. He provided girls for the proposed five-star hotels and luxury resorts that were to lure the big Asian money. When the Asian tycoons never materialized—they were too smart to flock to icy, frigid Vladivostok, even if it meant a taste of exotic blond sexual delicacies—and a glut of blond ladies were left languishing in the front rooms of Vladivostok's seedy casinos, it was Naddy who decided if the money won't come to the girls, then he would bring the girls to the money. The Nipples and Vodka Express was born.

The Russian girls were the first white women to work in Bangkok's sex industry, and they immediately commanded prices even higher than the top Thai escorts. Asian businessmen apparently were willing to pay a premium for Caucasian, preferably blond, ladies. It was a status symbol for them, and they paid handsomely for the privilege. Soon, the Thai *jaopor* who had agreed to let Naddy bring in the ladies began to regret the relatively light tithe they were extracting from the Russian newcomers. Not only were they getting shortchanged by the Russians, but the Russians were also cutting into their core prostitution and escort-service businesses.

For Naddy, this was the best of times. Business was turning out to be more lucrative than he had ever imagined. He brought in several fellow *bandity,* began setting up girls down in Pattaya as well as in Bangkok, and within six months had built a bankroll of several hundred thousand dollars and was making plans to expand his business to Koh Samui and Phuket, two resort islands popular among visiting foreigners. His Sathorn penthouse had a view of Lumphini Park, and downstairs in the garage was a white Mercedes E320 he leased from a Thai dealer only too happy to roll a Benz off the lot in Bangkok's crashing economy.

For the first time in Naddy's life, he felt he could have anything he wanted. He even felt he could show up at a Patpong bar, get a little drunk and embarrass the local lady-boys who had humiliated him the first time he fell for their act in a Bangkok hotel room. Even if he went over the line and insulted a lady-boy or one of the bouncers, he reasoned, his connections with his Thai *jaopor* partners would keep him safe. After all, hadn't he been paying tens of thousands of dollars in U.S. currency as protection?

Trey had decamped from the Federal just a few days after arriving in Bangkok and moved in with Song and Bin and four other girls in a relatively modern flat—the Thai version of a convenience apartment—in a four-story ferro-cement building off Sukhumvit Soi VI. The girls slept there on foam beds with intricate Chinese-made white lace sheets when they weren't successful in picking up a foreign customer and returning to his hotel. They had their pork and basil with chili sauce delivered in white Styrofoam containers when they woke up at five or six in the evening. They also had drinks delivered, beer in bottles or cherry sodas that came in plastic bags with straws poking out of them.

A few nights after I arrived, while the girls trolled the bars looking for customers, Trey and I stayed back at the apartment. We were joined by Cameron, a pink-faced, chubby Australian with long graying hair. He wore a safari shirt tucked into a pair of jeans and a pair of sand-colored boots with thick tread. He was a journalist, he told me. But he was vague about what publication he actually worked for. From what I could gather, he did the oc-casional piece for an Australian wire service, which seemed even less rewarding than writing for Inflight magazines. As soon as he sat down, greeting Trey with a hearty "G'day, Robocop," Trey or-dered beers and Cokes in bags from the boy in the hall. In fact, I had noticed that Robocop was buying pretty much everyone drinks—the hookers, the Filipino band at the King's Corner, even the bartenders. All with the magazine's money. Before the drinks even arrived, Trey sent Cameron out with eight hundred baht to procure for us a film canister full of grainy brown heroin. Cam-eron returned sweating half-moons in the armpits of his safari shirt but with his balled fist around the plastic container of dope.

We poured the heroin into loosened-up cigarettes that made a sizzling sound when we lit them, the bitter fumes leaving a faintly medicinal aftertaste. For Trey, who had been grinding away on speed tablets for several days in a row, the effect of the opiate was to make him less aggressively voluble—he was actually capable of listening when Cameron spun out his stories of gun-fights in Patpong bars and foreign drug dealers hung from a tres-tle bridge in Pattaya and meth factories along the Burmese border and this Russian pimp who had been beaten to a pulp and left for dead. This whole world, the way Cameron told it, sounded fantastic and rich and full of great subjects. And I could see Trey taking all this in, these ideas that he and I both knew were good magazine stories. He even had a yellow legal pad on which I assumed he was scribbling story ideas. These were sexy stories we could sell to English and American magazines. One could make a living here as a writer, I realized. There was a lawlessness to this place—or was it just that we were too stoned and foreign to even understand the laws?—that lent itself to the kinds of stories young men are attracted to.

We smoked that brown heroin for six hours. You can't really sleep on the stuff; you nod a little, but then some demon in the dope kicks you awake again. You sit up almost with a start and then slowly begin somnolently drifting away. And you have little snatches of dreams, like you're able to peek into your subconscious for a moment or two and sneak a glimpse at the pipes and wires and hissing furnace of your own intellectual steam room. Mrs. Langston, my second-grade teacher, was there for an instant, standing in front of a chalkboard, her gray wool plaid skirt hiked improbably, disturbingly, high on her veiny, pale legs. And here was Mick Jones of the Clash, explaining that Protex was a brand of British condom. The whole time I'm thinking, This is pathetic: you mean this is what I think about when I think I'm not thinking? I sat up on the foam bed, resting my arms on my knees as I sipped soda from a baggy. Cameron was asleep, his fleshy pink face now vibrating with his thick, mucusy breathing.

Finally the girls came back home, clomping down the hall in their chunky heels, carrying their little black purses and almost shouting in their nasal, angry Thai voices. There were a half dozen of them, Song and Bin leading the way. Song pumped her fist once, cheering for Robocop, who roused himself and swallowed two more of the ethylamph tablets in an effort to stay awake. The girls had turned over the cardboard box that a CD player had come in and put it to use as a makeshift card table. They had broken their flimsy coffee table during another card game. Song had been slapping down her trump cards so hard the table actually snapped down the middle of the cheap veneer wood. It now languished in the corner like a passed-out whore.

The card game that started up now, as the girls unwound from their night of dancing and fucking, was the usual high-stakes, cardboard-banging affair. They played a game similar to hearts, with more side betting and a contract system similar to bridge, but by these rules, alliances could form and sunder midgame. It perfectly suited the catty nature of the girls, and watching the dazzling speed at which they shuffled, dealt, bid, bet and played was yet another lesson in human efficiency. If Song and Bin had wrenches or spot welders instead of cards in their hands, they might have assembled a car in a matter of minutes.

If you had to choose one of them as the more beautiful, I guess in terms of pure aesthetics it would have been Song. She was the more Chinese-looking of the two, with her perfectly oval face and long black hair. Each eye was like two crescent moons attached at the tips; her nose was small and perky—obviously the result of some cosmetic surgery—and her lips were almost preposterously fleshy, so bulked up on collagen they were like the features of a cartoon sexpot. In fact, with her surgically enhanced breasts and that overtly erotic mouth, she reminded me of the human equivalent of one of those bird species where one gender is gaudily plumaged to attract a mate.

The girls seemed to listen to Song, who had managed to rent this flat and shook them down every week to pay the rent. And Song, tall for a Thai woman, could be menacing or, conversely, portentously taciturn when she didn't get what she wanted, shaving her long, artificial fingernails with a straight razor and pointedly ignoring whomever had fallen out of her favor.

Bin, on the other hand, was more gentle, retiring, quiet, but in her arch way she was sexier than Song and everyone knew it. While Song had all the overt characteristics that were supposed to add up to sexiness, somehow they seemed too contrived and the sum ended up less than the parts. Bin was natural and comfortable with her looks. Her face wasn't as perfectly symmetrical as Song's, nor had her nose been surgically shaved to such pixieish proportions, but in the imperfection there was a cruel cast that drove foreign men wild. Bin was less talkative than Song, more prone to smoking Krong Tips and popping the knuckles of her long fingers while Song bleated away in her obscenity-laced Thai. I began to look at the two of them this way: if Song was Butch Cassidy, then Bin was the Sundance Kid. Everyone knew

Song ran the gang, but without Bin there really wasn't any gang at all.

Trey had finally fallen asleep, his hands tucked between his knees as he curled up into a fetal ball. Next to him was his yellow legal pad. I pulled it over to read what he had written there, but instead of notes on the kickboxer or story ideas or maybe something about this Russian pimp he kept babbling about and that Cameron had been describing, he was halfway through composing a garbled note to the famous editor in New York, asking for more expense money. Research was going well, Trey assured him, but it would take a bit more time and money. There were officials to be bribed—Trey spelled it "brided"—and he often had to take the kickboxers out to sing karaoke—he spelled it "Kirioke." The letter made me wonder what Trey had actually been doing, if he had done any research at all. Had Robocop just been sitting here getting loaded and hanging around with Thai hookers? I stood up to leave, and Bin followed me out into the hall. She had taken to giving me special attention whenever I showed up at the King's Corner, sitting in my lap or grabbing me from behind when I was about to make a pool shot. Bin, in her quiet, determined way, seemed to have decided that since Song had staked a claim to Robocop, then she should have me. I was flattered by Bin's attention, and when she spoke to me or refilled my Coke glass, it seemed it was because she genuinely liked me and not because she saw in me a potential revenue stream.

When I came out of the communal john, there was Bin, standing in her crisp white T-shirt and black jeans with her skinny legs, and she was smoking a cigarette that she now discarded, exhaling smoke and snuffing the butt on the floor. Being alone with her always made me a little uncomfortable.

"Look." She handed me a stack of photographs of herself in a cutaway one-piece bathing suit. She was posed on a white platform of some kind that looked almost like a gigantic wedding cake. Where could these have been taken, I wondered. In each of them Bin had one leg extended slightly farther forward than the other and stood with her hands on her hips, smiling for the camera and demurely tilting her head down. All the photos were virtually identical.

"Um, very beautiful." I didn't know what to say.

Bin took them back, nodding as if she had made her point. "Do you like me?" she asked.

I nodded. "Of course."

She wanted to come with me, she explained. She wanted to be with me, she told me, she wanted to love me.

And she was such a handsome girl that I was shocked when I told her I wasn't in the mood right now. Maybe later. And it was true, right then, I just didn't feel like it.

When Naddy regained consciousness, he remembered he had been at SuperPussy; he recalled busting the balls, literally, of a lady-boy, and stumbling out of the place searching for the keys to his Mercedes, and then he recollected a searing pain in his shoulder, several blows to the back of the head, something sharp and stabbing in his ribs, and that was it. Now he could barely move. He had a limited range of motion in one arm and one leg, could breathe with difficulty and felt persistent stinging sensations in his ribs and chest. His head was totally numb, as if wrapped in a gauze sheet. And he was blind.

The doctor told him he would regain his vision shortly, that they had laid wraps around his eyes until the swelling went down and they could make a decision on whether to graft skin or to attempt to stitch the remaining skin. Meanwhile, even through the massive doses of Demerol they were intravenously dripping into his vascular system, Naddy realized that he needed to be moved. Whoever had beaten him up, he guessed, must have left him for dead. When they found out who he was, and that he had survived, they would come back for him. He demanded that the doctor arrange an ambulance. When the doctor refused, he called two of his underlings, who brought a black satchel filled with purple and red Thai currency from which Naddy removed ten thousand baht that he stuffed in the doctor's apron. He was moved that day to Samrong General Hospital. Each day of his lengthy convalescence, he was transported from hospital to hospital, from Samrong General to Bangkok Christian to St. Louis Hospital, then back to Samitivej. As Naddy recovered, he had a regular nightmare that #35 was standing over him with a straight razor, cutting his pinky off to remove his ring.

When the swelling around his eyes had gone down and the wounds around his mouth and cheeks were healing, Naddy was shown several different options for how he wanted his eyes, nose and mouth reconstructed. His previously handsome face was now a fleshy blur of mangled lips, flaps of red, pustulating flesh and discolored abscesses. It would be a matter of skin grafts, hair transplants and some simple facial sculpting. The physicians assured him they could make him more handsome than he had been.

On a typical night at Spazo, a dimly lit wood-paneled nightclub near Bangkok's embassy district, the crowd of women by the bar is uniformly young, expertly made up and strikingly turned out in tight-fitting red and black leather skirts and bodysuits. With their long cigarettes, tall drinks and bored expressions, they are Czarist catwomen on the prowl for convertible currency.

The Russian girls know enough to stay away from Patpong. It was made clear to them by Naddy and his partners that the strip of bar and hustle venues was exclusively the domain of Thai working girls, boys and lady-boys. The Russians were set up at several bedroom motels or at one of the nightclubs where they would be able to operate out in the open.

The first few flights of Russian ladies to descend on Bangkok were savvy working girls who had acquired their trade in Russia's wild, wild east. They were professionals handpicked by Naddy and his partners for their looks and loyalty. Bangkok was an excellent opportunity for these ladies, a capital city ripe with new Asian money and connected via cheap flights to the rest of the world. If the girls played it right, they knew, then Bangkok could be the first stop on a long and profitable trail to a life of hard currency and easy living.

I had rented a spacious room with a small kitchen and veranda and private entrance in a bungalow off Banglamphu, on the river not far from Kao San Road. A short, elderly Indian woman who wore a blue dress like a nurse's uniform had let me the room for $300 a month. That reasonable rent, however, was belied by the fact that Miss Kuda charged extra for everything. Did I want a phone? My laundry done? Electricity? Running water? A mailbox? A front door? A padlock on that front door? A key to that padlock? Each of these was added on so the actual rent I paid was close to double that agreed upon. Her most attractive attribute as a landlord renting to *farangs* seemed to be her total indifference to her tenants' depraved behavior.

The rooms and bungalows all opened onto the same dirt courtyard, which had a desiccated bodhi tree in the middle and a few dusty, flowerless orchids in pots. I didn't see much of the other tenants, who were evenly divided between earnest young *farangs* who made a living teaching English and spent the rest of their time studying Thai, and older, dissipated foreigners who slept all day and brought home an endless series of whores in the late evening. Sometimes these girls would hang around for a few days, soaking as many baht out of their customers as they could, until the rate of return for each suck or fuck had diminished below the girls' own perception of their orifices' economic value.

My own neighbor was a short German in his sixties with a beard and mustache and wattle that hung from his neck and swayed as he walked. When we met, he told me he had been a sailor, a *kriegsmariner,* who retired here because his pension D-marks went a lot further in Bangkok than in Bremen. Kluter walked with a bowlegged shuffle, his extensively tattooed legs and ankles and sandaled feet making skidding noises along the dirt courtyard. It was pathetically obvious why he was here: the girls. Where else could a skinny, ugly, degenerating old German soak pick up a different girl every night and still afford to keep a roof over his head and eat three square meals a day?

"I am still strong," he said, flexing pale, flabby arms so that the anchor and mermaid and rum bottle and pirate ship and iron-cross tattoos didn't seem as distorted on his distended flesh as when he was at ease. But he was so skinny. And in the two weeks I'd been there, it was obvious he had lost even more weight. "I have better things than food for spending money on," he said, smiling and pumping his hips.

Indeed, his favorite girl was a dark-skinned Cambodian with sharp eyes, a flat nose and pronounced canines that made her look vaguely lupine. She was small and skinny, with tiny breasts like balled baby fists, and I didn't like to wonder about how old she was. Put it this way, in the States, I would have assumed a girl like this was still in junior high. Sometimes I would still be awake, sitting on the balcony nodding off from the heroin I'd been smoking or just bullshitting with Trey, when I'd see Kluter returning with his Cambodian girl. In the dark, you could barely make her out because of the variegated shadows cast by the bodhi tree, but you could see her eyes, white, cunning, appraising. They were the eyes of a thief.

I already knew, however, that Kluter had nothing worth stealing. A footlocker with a few old sailor's uniforms, a half-dozen terribly stained cotton polo shirts, his filthy trousers—Kluter refused to pay Miss Kuda any of the extras she used to pad the rent. There was also a Chinese-made Silverstar television and an old cassette player, and that was about it. Or perhaps I hadn't the stomach to take a real look around. His little room stank, of feces and sweat and urine. The sheets were flecked with old gray pubic hairs, blood stains and brown fecal spots all sprinkled over a backdrop of piss-and-jism yellow. How many hookers had he banged on those sheets? Kluter didn't know. He asked me to stay for coffee. He showed me how he used an old sock as a filter. I politely declined.

Bangkok was turning out in many ways to be a repeat of

Tokyo. My first assignment had been with *Sawasdee,* Thai Airways' Inflight magazine, a thousand words about Bangkok's insect markets. I had written it in about two days, going down to the market one afternoon and then visiting the bug mogul, who actually distributed most of Thailand's edible insects from his Chitlom offices. The story had paid only $500, but I felt I could probably resell it to one of the Japanese Inflight mags so it would net another $1,000 or so. Still, I was grateful for Trey's generous expense account, which allowed us to dine out and run a long tab at the King's Corner.

One afternoon we went to a go-cart track out past Sukhumvit, off the airport highway. Trey rented the little two-stroke powered steel-framed midget cars for all the girls, plus Cameron and me. Predictably, the girls were the best drivers, taking the kidney-shaped course with fighter-pilot-like efficiency, leaning into the curves with cigarettes dangling rakishly from their bubble-gum-pink lips. After a few laps I realized the driving wasn't as fun as it looked before strapping into one of the cars. I had imagined something more like bumper cars, where you tapped the other drivers in what was essentially a harmless arcade game. This was something else, the cars were hot and noisy and stank of gas, plus they seemed genuinely dangerous. I felt on several turns that I was perilously close to tipping the little red buggy. It was impossible to keep up with Song and Bin, and after being lapped by them for the second time, I drove into the pit lane, turning my car over to the attendants. I went inside and sat at the bar, watching them drive while eating a chocolate ice-cream novelty. Bin soon pulled in and came to join me.

"Finish?" she asked.

I nodded.

"I'm sorry we all passed you," she said.

I told her I had fun anyway.

"Robocop likes it." She pointed outside.

Indeed, Trey was now spinning by on the nearest of the track's curves, fist pumping in the air as he passed Cameron, who, being the heaviest of all of us, was relegated to the slow lane.

"Robocop is handsome," Bin told me.

For some reason I felt a pang of jealousy. But why? About a hooker saying my friend was handsome? Who cared? Was I that competitive?

"He's more handsome than you," Bin said matter-of-factly, without even looking at me.

I felt betrayed. Bin was the one who was supposed to like me. Trey had Song. He had the glamorous assignment from the famous magazine. Now even Bin had decided she liked him best. It only made sense, I supposed. When you're on a roll, you're on a roll.

"But I like you better," Bin said, turning to me. "Sometimes you look mean, but you also look strong. I like strong men."

I thanked her. But I didn't feel strong. I'd just revealed how much of a wimp I was on the go-cart track. I bought Bin an ice-cream novelty, which she ate a few bites of but then seemed to forget about as soon as she lit a cigarette. At that point, the outing to the go-cart track began to feel like a bit of a date, the conversation rotating back around to Robocop and then to the ice creams again—we really didn't have much in common. She was actually an ethnic Lao, sort of a poor cousin to the Thais, from northeastern Thailand, near the Lao border. Her first language hadn't been Siamese but a sort of twangy northern Thai-Lao hybrid. Her family still lived in a village named, it sounded like to me, Me So Sorry. She told me about her brother, who was still in school. He was angry at her and wouldn't speak with her anymore. Was it because she was a hooker? No— she shook her head—because she stopped sending money home. For the first time, as we talked, I could sense something vulnerable about Bin. I understood it was terribly important to her that we be together, that it meant something beyond just sex or money.

Bin and I went back to my bungalow from the go-cart track. It was early evening, and as the taxi was making its way back along Rama IV, she told me she was going to take a few hours off from work. She said I didn't even need to pay her. And when she told me that, she was looking deep into my eyes, like it really meant something.

Kluter was on his way out as Bin and I exited the taxi, and he gave me a big, openmouthed nod as we walked up the dirty path. Finally, he seemed to be thinking, this guy gets it.

Once we were in my bungalow, and Bin and I began kissing, I was surprisingly uninspired by the feel of her tongue and her lips. Usually I incline to overexcitement, to losing steam a little too early in the encounter. However, with Bin, I felt only the faintest stirring. I assumed my initial apathy would pass as soon as she began rubbing her hands against my army shorts, clutching me in her red-fingernailed hands. Instead I remained in repose. This had happened to me before. Once, in Tokyo, I had dated a very pretty Canadian photographer who for some reason didn't arouse me. I had even discussed this with Trey, who ascribed it to something he called pheromones. Everybody has a certain smell, he told me, comprised of these pheromones. You might not even be aware they're there, but if they don't tickle your pickle, then there's nothing you can do.

Now Bin had slipped off my shorts and underwear, and despite her oral ministrations, which were vigorous and, from a technical standpoint, first-rate, I was still flaccid, or at best half engorged. Perhaps if she took off her clothes. I needed visual stimuli. I stood up from the wood-frame bed and reached for her black tube top. She held her hands over her head and allowed me to wriggle it off her. She climbed out of her bra rather than having me unstrap it—a gesture I figured she'd learned to save precious time that clients would otherwise spend struggling to unclasp it.

Those breasts were the best that Asian surgery could produce—I'd seen them before back at her apartment, but now, with them jutting out before me, almost superhumanly perfect but still inspiringly mammalian in their roundness and firmness and their perfect, half-dollar-size nipples, I knew that this was what got men hard all over the world. Yet I was still not responsive. She set back to work sucking me off. Her mouth was lusciously moist, she swabbed her tongue up and down the shaft, but it may as well have been happening to the penis of the guy next door for all the good it was doing me. Why was this happening? She was a lovely woman here, offering me her sexual services, and yet I was incapable of anything beyond this little, pudgy, half-cocked erection. What the hell was wrong with me?

I began to grow impatient with my own inaction. And Bin's eager ministrations now began to feel irritating rather than pleasurable. I pushed her away, shaking my head, shrugging. Nothing doing. She tried to push back, forcing me down again, but this time I resisted and stood up, pulling my pants up from my ankles.

"No go," I told her.

"We can get you something," she suggested. "Some medicine."

"Maybe."

"I'll go get some," she volunteered. "I'll be right back."

No. Whatever mood we'd created had now been lost. I didn't want to resort to artificial stimuli, whether what she had in mind was manufactured by Pfizer or by a local brand with a name like Imperial Federation of a Hundred Lucky Tigers. When this had happened before, the Canadian photographer had been game enough to sleep over at my apartment and give it another try in the morning. She'd even gone on another couple dates with me, although by then it was clear that without the sex, there wasn't much reason for us to go out. I assumed Bin would hang around and perhaps we'd give it another try later. Maybe if we took a nap and then woke up, it would all just naturally work out.

But when I refused her offer to find a medical treatment for our problem, she began to sulk and grow increasingly embittered. That I didn't want to seek an immediate solution struck her as a rejection of her charms. But she was on to something. What was wrong with me? Could it be those pheromones again? That seemed unlikely, twice in six months at my age. I was still in the prime of my life, I'd had no lousy wounds, I shouldn't be wrestling with this sort of problem. By now I should have been taking advantage of Bin's generosity by banging her senseless. (I hated to think that I had once again come up short when compared to Trey. Song no doubt would have already filled Bin in on the wonders of Trey's amphetamine-enhanced performance.) Perhaps it was the dope I was smoking, the heroin I had been mixing with my tobacco. But that had never slowed me down before. In fact, quite the opposite: a mild dose of opiates in the past had allowed greater duration in my performance.

Bin was now gazing at me speculatively, as though asking herself the same question. She had pulled her bra back on and was turning her black tube top right side out. She was a professional, a working girl, and having a freebie metaphorically reject her sexual favors was an implicit rejection of who she was.

"You don't like me," she said. "You hate me."

"No, no, I like you, Bin. I think you're wonderful."

"Then why? Why are you not strong?" She held her arm up with a balled fist to illustrate what an erect phallus might look like, in case I didn't know.

"I don't know, Bin." I shrugged. "It happens. The more we talk about it, the worse it gets."

She shook her head and lit a cigarette. "I go now."

I told her I would meet her later, at the King's Corner. "I don't care," Bin said as she left.

I followed her as far as my porch, where I stood watching the circular motion of her trim, muscular ass as she tromped up the driveway. I felt awful.

Kluter had returned home and was also sitting on his porch, drinking a Kloster and shaking his head, watching Bin go. "Very nice."

He looked like a skeleton sitting there, pale and skinny beneath his stained white cotton shirt. I hadn't taken a good look at him in daylight for a long time. His face was drawn and sallow, with the shadows cast by the ridges of his eye sockets almost obscuring his metallic blue eyes. He was smiling, though, a big toothy grin that revealed his brown, receding gums.

I felt so inadequate that I wanted to confide in someone. I asked him if he'd ever had, you know, erectile dysfunction.

He didn't understand the question.

"Impotence."

He shook his head. He still didn't get it.

"No lead in the pencil. Mister Softee. A limp biscuit."

I made several gestures with my fingers to demonstrate a penis in repose, but nothing made any sense to Kluter.

"Penis kaput," I said.

Kluter sat up, suddenly concerned. "Kaput? With that one?" He gestured up the road after Bin.

I nodded.

"Oh *mein* God." Kluter banged his forehead, appalled at the waste. "You should have sent her over here. I would have fucked her for you."

He was supposed to be one of the best plastic surgeons in Bangkok, a gentleman employed by lady-boys who wanted to feminize their features or have a sex change done. He was duly accredited, properly licensed, board certified, in short, Naddy was assured by his attending physician at Samrong General Hospital that Dr. Wacharachaipong was no Chink scalpel cowboy. The doctor was capable, Naddy was told in a conspiratorial whisper, of making "a fish look like a dog."

Dr. Wacharachaipong may indeed have been a whiz at reconstructive facial surgery, at reducing Adam's apples or shaping faux clitorises. What he did not know how to do was reconstruct *Western* facial features. All his previous operating experience had been on Thai people, on Asian faces. Naddy was his first *farang,* and the resulting surgery left the Russian looking like a badly conceived admixture of Caucasian and Asian features. With his immense head and his new, small, almost effeminate eyes and pert button nose, Naddy resembled a Down's syndrome child grown into middle age. It was a mistake, a genuine plastic-surgery disaster. After performing the operation, even before the wraps were off the patient, Dr. Wacharachaipong discreetly flew off to attend a symposium in Switzerland.

Naddy the Pimp could live with a face like an aging Japanese comic-book character; what he could not live with was the knowledge that the punks who had worked him over were still out there, alive, breathing the same rank Bangkok smog as he. As soon as the threat of infection receded, Naddy checked out of his last hospital and was driven to a new apartment near Sukhumvit Soi III, where he ordered all the mirrors stripped from the bathrooms so he wouldn't have to look at himself while he set about brooding on his revenge. Throughout his convalescence, he had made sure the weekly payments to his *jaopor* had never stopped. He still had good money coming in from his girls, who were maintaining steady earnings despite the recession that gripped Thailand. Pussy, unlike real estate, never slumps. But what was the point of socking away a fortune if a few uppity Thai boys could beat the crap out of him and live to tell about it. He had lost face, literally, the ultimate Asian insult.

His underlings had discovered that the four bouncers who had come after him were no longer at the bar, nor was #35, the lady-boy. Obviously they had found out who they had fucked with, heard that Naddy had lived, and elected to vanish rather than die. Naddy, never a man to employ conventional methods, felt a direct approach to finding his attackers would be best.

Accompanied by two massive Thai bodyguards who flanked him as he strolled down Patpong, Naddy returned to SuperPussy carrying a bowling-ball bag. He climbed the stairs and strode to the cashier, beneath the stage crowded with undulating bikini-clad girls. He gazed around the darkened, cavernous bar. It was early in the evening, before the bar became crowded with customers, and Naddy's presence, his large, oddly distended face with its sagging lips and sad eyes was the center of attention. The manager and the new bouncers exchanged whispers and confused glances. No one was sure what to do. Clearly this was Naddy the Pimp. But why was he here?

Naddy set the bowling-ball bag on the bar and began removing thousand-baht-bill stacks of currency as thick as waterlogged paperbacks, piling ten silver and blue bundles on the bar. One million baht ($40,000) stood under the club's black lights like a purple monument to greed, danger and opportunity. All the attention shifted from Naddy to that pile of currency, more money than anyone in the bar had ever seen at one time. Naddy, employing one of the massive bodyguards as a translator, told the now silent crowd that this was the reward for anyone who told him the whereabouts of the four bouncers and #35.

Trey never actually seemed to be working on the kickboxer story. Once in a while I'd see him with his notepad propped on his knees, seated at a table at the King's Corner. He'd read me a sentence or two he'd been working on. They were clever sentences, funny, full of references to epochal American sporting events: the Thrilla in Manila, the Immaculate Reception, the Shot Heard Round the World, and with zingy twists on familiar sports clichés: his kickboxer's opponent, who wore cologne, entered the ring by mounting three steps in a cloud of must; his defensive strategy was to take two lefts but never a right, and Thai kickboxing, of course, was a game of clinches. But you needed hundreds, perhaps even a thousand, good sentences to make a fine magazine article, and from what I gathered, Trey had written about a dozen.

Not that it seemed to bother him. When I asked him about the story, he seemed breezily confident that it would get done. Trey had always been that way, even in Tokyo, optimistic and upbeat about his prospects even when they seemed no better than mine, and I was generally more circumspect and pessimistic about the likelihood of a positive result from all my proposal writing, querying and reporting. Magazines were a terribly fickle business, and it was proving very difficult to break into the top markets. The U.S. had just gone through a period of intense fascination with Japan, and that had been a great help to both of us. But with that now waning, as Japan began to seem less of a threat to the West, it was imperative that new territories be discovered and mined. Trey was right about that. For example, this

Russian pimp story that was by then making the rounds of the *farang* community in Bangkok was exactly the type of thing that seemed salable in the West. Trey and I talked about it frequently, exchanging pieces of gossip we'd heard and little factoids we'd gathered from acquaintances. This Naddy was fascinating, representing the confluence of so many trends: Russian destabilization, the appearance of Caucasian hookers in Asia, the Russian mafia becoming a player in the Far East. We discussed how the story might be written, from whose point of view it might be told, even what the scenes might be. The tacit agreement was that Trey, because he'd gotten to Bangkok first, would get to write this one. And that became a source of some contention between us. He already had the big assignment from the big American magazine. Wouldn't it be fair that I should get the story of the Russian pimp? It sounded like grousing on my part, but it was hard not to feel jealous of Trey, sitting there in the hookers' apartment, his notebook of clever sentences balanced on his knee as he pulled open another Ampo-Dentinil capsule and chewed some more speed. Trey had always had a Panglossian perspective on his life and writing in general, but now his optimism—or was it the speed he chewed all day and night?—seemed to have inflated his ego to Maileresque proportions as he surveyed his sordid little domain. He dismissed my occasional advisories that all wasn't as swell as it seemed by waving a hand imperiously in front of his face. Measured realism had no place in this world of hookers and speed and big ideas for big magazines. (Or was it our conflicting preferences in drugs? I was going through a phase of tending toward downers, opiates and benzodiazepenes, while Trey was committed to uppers. Our pharmaceutical paths had diverged.) Yet there was no getting away from it. Maybe he was right, maybe taking liberties and thinking big resulted in big stories. My cautious approach, after all, had gotten me where? Into the pages of myriad Inflight magazines. Trey, with his kooky, speed-fueled passion, now seemed on the verge. And I hated myself for being so petty, but I couldn't help it.

Starting as a writer is so hard—it might be the only thing

harder than keeping going as a writer—and from my vantage point, Trey had ascended some crucial next step that had to be mounted if you were to ever make a living and a career in the business. With his kickboxing piece, he would have a major feature in a magazine that mattered, which would then spawn other assignments that would magically elevate him from the tawdry world of Inflight magazines. While I, in my saturnine jealousy, foresaw being mired in the second-rate world forever.

Sometimes, sitting in the girls' apartment while Trey was rewiring on more speed, I would feel almost like fleeing, as if being with him reminded me too painfully of my own shortcomings. If only I could think positively, like Trey, be optimistic, embrace the future and feel confident about my prospects. I should face the future open-armed and welcoming, rather than beady-eyed and suspicious. "More like Trey, less like Karl" began to reverberate through my consciousness.

And making me even more uncomfortable was the fact that Bin now seemed to hate me. It wasn't just that she was disappointed or hurt or saddened by my inability to perform. She held it against me. She never gave me another opportunity to make good, nor did she pay any more attention to me outside of hissing Thai vituperations in my direction. The other girls had also taken to looking at me askance, and once Song even said to me, sneering: "You're no Robocop."

If, in my own eyes, I had dropped into second place in the two-way race with Trey, in the girls' eyes I had fallen into a different category altogether. I was being chastised for my nonperformance and had been relegated to some sort of despised eunuch status. A pariah. A half-caste.

"Bin was terribly insulted by what happened," Trey explained to me one afternoon while the girls were noisily playing cards. "She was hurt."

"It wasn't her fault," I said. "But I mean, it wasn't mine either. It's the pheromones."

Trey looked at me curiously. "Pheromones?"

"Yeah, you know, you told me about them: they're like these

undetectable little sense molecules that tell you if you like someone or not."

Trey shrugged. "I guess."

He went back to writing in his notebook. Then he looked up,
wrinkling his brow. "You know, I'm usually not into guys."

"Okay." I nodded. "So what? What does that have to do with
anything?"

He put down his pen. "You don't know, do you?"

"What?"

"These are all guys," he said, indicating the girls playing
cards.

"You mean—"

"It's true. All dudes. All transsexuals."

I looked over at Song and Bin and the rest of them. Suddenly
a few things began to make sense. Their surprising height, for
one thing, their long fingers, the fact that I'd never seen any of
them naked, the teutonically vigorous pool sharking and the
macho, chest-beating card playing.

I felt I'd been labeled impotent under false pretenses. But it
turned out that was what made it all the more insulting to Bin,
that in my estimation she'd—or he'd—come up so far short as a
woman that she/he was unable to sell me on the idea where it
really counted, in the sack.

As for Trey, it didn't seem to bother him. "I mean, in some
ways it's the same," he said. At least two of the orifices, he reasoned, were basically identical. And as for the disparity regarding
the primary sexual orifice, these lady-boys were so skilled that the
absence was easily overlooked. But how was this different from
being gay? I asked.

Trey shrugged. He hadn't given that much thought.

"I mean, look at them," Trey said. "They clearly *aren't* guys."

And he had a point. They existed somewhere in between,
which meant that Trey was also somewhere in between. Or
maybe not. But in this instance, my own squeamishness regarding women with dicks was yet another aspect of my general per-
sona of party pooper in chief. I was the inveterate prude, so out

of step with the groovy new way of living Trey had discovered here in Bangkok. Life wasn't about smoking heroin and banging girls; it was about chewing speed and fucking transsexuals. What was wrong with me? Didn't I get it? More like Trey, less like Karl.

I decided I would run all this by Kluter. If even he wasn't put off by the idea of a sex partner with a penis, then maybe I was behind the times. This was a new era, after all, and maybe it did require adjustments and reorientations. But I hadn't seen Kluter in a few days. He always kept erratic hours, heading out to pick up a hooker at whatever hour he fancied. You never knew if he was in his little bungalow, pumping away on some fifteen-year-old he'd dragged out of Thermae.

Once in a while I'd seen his regular squeeze, the Cambodian hooker with greedy eyes, walking to or from his bungalow. And one afternoon I saw her walking out cradling his television between her arms while a Thai kid with long hair sat revving a Yamaha four-stroke Vega. Alarmed, I called out to her, but she began trotting and hopped onto the back of the bike, somehow managing to prop the TV on one knee as they sped away.

I walked back to Kluter's bungalow and knocked on one of the cedar posts that held up the fiberglass-roofed porch. No one answered. I climbed the steps and, carefully pushing the slightly ajar door farther open, I was overwhelmed by a putrid, fecund vinegar smell. It wasn't the smell of death, but it was clearly decay. Kluter lay on his filthy mattress, his breath wheezy, his shirt unbuttoned to reveal, amid his tattoos, festering sores and lesions. When I called his name, he didn't respond.

My first impulse was to turn around and close the door behind me. If even his Cambodian squeeze couldn't be bothered to lift a finger on his behalf—in fact, she seemed to take Kluter's illness as an opportunity to commence looting—then why should I bother with figuring out the Bangkok equivalent of 911? If this priapic old kraut had banged himself to death, whether by AIDS or some even more sinister STD not yet diagnosed or analyzed, then what problem was it of mine? I imagined myriad complications: paperwork, police interrogations, trips to the German embassy, a visit to the morgue. Did Kluter even have a family, some German equivalent of next of kin who could at least dispose of the body? Or would this all be my responsibility?

He was wheezing away on his rank sheets, his every breath filling the little bungalow with his sour effluvium. He wasn't dead yet; I realized I had to do something.

I went to find Miss Kuda. I walked across the courtyard to where she sat on a covered wooden platform, waving a cedar hand fan in front of herself.

"We need an ambulance," I told her. "For Kluter."

She didn't budge. I could see her quickly running through the calculations, figuring if there was any margin in calling for an ambulance. Or would it be more economical to wait? Was Kluter worth more to her dead or alive?

"Someone already took his television," I informed her.

That seemed to tip the scale in favor of keeping Kluter above ground. With a pulse, he would at least pay his rent. Dead, with no TV, who knew what he was worth? She shouted something to one of the maids, a woman with a faint mustache who ran the counter where they sold soap and bottled water. The maid nodded, and as far as I could tell, the game of telephone seemed to end right there.

"We need it now," I said.

Miss Kuda nodded.

"Now."

"It's coming," Miss Kuda assured me.

I shrugged. I had done what I could. If Kluter died, it was now officially out of my hands. Miss Kuda could deal with the fucking body.

But as soon as I was mounting the steps to my bungalow, I heard the hoarse whining of sirens cutting through the thick Bangkok smog. Actually, more than one siren could be discerned.

Two ambulances from two different hospitals arrived almost simultaneously. I don't know if they had even been called or if, like carrion, they had smelled Kluter's imminent passing. No matter, they had arrived, leaving me hopeful that Kluter would receive the best medical care Thailand had to offer. But instead of sliding out gurneys and preparing IV tubes, as I had seen paramedics do on television shows, these fellows stormed out of their minivans and began shouting at one another as if diving back into an old domestic spat. I walked over to where the two competing paramedic teams—one in blue uniforms, the other in yellow—stood facing off, loudly debating in Thai and gesticulating vigorously. Finally the driver of the first Toyota Hi-Ace walked up to the leader of the other group and shoved him in the chest.

I trotted over. My appearance on the scene momentarily stopped the squabbling. They had come for a sick foreigner. If that was me and I was running around, then perhaps there was nothing to fight over. In unison, the two factions turned toward Miss Kuda, who hurriedly reassured them there indeed was a dying foreigner on the premises.

"Who was first?" the driver of the first Hi-Ace asked me.

I honestly couldn't say. They had both seemed to arrive in the same cloud of dust and exhaust. I knew, however, that I had to pick one ambulance or these two teams of medical professionals might just choose to slice Kluter in half in order to split the lucrative *farang* billing. I pointed to the driver who had asked and said, "You. You were first."

That seemed to settle matters. I may not have been a sick foreigner, but I was a foreigner and presumably was somehow connected to the one they had come to pick up. The disappointed team retired to their van and started the engine, tearing out of the gravel and macadam driveway so that a spray of pebbles rattled along the side of the chosen ambulance.

A gurney was duly produced and rolled back toward the bungalow, where I showed them Kluter's dissipated, prostrate form. With surprising delicacy, four of them lifted Kluter and hauled him from the shack, down the steps and onto the gurney. Thinking quickly, and before Miss Kuda could appraise Kluter's worldly possessions, I rummaged through the bureau drawers, looking for Kluter's passport or some sort of documentation. I couldn't find anything. When I looked up, there was Miss Kuda, smiling, and I knew that she already had Kluter's passport, and if he didn't recover soon that red Reichspass would soon find its way onto the black market. Would, in fact, probably be sold to someone like Naddy the Pimp.

I suddenly wanted to get out of there. To go back to Tokyo, far from greedy Miss Kuda and decaying Kluter and bemembered Bin and even from wired, peppy, upwardly mobile Trey. He could have this place, I decided, perhaps I didn't have what it took to make it here in Bangkok if what was required was a murky sexuality and boundless enthusiasm. Tokyo, with its corruption so institutionalized it didn't even seem corrupt, and its docile people and girls who were girls, was perhaps more my speed. More like Karl, less like Trey.

Maybe I'd even get a job at a wire service.

I told Miss Kuda that I would be leaving. She squeezed an extra half-month's rent out of me, but she didn't seem unhappy to see me go. I was, after all, the only person besides her who could put up a competing claim to Kluter's remaining possessions.

Within a week, the first of SuperPussy's bouncers, a former kickboxer, was found along the banks of a Bangkok canal with a bullet between his eyes and severe contusions about the head and neck. Another was discovered executed in the same manner in his squalid Bang Phlad apartment. A third was found slumped over the handlebars of his Honda motorcycle, shot through the mouth after being bludgeoned about the head and neck with a blunt object. The fourth vanished and hasn't been heard from since.

Number thirty-five had also disappeared.

No one knew who gave away the whereabouts of the bouncers and the lady-boy. And police have never bothered to link the murders. (Bangkok has one of the highest murder rates in the world.) But for the *jaopor* who pay attention to such matters, it was clear who was behind the killings. These killings were a message, and that message was don't fuck with Naddy the Pimp. Even if Naddy himself hadn't pulled the trigger or wielded the cricket bat, he could have easily hired the muscle and hit men to do the dirty work for him. (There are between two and three thousand hired killers in Bangkok with the weapons and training to carry out professional hits such as these.)

But a funny thing happened just as soon as Naddy got his revenge: he too disappeared. His vanishing coincided with a police crackdown on Russian prostitutes that had the Thai immigration holding cells bulging with Russian ladies. "Suddenly, we had a flood of pretty young Russians," a sergeant major at the Immigration Investigation Division told me. "The police suddenly made it priority one to hunt Russians for visa violations."

The powers that be, ranging from the Bangkok police to the *jaopor* who run the prostitution industry, were tired of Naddy and his girls muscling in on their territory.

"What Gennady didn't count on," a Russian national who used to work with Gennady and now lives in Tokyo later related to me, "is that the Thai *jaopor* who run Patpong weren't going to take kindly to a *farang* knocking off their employees. He forgot that he was only a guest in Bangkok, and was there only as long as his *jaopor* wanted to put up with him. When he went out of line, that provided a neat solution to their problem."

Though the Russian girls are now back in Thailand, their numbers are diminished and their presence is certainly more low-key. Tamara, a Russian prostitute who came on the Nipples and Vodka Express, applies this wisdom to Naddy: "Naddy was here and now he is gone. That's it. End of story. I am here to make money and the money is still here."

There are rumors that Naddy is back in Russia, or in Shanghai, or in Macao. There are also rumors that he is dead, a corpse in the sediment of one of Bangkok's canals.

There is also a rumor that at one of Patpong's bars, there is a striking lady-boy who wears #35, and if you catch a glimpse of her right hand, you will notice she wears a bizarre platinum ring with a cobra-head setting and emerald eyes.

Trey did finally write his kickboxing story. But unfortunately for Trey, the Harvard MBA kickboxer decided to write his own story and, through a New York literary agent, circulated a book proposal with a sample chapter that was soon published in an even more prestigious magazine than the men's magazine that bought Trey's story. The men's magazine, not wanting to run a story that suddenly seemed stale, passed on the piece, paying Trey a 25 percent kill fee.

Still, Trey should have been able to work for them again. But there was a dispute about his expenses. He billed the magazine for $11,000 but could produce receipts for only about a third of that. The rest had been spent, presumably, on hookers and drugs. Trey was dismissive when he returned to Tokyo and the famous editor's not famous assistant called him, telling Trey they weren't going to put through his expenses unless he came up with better documentation. "Don't all gonzo magazine writers do this?" Trey asked me at one point while he was forging Thai receipts he'd bought at a Bangkok stationery store.

One night two years later, I saw a hearty, well-built German with blond hair who I swore looked like a younger, healthier Kluter. I was at Angels, a bar on Sukhumvit Soi IV where hookers picked up foreign clients. For a second I thought it might be Kluter's son—if he had one—but as I circled the dance floor to get a better look, I realized it was Kluter himself. Whatever disease he had, it apparently was in remission, and he looked about as vibrant and undissipated as it is possible to look in a Bangkok pickup bar.

I walked over to him, smiling, reaching my hand out. I was genuinely glad to see him. "You're alive," I shouted over the bleating house music.

Kluter looked up at me, confused.
He had no idea who I was.

Trey eventually sold the Harvard MBA kickboxing story to an Inflight magazine. He never did write that story about the Russian pimp.

I'm still working on it.

THE GAME

The *sakura*, or cherry trees, are blossoming early this year, although no one in Tokyo is in the mood to admit it. The annual round of boozy cherry-blossom-viewing parties has already been scheduled for next weekend, so the parks are curiously empty today, despite the fact that by next week the petals will already be falling from the trees, skirling into cups of plum wine and sake, as drunken revelers finally concede that spring is upon us. But as I cut through Arisugawa Park in Nishi Azabu, skirting baseball-capped Japanese kids chasing one another with plastic ray guns, I stroll amid cherry trees in lovely, pinkish-white bloom, canopies of petals wafting in a tropical-tinged breeze against a gentle azure sky. I'm on my way to meet Nigel and Dina. They are living the life I want to live. They have turned their backs on the conventional routes to career and success, hewing their own futures out here on the Asian frontier.

"All right, mate," Nigel told me over the phone when I asked if I could accompany him and a few friends on their upcoming travels. "But if you're not cool, we give you the sack."

Draw a triangle whose three points are Tokyo, Goa and Bangkok. Approximately one hundred thousand Americans, English and Australians between the ages of eighteen and thirty-five ride a circuit of work, travel and partying within that triangle. Unlike the hippies of a previous generation, this Far Eastern subculture lives a cycle of work and play that results in constant motion between cities and countries. As the nations of the Far East ride capitalist cycles of boom to bust to boom again, it has become possible for young, adventurous Westerners to stay for a few years in these exotic locales, moving about and living well by earning the money they need as they go. A few of them, like Nigel and Dina, have made or inherited prodigious amounts of money and have effectively cashed out of the various rodent races run in the world's rat traps and are living on the circuit, as this travel route has come to be known by its denizens.

In a previous life, Nigel was a Barings-cleared trader on the Hong Kong futures exchange, which meant he and his partners kept their margin accounts at Barings Securities. When that firm collapsed in 1995, Nigel and other Barings-cleared traders were barred from the floor of the exchange. Nigel watched the subsequent market panic from the observation deck as his partners' equity vanished into a mass of liquidation and litigation. Though his personal assets were safely deposited in dollar-denominated bank accounts, Nigel decided then, as he watched the blue- and yellow-jacketed traders scampering across the pit like children running from an insatiable ogre hungry for their money, that he was done with this life. "Been living on the circuit ever since," Nigel says, "on the cream"—meaning the good life.

Other riders of the circuit earn their travel lucre in Tokyo, Hong Kong and Shanghai, as brokers, traders, journalists, computer programmers, English teachers, models or hostesses and party and unwind in Koh Phangang, Koh Tao, Borakai, Bali,

Goa, Kashmir and Kathmandu. They have blazed a bizarre and energizing on-the-go lifestyle, as comfortable in Koh Tao bungalows as they are in Tokyo skyscrapers.

These are the people you see for a few moments in hotel lobbies or in line at Don Muang airport, the people you find when you've been traveling for a week and feel like you've arrived somewhere exceptional and remote and then you see that not only are some other Westerners there but they've already rented the best cottage.

These riders of the circuit have become a common sight. In their well-cut suits and designer outfits, hauling Prada bags—or knockoff Prada bags—and Halliburton briefcases, tapping away on notebook "Tosh" (Toshiba) computers, they are the flesh-and-blood embodiment of those commercials you see featuring young, handsome Caucasian executive types winging around Asia, checking in to first-class hotels and conversing in vernacular tongues. Nigel, who continues to dabble in options trading via offshore bank accounts, considers his generation of Occidental Asia hands the first to truly make a playground of the Far East. "I love the idea that I can skip from Tokyo to Hong Kong to Bangkok all in one day," he says.

He assembles his reality out of different bytes from different cities. A friend calls from Hong Kong and he goes. Or Jakarta. Or he hits the islands for a few weeks. And as the continent gets wired, uplinked and digitized, there will be no reason to have a home at all. Home will be where the hard drive is. "This is the game that changes as you play," Nigel says, echoing a common saying uttered by riders of the circuit, "and I just hang on."

But with adaptability comes a price, and if you become comfortable anywhere, then perhaps you are at home nowhere. "It gets a bit messy at times," says Holly, twenty-four, an American who has been living on the circuit for the last three years, supporting herself with part-time promotional work in Tokyo for Sony. "It becomes hard to form lasting attachments, because at the back of your mind is the suspicion that this really cool person might exit your life next week."

My new companions all know how to sleep on airplanes. It is as if the smell of jet fuel is a tranquilizer that puts Nigel and company under, blissfully anesthetizing them for flights long and short while I sit awake, squirming in straight-backed chairs counting down the minutes until destination.

There were a few things I had planned to do in Tokyo. There are friends I haven't seen in over a year. And, most important, my grandmother is a spry, alert ninety-two and I had hoped to hop the Tokaido train line down to Yokohama to see her. But then I ran into this crowd, Nigel and Dina and Jason—a male model— and Tamara—a five-foot-ten-inch strawberry blonde who quit a job with Microsoft to move to Asia. And they were doing what I wanted to do, living on the circuit, mingling and jet-setting in a world of beautiful kids without a care in the world, who know the good spots and the right clothes. Okay, I admit it: they're the cool kids, and I always wanted to be just like them.

Visiting my grandmother sort of went out the window.

The flight from Tokyo to Bangkok is six hours, slipping along the Chinese coast until the lush islands of the Gulf of Siam and then the smog-choked metropolis of Bangkok slide into view.

The whole flight down I am excited, feeling like I am molting, revealing a newer, more vibrant skin that will enable me to experience life to the fullest. And this is no down-market expedition I've signed on with. Nigel and Dina have the connections and the money to stay at comfortable hotels and are veterans at living the good life. They have made deals with hoteliers, restaurateurs, telephone companies and Internet service providers that allow them to live out here in relative comfort and style. But this life isn't about cutting a deal, getting the best rate, striking a bargain. It is about discovering who you are when all your cultural and societal shields are removed. You can't hide behind some title or position; no one will treat you with any greater deference because of your posh college or impeccable bloodlines. All that is stripped away, and you are left with yourself and one simple, Gatesian question: What do I want to do today?

Bangkok is hot and damp, and the air is so thick with exhaust that I can feel bits of grit between my teeth. By evening, however, balmy breezes skidding up the Chao Praya River from the Gulf of Thailand lower the heat to below body temperature and make this courtyard at the Tak Sura restaurant tolerable. Bodhi tree branches descend in broken arcs to where we sit around a splintering wooden table. A bucket of ice melting in the tropical heat, a bottle of Mekong whiskey and sweating bottles of Coca-Cola are gradually festooned with pink bougainvillea petals falling from the trellis overhead.

We arrived in Bangkok this afternoon. After checking in to the Sukhothai Hotel, a gaudy, postmodern, nouveau-Asian temple to speculative excess and economic optimism, I swam a few laps in the deliciously chilly pool. I had climbed from the water and sat on a chaise longue, marveling at how I felt wetter out here in the humid air than I did submerged, when Dina came downstairs in a white bathrobe. She shed that linen layer and dove sideways into the pool, like a synchronized swimmer at the start of her routine. In precise, measured strokes, she swam back and forth, finally climbing up the wooden ladder to where I lay watching.

She took the chaise next to me, dislodging water from her ear by tapping the side of her head near where the pool's chlorine had tinted her blond hair green. I watched the flesh of her arms and her Balinese warrior tattoos jiggle as she let down her hair and shook it out. When dry, Dina's hair hangs straight as a glacial waterfall, sheer and dangerous, framing a sun-filled, blue-eyed, dramatically cheekboned face whose small mouth is given to grinning mischievously or smiling sympathetically. In her left ear she wears a diamond the size of a Spanish peanut. Smiling now, she slipped on a pair of Persol sunglasses and sat back in her chaise, her expression becoming impassive.

Dina's money came the old-fashioned way: she inherited it. Knightsbridge heiress and London nightlife refugee, she's been out here four years, acquiring her intricate warrior tattoos and a wide-ranging knowledge of how to live on the circuit. She possesses the charm and allure of having turned her back on precisely the lifestyle most first-worlders are seeking; luxurious financial freedom is her birthright. She drifts in and out of her friends' lives. She flies off to Hong Kong fortnightly to see classmates from Cambridge who have been posted there. Or she takes off to Tokyo or Delhi, to visit any of a long list of acquaintances, friends and associates. One has the feeling as she undertakes these voyages that she is some sort of Mother Teresa of the e-generation, bringing solace and relief to mind-blown ravers throughout the Far East.

For Nigel, there were errands to run upon arriving in Bangkok: he needed updated SIM cards for his Philips cell phone. Through a friend in Bangkok, he'd had his British Telecom cellnet phone modified so that the memory chip automatically reloaded after each call, allowing for unlimited free international usage. He also wanted to head over to an office building near Lumphini Park, where an old partner of his was working for an American vulture capitalist buying up distressed Thai assets on the cheap.

His partner was long gone, however, over to Bangalore, India, where capital-hungry software start-ups are giving Silicon Valley a run for its seed money.

When Nigel returned to the hotel and joined Dina and me by the pool, he seemed distracted, sitting quietly for a moment on one of the chaise longues. Nigel has golden hair mingled with clay-colored strands, a cleft chin, stern lips programmed for easy smiles and dewy, morning-colored eyes. His manner today was worldly, tired, anxious about some unknowable future as his thoughts returned to his former partner who had stayed in the life Nigel had left behind.

But by the time he emerged from a brisk swim, he was his old self again. "Fancy a tuk-tuk race?" he asked me.

Tuk-tuk races are simple. You hire two of the garish chrome and neon blue, three-wheeled, open-air, 250cc motorized rickshaws, explain to the drivers where you want to go and proffer a purse of four thousand baht to the winning driver, to be paid by the losing passenger. During dinner, Nigel and Dina had laid out the route for the race: up Thanon Rama IV, along the canal and then down Lan Luang to the Democracy Monument. Total distance: about four kilometers. Nigel guessed the running time in sparse Sunday-evening traffic would be about eight minutes, six if we sprang for four-thousand-baht purses.

"For four thousand," Nigel explains, "they're willing to flip the things."

By negotiating the fares up to triple what they would usually charge for the route, and then adding the four-thousand-baht purse on top, we find two amenable sixteen-year-olds with Krong Tip cigarettes dangling from their lips and malice in their eyes. The race is to be between Nigel and me. Dina shakes her head and laughs dismissively when I ask why she will not be participating.

"Both jockeys must be of equal weight," she says, shrugging, as if the matter had been ruled on by official tuk-tuk racing stewards.

Nigel, leaning forward and consulting with his driver, points to me and explains in broken Thai that there will be additional rewards for defeating me. I am hesitant to further encourage my driver, who has donned sunglasses for the evening race and is gunning the high-pitched engine, sending plumes of exhaust through the upholstered rear of the tuk-tuk.

A gambler by nature—I had seen Nigel take the manager of the One-Eyed Jack's hostess bar back in Tokyo for a few thousand yen at backgammon—Nigel suggests side betting. I demur, shaking my head. I want to get the race over with and survive, ingesting as little of Bangkok's smog as possible along the way.

Nigel thoughtfully lays out one last ground rule. "If we both smash up, then whoever gets closer to the monument wins."

And we are off, the motorcycle engines revving like watermelon-size bumblebees. The drivers swerve between stalled rows of traffic, jump center-line dividers, ride into oncoming traffic, fishtail wide around tight curves, keeping the race close through densely populated city blocks of Thai traffic. As we whiz past noodle wagons, street vendors and bus stops, coming within a few inches of fluorescent-lit chickens and ducks hanging from iron hooks, I close my eyes, as I did during scary sections of roller coasters as a child. I want this to be over. I resent Nigel; this isn't fun, this is horrifying.

The sound of a tuk-tuk engine at full throttle is deafening, and the feeling of a tuk-tuk as it tilts upon two wheels to negotiate a turn is stomach-churning. Why has Nigel convinced me to do this? I open my eyes and sneak a glance at Nigel, whose tuk-tuk has fallen behind mine.

We are winning! I watch a signal up ahead go from green to red, and notice my driver crank the throttle one more time. He is running the light. He peers back at me with a gold-toothed grin that communicates he is not afraid of death, and takes the intersection at seventy miles per hour. The cars accelerating toward us from two directions are a blurry sea of yellow and red headlights, and the sensation is that of a suffocating, lighted tunnel closing in around me. A cacophony of car horns. Drivers angrily shouting in Thai. My driver whooping. I feel motes of exhaust mash painfully against my eyeballs. I am crying.

Then, just as we squirt from between the rows of traffic, I see up ahead of me the beige tumescence of the Democracy Monument, erected in the twenties as a granite embodiment of the ruling elite's lip service to democratic ideals. Never had any monument anywhere been a more welcome sight.

We have won. I slap my driver on the back, giving him the thumbs-up sign. Nigel's tuk-tuk rolls to a halt next to ours, beside the sidewalk tables of the Vigit Restaurant. His driver shouts something at my driver in Thai. A brief argument ensues while Nigel digs four thousand baht from his money belt. My driver, arguing the whole time, slides the eight purple five-hundred-baht notes into his polyester slacks.

Before I can climb from the tuk-tuk, my driver grabs me by the shoulder, holding out a wrinkled brochure featuring pornographic depictions of Asian women. "You want Thai lady?"

The island-festooned Gulf of Siam spreads out before us, green and rippling like wrinkled pool felt. After a short, turbo-propped hop from Bangkok to Koh Samui, we have hired a twenty-one-foot, Yamaha 400-horsepowered hull thumper to take us across from Koh Samui to Koh Phangang. Fishermen in long-tailed boats are heading back in to shore, their stooping, slender forms silhouetted against the late-afternoon sun so that they appear almost as the one-brush-stroke figurative renderings of ancient Chinese scrolls.

As we bounce across the foamy sea, I cling to the metallic railings of the boat. The strong tropical sun beats down upon me and I feel the powerful engines pushing me out, out, out, away from whatever was back there and toward my new future. I gaze at Dina and Nigel, and at Jason and Tamara. Nigel hunches down, rolling a cigarette. Jason lays his head back, gazing skyward through his Oakleys. Tamara has wiggled through the narrow forecastle of the boat so that she is leaning her head over the bow, watching the chop. Dina smiles at me, as if she is appraising me and has found in me some sort of good deal.

"How come you and Nigel aren't . . . you know?" I whisper-shout over the boat engine.

"We tried, once," Dina says. "Last season. In Goa. It didn't work out, was a bit . . . well, it's like we're too similar."

As Koh Phangang looms into view, vibrant green like an emerald in a turquoise setting, the water in the middle of the channel becomes more choppy, the waves crashing against the bow and sending up plumes of white froth that splash back over us. The boat gurgles to a halt, bobbing in the violent current. We listen to the sound of sofa-size waves pounding the port side of the vessel. I wonder if the engine is broken.

"You pay now," the Thai captain shouts.

Nigel hands over two thousand-baht notes, and the captain powers up the Yamahas and we're off again, slapping the waves all the way to Hat Rin.

The last time I was here, in 1993, I was working as a journalist in Tokyo and heading off to Thailand every chance I got. If I have matured in the interim, Koh Phangang has not. There are infrastructural changes: the island now has electricity, bungalows are well appointed with air conditioners and plumbing, and Chicken Corner, the main crossroads, has been paved. But Hat Rin, and all of Koh Phangang, may be defined more by what it is not. It is far from the tamed, tropical, down-market Tahiti that neighboring isle Koh Samui has become. On Koh Samui, condominium complexes and golf courses have sprung up, accompanied by prostitutes and hordes of German and Scandinavian tourists. Koh Phangang, on the other hand, remains an idyllic, hedonistic Eden where one can still find a secluded beach, a deserted cove, a splendid sunset that seems custom-made just for you.

We rent bungalows nestled between boulders, ingeniously constructed from coconut wood, planks of palm and bamboo. They are like tree houses, with stilts, posts and roof beams of solid, young bodhi tree trunks that suspend the bungalows over the tide pools so that at night you feel as if you are at sea, floating away on a solid, unsinkable raft. There is something luxurious about a solid wooden structure, from the softness of the woven-straw, tatami-like matted floor to the rustling sound that palm thatch makes in the gentle evening breeze. This little cabin is the sort of place I imagined myself ending up in when I decided to get away from it all. A simple, humble structure, Robinson Crusoe–like in its ingenuity but thoroughly comfortable, it manages to be the opposite of both a New York apartment's clutter and a Los Angeles ranch house's expanse.

Our porches face the sunset, a tangerine glow that slides down into the Gulf, over sampans and craggy islands. Okay, okay, I think to myself as I string a hammock between two beams on the front porch of my bungalow, I came out here to renounce that old life, to let go of all my worldly ties. Now just sit here and be.

Dina lies in a hammock on the front porch of the next bungalow. From where I have strung my hammock, I can hear the gentle creak of hers as she rocks back and forth. One bungalow over, Nigel has logged in, via his Tosh, satellite phone and IBM's Internet service—the ISP that seems to work best out here—to the Web, where he is checking his e-mail. The lapping of waves against the rocks and the gentle tapping of computer keys and a hushed, barely perceptible conversation going on somewhere add up to a soothing din. I just want to be here, my face warm in the afternoon sun, my belly full from a fresh mackerel that went from hook to grill in one hour, with my new good friends all around me. This is what it's all about: renounce the past, live in the present. Ignore for a moment the tapping of computer keys, the idea that I should be somewhere else, doing something else. I am trying to shake that need to achieve out of my bones, to will it from my psyche like a dirty memory. This is who I am now. A guy in a hammock on the Gulf of Siam.

I spin out of my hammock and clamber down the wooden stairwell to the boardwalk, following my shadow until I come to Dina's porch, where I politely knock on a beam—bungalow etiquette.

"Come up," she calls down.

Suddenly, I don't know what to say. I don't know the circuit's equivalent of small talk.

"Good fish, eh?" I say lamely.

Dina sets down the Japanese Marlboro she had been smoking—the Japanese Marlboros are conspicuously better than the licensed Thai version of the red-boxed cigarettes.

"It was nice," she says. Wearing a crocheted, belly-ring-revealing Issey Miyake top over a yellow, tan and black sari, Dina is curled on her side, a warm ball of caramel-colored flesh that seems to glow in the sun's dying light. She stretches out like a cat waking from a nap and checks her men's Rolex Daytona.

A bright, lime-green gecko skitters along the railing, its tail curling and uncurling like a beckoning index finger.

"Don't you ever get tired of all this?" I ask.

"What?" she says, her eyes brightening.

"This life," I say. "You know, living out here, the constant motion. I mean, is there an object to all this, a destination, is there someplace we're going?"

Dina gazes distractedly out at the Gulf, and I turn and follow her eyes and am dazzled by the vista of shimmering tips of tiny waves, dappled with a thousand shards of broken sunlight. A flock of slender black birds flies past at eye level, skimming the tops of the waves. A gentle, warm breeze floats in, billowing Dina's wispy blond hair, and I realize that somehow this is where we are going.

"Let yourself go," Dina says, drawing me in with her glance. "This is the game that changes as you play."

That night, I light a mosquito coil and listen to the rush of high tide beneath my bungalow. When I lie down on the surprisingly comfortable slatted bed, the sound of the ocean is a white-noise lullaby. I feel as if I am afloat in a warm pool of liquid proteins; I am sure a fetus hears a similar sloshing inside the womb.

There are tiny, bright green geckos running across my ceiling. They are gentle creatures, harmless, avid fans of sunlight during the day and mosquitoes at night. They rattle the underside of my shingled ceiling—saurian warriors devouring their weight in insects. In the dim moonlight I catch glimpses of them: bright, almost fluorescent green streaks darting across the ceiling. After an hour, I realize I did not properly light my mosquito coil, and that these geckos have been helpfully sweeping the cabin of insects.

There is a knocking at my bungalow. Silently, without waiting for a reply, Dina pushes open the wooden door and stands for a moment, silhouetted by the shimmer of moonlight against the sea. She is smoking a cigarette. She takes a seat at the edge of my bed. I sit up, bashfully pulling the sheet up around my chest. "You're cute, you know." She almost whispers this, haltingly. She is embarrassed. And I curse the darkness, for I wish I could see Dina blush.

Tokyo and my grandmother seem very far away.

Two days ago I stopped wearing shoes. Now, as I make my way to Mushies for banana pancakes and coffee and a two-day-old *Financial Times,* I go barefoot along the dirt path from Hat Rin Nai to Hat Rin Nok. I stop at the dock and watch a motorboat disgorge a quartet of Swedish girls wearing hiking boots and carrying backpacks. I am amazed by how pink they are.

I have fallen into a routine. Wake up at noon. Banana pancakes. Toothbrushing. A swim in the warm blue sea. Nap. At that point it gets hazy. There's another meal. And then there are parties. Every night a party. Occasionally I swallow white pills that alter my neurological perspective so that the music comes on very strong, the bass pushing up from the floor, through my knees and hitting home in my solar plexis. The DJs are celebrities in this world. Some trendy big-beat DJ in from London, or a trance DJ in from Ibiza or a drum 'n bass spinner from Goa.

We are lounging around a heavy teak table at Outback. Merican, the shaved-headed Hungarian refugee who owns the joint, is trying to convince Nigel to buy a piece of the club. It is a beautiful building, open-air, generously terraced, fashioned of tropical hardwoods worn smooth and gentle by the padding of bare feet. There are giant ceiling fans like DC-3 propellers hung from the beamed, thatched roof, cooling the crowds at the thick mahogany bar or having a boogie on the dance floor. We sit on the veranda, facing the cool sea breeze, next to a stone patio where a Japanese girl twirls a baton set aflame at both ends, tossing the fiery stick skyward and watching the pinwheeling flames as they cut a gyrating arc in the black island sky.

"Then I'll be stuck here." Nigel shakes his head and tells Merican, "If I buy a piece of this place, I might as well be married to you."

A girl named Dee, proprietress of London's Café de Paris and Madame Jojo's nightclubs, sits beside me, bemoaning her recent motorbike accident. Maple-haired with glowing skin and bugging-out eyes, she asks Nigel and Dina about Tokyo. When she hears her chum Simon LeBon of the pop group Duran Duran was in Tokyo at One-Eyed Jack's, she shrieks, "Oh, I'm gonna take the piss out of him when he comes in my club. 'Simon,' I'll tell him, 'I was there, I saw you pissed at that Roppongi hostess bar.' "

Nigel shrugs as he listens to Dee. "The girls at the club were all using his mobile phone to make international calls."

Dee grows pensive. "They shouldn't take advantage of poor Simon."

I am gradually coming to feel as if I belong out here. I have my friends, and as I look around the table at Nigel and Dee, and at Dina, of course, I become convinced that these are the people who matter most to me. Of course, by now the MDMA—the White Doves I've taken—make me trusting and faithful and obedient: oh, toss all that, it's a blur now and all I'm thinking is here we go, here we go, here we go. I put my head down against the teak table, fighting off a wave of nausea. When I look up, the world is warm and these lovely creatures are so cuddly. They are also the only people in the world right now who know where I am.

I have known them for ten days.

Merican turns to me. "How about you? How would you like to buy half of my club?"

I have known him for two hours.

Nigel returns to his bungalow, where he will jack into cyberspace for Wall Street's opening bell. He has taken to following the markets more assiduously, picking off the tiny profits to be had in the price movements between Tokyo's or Hong Kong's close and London's or New York's open.

Dina and I watch the sunrise over the Gulf of Siam from the wooden veranda at Backyard, a disco nestled in the jungle crowning a hill above Hat Rin. Backyard Dave, a legendary DJ on the circuit, helms twin direct-drive turntables, spinning a satisfying morning mix of sunrise music—aural orange juice to soothe frayed nerves, keeping the kids in batik pants and fluorescent wraparound jewelry and camouflage Versace shirts locked in little trance marches to nowhere.

I smile at Dina, who is wearing an orchid-print sundress and thick-heeled crepe shoes. Her face is radiant and beaming in the morning light, and I realize I have never seen her panic, have never seen her lose her cool. It is as if she possesses an inexhaustible font of mysterious inner peace. Nothing flusters her. She hops from destination to destination like some wayward location scout for the feature film that is her life, and she never seems to lose patience with those around her, to let down for a second her facade of tranquillity and peace. I envy her. I want to be just like her.

Later, Dina rolls a spliff and we come down together in her bungalow. And as the sun rises and the waves lap against the deck, we fall into each other's arms. It goes off surprisingly easily, this conjoining, because Dina's confidence and experience trump my eagerness, and she has a way of making it all fit together. Now I am really on the circuit. Now, I tell myself, I am really one of them.

Using Nigel's Tosh, I check my e-mail. One from my agent. Something about a contract. I don't bother replying.

We keep moving. The season is ending. Merican, unable to find a partner, has shuttered Outback until next season. Backyard has held its closing party. Soon, Koh Phangang will be too hot and the riders of the circuit will be on their way to their next destinations. I don't bother to ask Dina where we are going. She mentions another island, this one more remote than Koh Phangang.

By long-tail boat we pull out from Hat Rin, the graceful, stained-wood bow bouncing on the foam like a diving board after the diver has leaped. Comprised of fallen, shattered boulders like the sedative crumbs at the bottom of an old Valium prescription, the winding, inlet- and cove-ridden Koh Phangang coastline seems to offer unimaginable delights just around the next point or rocky outcropping. Come just a little farther, the stony voice of the island seems to say, and you will find that perfect beach, that secluded cove, that idyllic palm grove by the sea.

Dina, her blond hair gelled and pulled back, sits at the helm of the boat, her sunglassed face serving as our prow. What does she want? What do any of these riders of the circuit want? Paradise? That's too easy: Goa. Lomboc. Koh Tao. There are plenty of lovely spots where the beaches, and parties, go on forever. No, the essence of the circuit is movement. The traveling is an end in itself. Tokyo to Bangkok to Koh Phangang to Kathmandu to wherever and then back to Tokyo for another round. There is in this relentless swirl of cool places, great-looking boys and girls and toxic substances, somehow the idea that if you just keep swirling, don't stop the dance, then you will be young and pretty and clever forever.

Studded with beautiful beaches, secluded inlets and lush jungle streams, Koh Tao breaks your heart because you know it is too pretty to remain undeveloped. The jungle has that pristine green color that juxtaposes with the ocean's faded-denim blue to create, for an instant, the illusion that you have finally found the perfect tropical island. Though the population of Koh Tao has mushroomed from 750 in 1993 to five times that today, it is still the least developed and most splendid of the Surat Thani province islands. Renowned as a destination for divers and snorkelers, the island is currently the closest thing to paradise Thailand offers.

As we scamper down the gangplank to the landing at Sai Ri and climb aboard a taxi that will take us to Tenote Bay, I blink furiously because of the dust in my eyes, wipe sweat from my forehead and neck with a bandana and wonder at how easy it is to forget when you are living in New York that such places as this exist.

The dirt road that winds through the hills has been gutted by recent rains. The driver must pick up speed at the top of each hill for the momentum to reach the top of the next. The jungle closes in around us; we are driving through an emerald tunnel. When we pass through a particularly thick grove of vine-shrouded bamboo, several dozen tiny praying mantises appear in our hair and our luggage. We laugh as we flick them from the truck and pick them from each other's hair until we pull up at Tenote Bay.

This half-moon of brown, green and blue coral teeming with manta rays, turtles and schools of tropical fish is a metropolis of aquatic life set amid a perfect, palm-tree-dotted, white-sand beach. An island of relaxing and mellowing out, Koh Tao is the opposite of Tokyo's moneymaking bustle, Bangkok's smoggy hustle and Koh Phangang's "Take two E's and defibrillate me in the morning" vibe.

I catch a glimpse of myself in the mirror of my bungalow, a quiet shack nestled on a hill in the shade of a swaying palm tree a few yards from the beach. I am skinny, my hair is long and there is a wildness about my eyes. I look feral.

Nigel, Jason, Tamara, my fellow riders of the circuit, have come to seem like my family—in just a few weeks I have come to feel I have known them forever. They are my universe, and that other stuff, my grandmother back in Tokyo, my friends and family in the United States, has all started to seem very distant and insignificant.

And Dina has come to replace all my worldly attachments. As long as she is near, then I feel secure, that my presence on the circuit is validated. That a woman as lovely and gentle of spirit as

Dina has chosen me serves only to confirm in my mind the correctness of my decision to pack in my old life. She is an avatar, a sign from God that I have done the right thing.

As I walk across the hot sand in a pair of pink flippers, adjusting my snorkel, I think to myself that I need only to be where I am now. This beach. This hot sand.

But then someone tugs on my hair and I turn around. Dina, wearing a gray and orange one-piece swimsuit with buckle shoulder straps, carries a mask and snorkel.

We are in the water, gazing down at the submerged space station of coral and schools of green- and brown-striped fish and a slender turtle darting amid giant, spidery-legged star fish. Dina sheds her mask and dives, her blond hair streaking behind in the pristine water. I shake off my mask and, clutching it in my hand, dive after her to where she has found, of all things, a Japanese hundred-yen coin.

But sometimes I do think about my grandmother. Ninety-two years old. She is nearly blind now, squinting to read with her one good eye.

At night, a crowd of us gathers under the palm-canopy roof of a little café on the beach. A gentle, ambient CD is slipped into the bar's tinny sound system. And after the generators shut down for the evening, we light candles that flicker in the sea breeze. We play Pictionary, translating those words—isthmus, earwig, pendulum—that the nonnative-English-speaking players have trouble understanding. The games dissolve into good-natured banter and cheerful laughter. I sneak glances at Dina's face glowing in the candlelight, her light dusting of freckles invisible beneath her tan. Nigel usually breaks away from the evening early to find a backgammon partner or check stock quotes.

But this evening, as I draw a skier, an island, a radio, a plumber, a pipe, and Dina gets them all before the sand runs out of the top of the hourglass and we win the game, I am as happy as I have ever been. My old life seems very far away.

I want to stay out here forever.

It is delicate, the balance that keeps a group of travelers on the circuit together. They need to all get along, of course, but there must also be a sense of purpose, of discovery, that in one another and our mutual enjoyment of the places we are visiting, we are adding value to one another's experience. It takes a special mix of people, each providing his or her own traits that coalesce into the fuel that keeps the group's motor running. Jason and Tamara, Dina and I and Nigel, somehow we work as a group. Without any one of us, the dynamic would change. Nigel is the leader, I now realize, he provides us with a sense of direction. It is Nigel who can make us feel as if a communal decision has been reached to move on, he takes the initiative and forms consensus, or creates the illusion of consensus.

While Dina naps on a hammock, Nigel and I climb several hundred meters up a narrow stone staircase to a thatched restaurant overlooking the bay. We sit on chairs carved from driftwood, ordering fresh swordfish mogenaigais and Kloster beers, and watch the bay turn a golden color as the sun, making a dramatic last stand atop a jungle hill, shoots out a burst of yellow rays. Nigel has become pensive; he's not the garrulous fellow who invited me to join him on the circuit. I suspect that despite his bravado about riding the circuit and this being the game that changes as you play, there is deep within him the businessman's or broker's sense that there should be some kind of order, that life is not a random sequence of events but rather a quantifiable and predictable series of possible outcomes, each of which offers its own risk/reward ratios. It is his way of thinking, and I can see that sometimes he struggles with his decision to renounce his old life. Hence his evenings hunched over his Tosh, making his small trades, picking off opportunities in capital and debt markets around the world. It's Nigel's way of keeping a hand in, staying in touch with what he left behind.

"What are you gonna do when you're forty?" I ask him.

He shrugs. I can see it is a question he doesn't want to think about. "That's twelve years from now."

"Well, then what do you think you'll be doing?"

"Having a fish curry on the beach." Even though he is smiling, I can see that he does not believe his answer for one second.

Walking by Nigel's bungalow the next afternoon, I see that he has packed, his duffel bag and his Halliburtan hard cases are lined up on his balcony. Surprised, I ask where he is going.

He tells me he is going back to Hong Kong. He's been offered a position by one of his former partners, as a currency trader. He'll have a desk. And a home. He'll wear a suit.

He can't look me in the eyes as he tells me this.

And now that he is gone, there is a vacuum, and none of us knows how to fill it.

We stay in Tenote, but the delicious languor of weeks past now seems torpid inertia. We do not know where to go. We watch as other riders of the circuit arrive and depart, posses of kids in Oakleys and Versace camouflage prints, and I can see that what is going on is we are checking out other groups and, somehow, auditioning for them. Our gang has psychically splintered. Nigel, in his quiet, stolid way, held us together. And now we will have to find new cliques. Another band of merry ravers, a new crew. Jason and Tamara, both attractive and affable, will have no problem finding traveling companions. As I look over the incoming and outgoing riders of the circuit, I hate myself for wanting to fit in, for wanting to be counted among the cool kids. What was the point of leaving my old life and those pressures of conforming if out here I just discovered a new dress code and required set of behaviors? Warrior tattoos. Long hair. Teva sandals. Versace camouflage shirts. Oakleys. Get something pierced. If I want to ride the circuit, will I have to succumb to a new aesthetic every bit as constricting as a tweed suit?

Dina and I are discussing our next move while sitting on a craggy rock over the bay. When Nigel was here, we never had to discuss where we were going. We just went. Now we are weighing options, striving to reach some sort of agreement about when we should go. Dina has become uncharacteristically quiet, leaving me to do most of the talking about schedules, departure times, possible flights from Koh Samui to Bangkok, from Bangkok to Kathmandu. Dina just nods, as if she feels it's wrong to have to discuss so intricately and deliberately where we are going.

"Let's talk about this later," she says, wandering over to the other side of the boulder and clambering down to the beach.

I dive into the water, adjusting my snorkel. I see a snake, white and dark green, slithering between the coral. Resisting the urge to panic, I paddle farther out into the water, admiring the schools of blue, green and yellow fish, each of them darting this way and that through the reef, finding, with each seemingly random turn and veer, just enough of whatever it is that sustains them.

In the spring, the riders of the circuit migrate north, compelled by equatorial climatic conditions and the monsoon season to seek out the temperate Himalayan foothills of the Hamachal Pradesh, Kashmir and Nepal. I have come north with Dina, assured by her that I would love Nepal, that Bali was too hot, and anyway, who wanted more tropics? But as I wind through the narrow streets of Kathmandu's Durbar Square, between Maju Deval and Trailokya Mohan Narayan Temple, dodging Nepali shoe-shine boys and Sherpa guides and bemoaning the fact that I have only one light wool sweater with me, I begin to wonder if I am losing a sense of myself. I feel I am playing a role, pretending to be carefree and footloose, when really I am neither of these things. These magnificent, immense triple-roofed temples with erotic carvings and elaborately painted roof struts, and those at Patan and Pokhara and Bhaktapur and even the splendid Himalayas in the distance and the possibility of a trek up Annapurna or a river-rafting trip in Chitwan, all of it has taken on a movie-set-like aspect, as if all these beautiful buildings and lovely vistas are just facades and painted scrims, and my fellow travelers and companions are also actors, paid extras hired to flesh out my trip. There is in this life of constant motion an inherent superficiality. What is the point of finding where the real depth lies if you're shipping out next week? You use a place, drain it of money and/or fun and keep moving, and if you use a place, you will use people. It becomes predatory, take what you can when you can and move on, because who knows where you will be tomorrow? The restlessness is not a by-product but a necessity. If you don't keep moving, you risk putting down roots, and if you put down roots, you have to get to know people, let them get to know you, and that is risky and boring and what's the point of that when there are great-looking, really cool boys and girls waiting on the next beach, at the next rave, in the next city? I have noticed there are no last names out here, everyone goes by a first name or a nickname; Jason, as he and Tamara were shipping off to Kashmir, even refused to tell me his last name, for fear that at some point, in some hazily imagined future, whatever he was doing would come back to haunt him. When I asked him what he was doing that could possibly be used against him, he shrugged. "You never know."

You never know, and you never trust anyone. You become like Nigel, a backgammon-hustling guru manqué, encouraging everyone to stay in the moment while scheming a way to get back into the financial markets. Or you become like the girls hostessing in Tokyo, making money for one more round of the circuit, tired of it all and bored with the life and sick of Asia already but no longer knowing what else to do.

"You can't go back and just work at some office," Nigel used to say before he went back to work at some office. "After you've been living on the circuit, let's face it, you're spoiled. How are you going to keep the boys down on the pub when they've seen Bangkok?"

It is New Year's Eve, 2055 of the Nepali calendar, and swirls of young Nepali boys, drunk on Tiger beer and Jack Daniel's, dance in the street to chanted ragas. They pump fists, shout "Happy New Year" and offer foreign women free massages. At Old Spam's Space, a generously courtyarded Thamel bar and nightclub, students of rival universities glare at one another and mingle uneasily. While a band of withered Caucasians twangs out a junkyard version of "Brown Sugar," Nepali blood runs hot as causes are found for numerous disputes: New Year's, apparently, is a time to settle old scores. As fistfights erupt around the stage, at the bar, next to our table, I look at Dina and notice something missing in her eyes now, a brightness lost, the blue eyes that were so full of mischief are now tired. Since our gang broke up, she hasn't been the same.

That night, after Dina goes to bed, I take a *tempo* to the Everest Hotel and play blackjack with Israeli army veterans and Japanese businessmen in a huge casino that reminds me of a high school basketball gymnasium. My fellow gamblers are intent on their cards and their Scotch; the game is joyless. I play blackjack like a robot, sticking when the dealer shows a five, doubling down on my elevens. This numerical enslavement to statistical probabilities is the opposite of the freeing-up of the soul I had hoped to find on the circuit. I begin to play irrationally, hitting on sixteens, splitting fives, doing everything wrong. I end up winning a few thousand rupees. Proof I shouldn't do things by the book.

When I return to our teak-and-mahogany-appointed cottage at the Kathmandu Guest House, toting a box of fresh croissants, I notice Dina's steamer trunk and Prada bags are gone.

I find a note on the nightstand, weighed down against the air conditioner's breeze by a hundred-yen coin.

> *This is the game that changes as you play.*
> *Bye—*
> *dina*

I go to Tokyo to visit my grandmother.

STANDARD DEVIATIONS

L aney had had jobs before. Short stints. A few months tending bar in Tokyo. A couple weeks riding around Los Angeles in a van with other aspiring male models. But really, since graduating from Pepperdine University with a business degree, he'd done nothing more to apply his academic skills than counting the take at the end of the night at RIP, the dive bar in Tokyo he'd worked in before hitting Jakarta.

Until now. This job, as an equity analyst for Falcon Securities, called on him to utilize his talents with spreadsheets, decision trees and inventory valuation—all the quantitative tricks he'd supposedly picked up eking his way through four, okay five, years of college. What his work actually comprised, however, besides hunching over a Sun workstation and Bloomberg terminal and squinting at flickering numbers, was sneaking into his bosses' never used twenty-fourth-floor corner conference room and gazing out the long-paned windows at downtown Jakarta's new luxury hotels and the shiny bank towers and the Indonesian

Parliament building that looked like a German army helmet, the whole smoggy mess shimmering with heat in the afternoons, and he would smoke the Marlboros provided for guests in a sterling cup emblazoned with the firm's bird of prey logo and marvel at how easy this job was. If he'd known that working in finance was like this, he would have signed on years ago and avoided the lost years bumming around the Far East. Not that he minded the Roppongi nightclubs or the German college girls down on Koh Samui or the Chinese diving students down in the Philippines. But this was somehow more exciting. Even the language of international finance and multimillion-dollar transactions was intoxicating: rips, riders, skinboats, squeeze. Fund managers called him all day from London, New York, Tokyo. He'd tell them stories about companies and powerful families: Indosat. Indofood. Astra. The Bakrie brothers. Two hundred million Indonesians. A burgeoning middle class that will be buying ever increasing amounts of rubber, plastic, fertilizer, whatever. They need cars, he'd tell them, gasoline. And the banks, well, the yarns he could spin about the banks. Tirtamas. Danamon. PSP. They borrowed in dollars at 7 percent and loaned in rupiah at 15 percent. With pegged exchange rates, this meant the Indonesian financial-services sector amounted to the surest bet in the world. He'd spit out some gibberish about single-digit price to cash flow, about sector growth rates, about the firm's political connections. About Madoff Dhar and the Asian tiger phenomemon. About 100 percent returns in dollar terms. About the Jakarta Composite Index being up 350 percent in just five years. And what could the money runner say but that he was going skinboat on Indosat? Every manager of every Global Emerging Equity Growth International Markets Fund was overweight Indonesia. Bigwigs came through every week. Barton Biggs. Julian Robertson. Mark Mobius. They met with central bankers and Suharto's family. And they bought.

Laney's job was to pick up the phone when these hungry fund managers called, and find some equity—any equity—to feed their greed. They had to have Indonesia in their portfolio. Now.

The firm made a fortune on its Jakarta shop. The sell-side bonuses piled up: Laney made more in a week than he'd made in six Tokyo months.

There were a dozen brokers like him on the sales desk, up from four local hires two years ago. The company seemed to take on any *bule* who came through with a business degree or a working knowledge of Bahasa. They sat in a glass-walled room along one side of the building, the air-conditioning turned up so that they carried their Armani and Gucci jackets to work and put them on before they sat down. The VPs sent over from New York and London wore English-tailored wool. The AC on their wing was cranked up a notch higher to accommodate their even spendier Savile Row suits.

Laney loved the camaraderie of the desk, the bullshitting and winking and high-fiving and the almost prisonyard-like macho posturing. Even the Indonesian guys, A students all of them—this may have been an entry-level position for an American business student, but for a Pribumi kid this was the big time—even they got into the trash talk about turning a fund manager into your bitch, and cracked up when someone ripped a loud fart.

Laney had arrived in Jakarta six months earlier, fresh from Tokyo, where, despite the girls and coke and even this stylish shearling jacket he had bought, he had begun to feel, for the first time, that life wasn't turning out as he'd hoped. Rangy and rugged-faced handsome with brown hair and blue eyes, Laney had looks that had always served to burn a trail through whatever adverse terrain he wandered. Laney possessed the attractive force of a potent man who seems indifferent to his power. That force, as palpable as the weather, had an atmospheric radius the size of a pub. It hadn't translated to photographs or videotape. His modeling career had ended weeks after it began. This despite the fact that the very same magazine editors who wouldn't book him wanted to bonk him. That would be a recurring pattern in Laney's life: girls liking him but doubting him. They were dismissive of him: any fellow who looked like Laney had to be a bit daft. But among men, Laney's manner could almost come across as diffident; his good looks didn't frighten away the rest of the boys.

Laney and I hadn't been close during high school. Laney never went through the awkward, long-limbed, pimply, chronic-halitosis stage that I was mired in for most of my teens. It seemed that one week Laney was collecting baseball cards and riding dirt bikes, and the next he was dating Rommy Mitchel and driving a Mustang. What you had to admire—even our teachers seemed to notice it and graded Laney on his own personal curve—was the effortlessness of his cool; he was neither calculating nor self-aggrandizing. It helped, of course, that you initially heard about Laney in the context of his being a stellar athlete, first as a fine Park League shortstop and AYSO center forward, then as a fluid surfer and casually stylish skateboarder and finally, by the time we were in high school, as an accomplished letterman volleyball player.

Laney was popular, of course, in the way that being well liked and the object of three dozen pubescent-girl crushes can make an otherwise normal kid appear to have rock-star attributes in the eyes of his less bitchin' peers. Certainly, by the time we were in high school, Laney had become one of those names—like Carrie Adair or Brit Linander or Rommy Mitchel—that were uttered with awe by the other kids in our grade. But Laney was the only dude whose name carried that sort of mysto freight. The rest of us feckless, gangly fifteen-year-olds could only speculate as to why it was that Laney already seemed to be accepted by guys three years older and how he was able to date Rommy Mitchel, a tight-bodied brunette whose last boyfriend had been the guitarist for Oingo Boingo, all this before Laney even had a driver's license. This was Laney, after all, with whom we had all played soccer and gone skateboarding, and suddenly he had been tele-ported to the realm of popular kids and their BMWs and hot chicks and the sort of life we imagined David Lee Roth was living while the rest of us were still pedaling over to Tim Thurtle's house on ten-speed Nishikis to score quarter ounces of mumbo.

To his credit, Laney never came off as arrogant. He always greeted me with his little head-bob-and-raised-eyebrow nod, the humble gesture always striking me as dependably American, almost small-town in its earnestness. (In Mr. Haddock's English class, I once overheard Bonnie Saucer and Brie Spitz oohing about Laney's little nod. It was yet another of his undeniably cool attributes.) We had more than a passing acquaintance, having played together on a half-dozen youth and tricounty soccer teams. If anything, as a teammate, he had been too unselfish. He sometimes gave up the ball when the best thing for the team would have been for him to dribble through the opposition and score. Instead he would cut through the defense, then leave the ball off for me or one of our teammates. What we then did with it was much less predictable than the good result you could count on from Laney. I can remember at least one sharply angled pass I received from Laney, onside in the penalty area, about four meters in front of the Mar Vista goal. I should have just struck the ball the first time, but in trying to control it with my left foot, I mistakenly pushed it too far forward so that it rolled harmlessly into the goalie's gloves. But Laney, alone among the half-dozen best soccer players in our town, wouldn't get upset when a less gifted athlete misplayed a ball. (Before one game against a team from Hollywood, Carlos Marzulli, a fiercely aggressive midfielder, threatened to stab me if I missed another easy goal. I took myself out of the game at halftime and had my father drive me home, claiming I had a headache.)

If Laney hadn't sat at the desk in front of me in Algebra II, we probably wouldn't have spoken for most of our sophomore and junior years. We were then occupying different realms. Laney was off in his world of good-looking girls and guys, and I was still playing Dungeons and Dragons and smoking crappy Colombian grass. For someone who clearly had better things to do than worry about the rudiments of the quadratic equation—if I had half the sexual possibilities that Laney appeared to, I never would have gone to class—he was a surprisingly good student. It was always a little frustrating for me that Laney didn't study and scored B's, while I with my equally poor work habits got C's.

Once in a while, if we both got to class a few minutes early, he would ask me how it was going. I would look up from the dungeon map I was drawing or the twenty-sided dice I was rolling to set up a new D&D character and tell him it was going all right. He would nod and look down at whatever I was doing and shrug. But again, Laney didn't seem condescending or supercilious, he would just do that little nod and turn back around and wait for class to begin.

By the time I was a senior, I had caught up some, becoming socially adroit enough to show up at the same parties as Laney, and we were able to resume a more thorough acquaintance. It was as if for him all my years of being too shy to talk to a female and spending all my time playing D&D had been magically eradicated. Or maybe he didn't think about it at all.

I don't know if what we had after that was a friendship; it was more a series of earnest conversations. He seemed to like talking to me, and we discussed different topics, mostly current events, history, politics. Though I still got barely passing grades, I did a lot of reading—books, magazines, newspapers: the only positive legacy of all that D&D was that it got me in the habit of turning pages. Laney was just discovering reading, or the idea that he was supposed to read, and he was wondering if there was anything more to it than the books he had read for his English classes— *Of Mice and Men, To Kill a Mockingbird, A Tale of Two Cities.* He had seen me in class with my monster manuals and *Lord of the Rings,* and I guess he now suspected that I knew something he didn't.

I didn't know anything, of course. Then Laney surprised me, he began asking me about foreign countries, different cities. I mentioned once that I was going to Japan with my family, to see my relatives, and that apparently set him to wondering. How was I going to communicate? What was I going to eat? I had been there before, and I told him you just sort of picked it up, the language, the food, it was easy. I don't know that anything we talked about ever stuck with him. But of everyone I went to high school with, he was the only one I ever saw in Asia.

We would end up hanging out in Tokyo, and I would eventually see him in Hong Kong and travel to Bali with him. He took to the region, in his phlegmatic, easygoing way. He came over to Tokyo after college, landing a contract with a second-rate Japanese modeling agency. He called me when he came to town, and we became closer in Tokyo than we had ever been back in Pacific Palisades. Perhaps that was more a matter of proximity, but somehow I was flattered that he seemed to now regard me as an equal. To me, of course, I was an imposter, nowhere near as cool as Laney and not in the same league. Hanging around with Laney, to me, was still like being with a rock star. The popular kids in high school retain that patina of supercoolness well into their twenties. Perhaps it fades badly after that, but during those years, Laney still possessed the same self-confidence that had served him so well back at Palisades High.

Laney hated to admit it, but it was true: he had been skating through life. The only area in which he had really excelled, Laney had confessed to me, was with women. When he was fourteen, he'd discovered that the reason his sister's friends always seemed to be hanging around the Brentwood split-level was because they enjoyed being close to Laney. Whatever image he was projecting out toward the world, Laney realized, it was likable. Both men and women enjoyed his company. And as he got older, that company turned to sexual congress with women. But not because he was good-looking—though he was, in a young Mel Gibsonish way—but because he was so easy to be around. With Laney and those blue eyes and that fleshy-lipped smile, girls could just sit there and be with him, on the couch, in front of the television, at the beach, wherever, and it would all be comfortable and natural and sweet. Not like it was with other boys.

He'd kept count in college: 102. There had been at least four dozen more since. But what Laney really adored wasn't the moist, impersonal action of a one-night stand but rather the frisson of budding romance that even the crawl up to a one-night stand could provide. For a few moments, while you were in a taxi from the club or standing together at the bar and you realized as your heads drew closer together and maybe you touched her neck or her side, there was this vast potential, a welling so great that it could contain all of Laney's force and desire. Too often, what it amounted to after that was just the mechanical act of rutting. In Tokyo that cycle of potential romance dissolving into a few nights of bonking had begun to seem like a downward spiral of less and less spiritual return and even diminishing physical gratification for each fuck.

He had come to Indonesia seeking a break. As his Garuda flight descended into Soekarno-Hatta, he could see the skyline glistening with dozens of partially completed glass and steel office buildings topped with immense cranes frantically swinging tons of concrete and steel into place like a breed of skeletal giants racing to reach the sun. The roads were choked with taxis and chauffeur-driven BMWs and Benzes. The air was already foul and besmirched with exhaust and factory exhalations. But in this bustle and filth, despite the newspaper boys and guitar-playing indigents who swarmed his taxi at every light as he rode in from the airport, Laney had sensed an energy and an opportunity, a backdrop against which he could reinvent himself. In Tokyo, he'd heard stories about the bubble, about the boom, about the good times he'd missed. And he'd seen the cranes idle atop unfinished office towers. But here in the Jake, he realized, he'd walked smack into a boomtown.

The next day, when his college buddy Bryn took him down to Plaza Senayan, where he saw the swarms of Chinese at the Tiffany and Joseph Abboud and Moschino boutiques and a rapacious sort of consumerism that he hadn't seen even in Tokyo, it confirmed his feelings of the day before. He saw two Indonesian teenage girls—they couldn't be over fifteen—actually fighting over a Moschino skirt with a golden clasp. And the place was expensive as well, Laney noticed as he paid the equivalent of $50 for a lunch of oxtail soup and pasta at an Indonesian-Italian place furnished with old Javanese teak pieces.

Whole gilded sections of town appeared to have sprung up between blighted neighborhoods. Next to a swath of rotting tin-roofed wood shanties would be a block of boutiques, restaurants and department stores offering, for a few hundred air-conditioned square meters, a viable version of Miami or Tokyo or Hong Kong in the middle of this impoverished third-world capital. Bryn—same year at Pepperdine as Laney, same lousy grades—was working for an English brokerage that was putting him up in a three-bedroom Blok M house with a swimming pool, three servants and a cook. It was the kind of place people paid a few million dollars for back in Tokyo.

That night, Bryn took Laney to a gathering of expats at his VP's house and introduced him to a few bankers and directors who gave Laney their cards and suggested he come around to see them. Laney had barely opened his mouth. He'd stood quietly in his one off-the-rack Ralph Lauren suit, swirled his claret and nodded as the expat financiers whispered to him as if it were a secret what kind of returns and growth the country was experiencing, and how all that return and growth had to be analyzed, traded and invested. That word was everywhere: growth. Phenomenal growth. Unprecedented growth. The kind of growth that happens, said a VP from Boston, when a few hundred million people suddenly realize they want their MTV. Someone had to provide the capital for that build-out. "Why not us?" a banker from London told him. "Why shouldn't we get rich right along with the natives?"

Laney couldn't think of a thing wrong with that.

The next day, during his first trip to the Falcon VP's office in Tower One of the Jakarta Stock Exchange, he'd realized how badly he wanted to participate in this orgy of wealth creation. From listening to Bryn and his friends at that party last night, it sounded like all you had to do was sit down, log on and start making a fortune. He wanted a piece. While he was waiting in the lobby along with a few other Caucasians and some Japanese fellows, all wearing fancy-cut suits and expensive wristwatches and carrying leather attachés, he'd felt embarrassed of his slightly out-of-fashion two-piece and the worn-out valise he'd borrowed from Bryn. He shot his cuffs to cover his plastic Swatch.

He shifted his weight while Mr. Chawling, the VP who ran the Falcon office, scanned his résumé—not much more than that biz-admin degree and few dodgy internships—and asked what the hell Laney had been doing the last two years.

"I've been a barman," Laney said, shrugging. "But if I had been doing something really great, you think I'd be here looking for work?"

Mr. Chawling was used to smart, quick, quiet Javanese and Chinese kids or American and British MBAs who pitied him for spending his career in this pathetic backwater. Laney was different. Laney was neither obsequious nor supercilious. "Here." Mr. Chawling wrote the name of a listed company on a piece of Falcon letterhead. "I'm gonna give you a shot. Tell me if this is a buy. Use my terminal."

Laney looked at the piece of paper. Astripa. He'd never heard of the company.

"Fifteen minutes," Mr. Chawling said, and walked out of the office.

Laney sat at the terminal, and after five minutes he had managed to call up a woefully inadequate set of financial statements. He managed to plug the numbers in to a spreadsheet and, after applying what seemed like the appropriate local interest rates, had been unable to extract anything like a free cash flow for the company. It was a dog.

Laney nodded as Mr. Chawling reentered the room. He hadn't gotten very far, Laney explained, but he didn't like what he saw.

"Wrong," said Mr. Chawling. "What does Astripa do?"

Laney shook his head. "Something to do with construction?"

"Birds' nests," Mr. Chawling said. "They have a whole plantation in Surabaya full of menageries of these little fucking swiftlets whose nests the Chinese can't get enough of in their soup. They're the number-one supplier in Indonesia—they have the exclusive government license—and they are soon to be number one in the U.S. and wherever hungry Chinks get a craving for the old-fashioned taste of bird's nest. Fifty-percent year-on-year growth. That's a strong buy."

Laney nodded. He'd blown it.

Mr. Chawling smiled. He was looking at Laney's half-completed spreadsheets and shaking his head at the quaint notion of interest rates somehow being relevant to recommending a well-connected Indonesian company. "Is this what they taught you in college?" he asked. "How to miss out on the most explosive economic growth in history?"

There was that word again: growth. Then he told Laney to come in on Tuesday. He'd start him as a junior analyst.

To celebrate, Bryn took him to Tanamur, a capacious cavern of a disco in the Tanah Abang section of town, where bar girls outnumbered the male customers ten to one. Laney, no longer concerned about husbanding his savings now that he had landed a job, bought drinks for a host of girls, Jujus and Titis ranging in color from a toffee brown to a balsa-wood beige. Regardless of the skin tone, Bryn was dismissive of them, referring to them all as LBFMs—Little Brown Fucking Machines. They were rent girls, Bryn told him, to be taken home and banged silly. Laney had seen his share of brothels and pickup joints, from Pattaya to Yoshiwara. This scene was different. As a joint, it seemed to possess that rarest of whorehouse traits: a plentitude of pulchritudinous hookers.

The girls, of course, were flocking to Laney. It is a phenomenon rarely commented upon, but Laney had noticed it in the past: that even in brothels, a man's looks, charm and sexuality are highly valued. Perhaps more so than anywhere else. There was a certain logic to that if you thought about it. What was the value system of a whorehouse? Sex is money. For the boys as well as the girls. In Laney's case, the girls could tell that this was a man to whom other females would ascribe a value. It's just the way hookers view the world: looks matter and sex matters even more. And in walks this guy embodying all the things these girls cared about, so they gravitated toward him as they would to their own reflections. They saw in Laney, this big strapping foreigner who they were sure would have a big cock, all the things they wished they possessed themselves: good looks and a cool sexuality. In his way, in this arena, Laney was like royalty.

He was giddy at the prospects laid out before him: not just the pussy lined up along the wood-paneled bar, but also the job and the money, the whole gilded potential of this town. What was that word? Growth. He bought another round of tequila shots for himself, Bryn and some girl named Cici. When the barmen set down the shot glasses, Laney slapped Bryn on the back and toasted, "To growth."

And he leaned back against the bar while Cici, a Batak from Medan with skin that shimmered like red rocks at dusk and long straight hair and a tight body with plum-size breasts squeezed into a little white dress, rubbed his crotch through his jeans. "Take me with you," she was saying, "I wanna go with you super bad."

Laney brought her back to Bryn's, along with a friend of hers from Jambi, in Central Sumatra. Bryn, shorter than Laney, was clearly less of a catch in the girls' eyes. The friend from Jambi lost out on some kind of argument with Cici and plopped herself sullenly on the rattan sofa. She wore imitation leather pants, a metal conch-pattern belt and a black T-shirt knotted at her waist. Leaning back on the sofa, she folded her arms, staring petulantly forward. When Bryn had gone into the kitchen, Cici said something to her in Bahasa, her syllables slithering as she scolded her friend for letting down the side. It struck Laney as a professional exhortation, a reminder that they had a job to do and were being paid to perform. And so perform this girl did, removing her top so that her large-nippled tits swung into view, and she cocked her head up toward Cici as if to show she was a good sport.

Bryn returned, carrying a couple of Diet Coke cans and a bottle of Glenmorangie. "Yeah, there it is, honey," he said, setting down the sodas and pouring them into glasses.

They stood in a trio, Laney, Bryn and Cici, as if they were an audience of the other girl, whose name Laney hadn't bothered to catch. As if to please this crowd, the topless girl swung her shirt over her head like a lasso and tossed it so that it landed in Bryn's face. Then she bobbed her fist up and down in the universal gesture of a cock sliding in and out of a mouth. Bryn shook his head, shrugged and unzipped his pants, pulling down his khakis and red-and-white-striped boxers so that he was standing in his blue shirtsleeves. The girl leaned forward, fished between the buttons of his cotton oxford, found what she was looking for and began methodically working on him, smearing her lipstick on his pallid member, staring up at Cici the whole time.

Bryn looked at Laney and grinned. "LBFMs." He shook his head. "The best." Then he turned back down to the girl. "Come on, lick my balls."

His first week, Laney had gone to Versace and bought two new wool and silk suits. There were five Versace boutiques in Jakarta, which struck him as odd considering the average Gembel's propensity to walk around in sandals and dirty dungarees. The riches of Indonesia's great boom, while plainly visible in select cantons, had hardly been dispersed evenly throughout the city. For every society matron who owned fifty-two pairs of Manolo Blahniks, there were a hundred shoeless indigents with outstretched wrinkled claws begging for 500 rupiah notes. For those lucky enough to be connected to the ruling regime or one of the elite families or business groups controlling the country, the spoils of this kleptocratic capitalist boom seemed boundless. The flowchart of companies that Laney had posted on the wall of his hotel suite was like a giant million-legged spider of firms interlinked and interwoven—the STTC Group was connected to the Raja Group, which was linked to the Bimantora Group, which was partially owned by the Schwab family. All you had to do was be on that chart, be the name at the end of one of those tendrils, and all the financing you could consume and political favors you desired would be bestowed upon you by the international community. With the fire hose of foreign capital gushing into Indonesia—$50 billion every year—there was no reason why they wouldn't all get their Benzes and Rolexes and compounds in Puncak. That was why, after all, a guy like Laney could show up and after forty-eight hours in town land a job paying him more money a month than he'd made in six Tokyo months. He had an expense account and club memberships, and the company arranged for him to stay at a serviced flat in a residential hotel.

The nights dissolved for Laney into this routine: squash or racketball at Club Olympus, a few drinks at BATS or another of the expat watering holes, then off to Tanamur or Tambora or Interhouse or another girlie-bar establishment, then back to his residential hotel, where he began every evening anew his quest to lose himself in rented female flesh. Laney found a certain release in the ritual of payment for sex. Even when the girls didn't ask for money, which happened once in a while, he would insist on paying them. It made a certain karmic sense to give something back to this country that was making possible for him a life and career he had never previously imagined.

It actually occurred to him one night, as a tall, lanky teenager named Momo who wore cutoff jeans and no underwear was dancing around his apartment to Primal Scream's "Surrender," that what he was pursuing was the final break between sex and romance. By paying for it, by evolving into a sexpatriate, he thought that he could transform into this sort of new man, one who didn't care about love, one who venerated what really mattered and what they talked about all day at the office: pussy and money. The money had made everyone greedy, from the VPs at his firm to the lowliest streetwalker down on Jalan Mahakam. They all felt entitled to a piece of the action. And it tainted them all, made them all somehow complicit in creating this atmosphere of venality and corruption that extended its leathery reach everywhere—from the beggars to the Suharto family themselves, everyone was furiously busy getting theirs.

He mulled this while Momo was bending over, pulling aside her faded denim to show him her ridiculously hairy pussy—she either didn't know about waxing or didn't care—and then turning around and blowing him a kiss. She had a face like a thief's. But this Momo who wanted everything and wanted it all now— earlier in the evening Laney had marveled at how she had gobbled the Elephants he'd offered her and then, in the taxi back, how eager she'd been to pull his stiffness into her warm mouth—was what Laney now aspired to be: a dirty, greedy cunt.

He was sitting at his desk on a swivel chair, raising the fingers of his left hand and sniffing at them every few minutes to see if that smell was still there. He hadn't been able to wash off Momo's odor, her underside's essence had adhered to his flesh and become part of him, and it was now leaching through onto his computer keyboard and his telephone handset. A vaguely briny smell, halfway between sweat and piss with a hint of musk, the odor wafted through his workstation. He wondered if his coworkers could detect it. Or would they just think it was the stink of the place, a little sex mixed in with all the money.

There was a new guy at the desk across from Laney. A graduate of some college in the U.S.—Michigan or someplace like that—Tommy was Javanese from a good family; his father had been a cabinet minister. He'd started a few days ago, wrinkling his brow as he scanned the Bloomberg and the databases, pulling down columns and rows of figures he was indexing and running through some sort of revenue-projection models. He'd been hired, Laney assumed, because of his family. The firm needed a few of these guys—rich kids who knew the right people at the right companies. They came into the office and took their places every day behind their terminals, but they hardly bothered to do anything. They'd read the Asian *Wall Street Journal* or talk on the phone and then knock off early for lunch and maybe some tennis. They weren't expected to field calls from fund managers; once in a while they would take calls from Indonesian companies that were seeking to get their shares upgraded. Implicit in their working arrangement was the fact that these privileged scions of the ruling class were biding their time before taking the helm of whatever corporation or federation had made their families wealthy. Not coincidentally, they were quiet and gracious and expected to be left alone.

But this Tommy was different. For one thing, he was wiggling his nose as if he could detect the stale pussy in the air. Laney, who rarely smoked, wished he had a cigarette or something to hide the stench. He kept his head down, pretending nothing was wrong as he scanned the wires.

"Something stinks," Tommy said.

Laney shrugged. "Open a window."

"Like something died," Tommy said.

Laney ignored him and studied the Bloomberg. The Lakers had beaten the SuperSonics. The Bulls were on a six-game winning streak. He got up to check if the conference room was empty. He could take a break, go for a smoke. But upstairs, Mr. Chawling was speaking animatedly into the speakerphone while another VP gazed out the window. Laney wondered for a second if he could go in and pluck a cigarette from the cylinder but thought better of it.

When he returned to his desk, the phone was ringing. An emerging-markets guy from San Francisco, a fixed-income specialist looking for a little Asian yield, short maturity, high liquidity—he wanted to get out of it at the end of the quarter. Laney hadn't been working on fixed income. But how different could it be? He scrolled down his trading screen to see what the firm was recommending: Astra, Indofood, Telkom, Steady Safe. He scanned the yields: two seven-point-fives, an eight and a nine. All dollar-denominated. He recommended the nine, assured the specialist the market was highly liquid—he had no idea if this company's bonds ever even actually traded—and that the underlying fundamentals were good. A Moody's upgrade was imminent. Cash flow was excellent.

"I'm looking at the financials right now," Laney was saying. "This is proprietary data."

After he hung up, he saw Tommy staring at him. "What?" Laney asked.

"Man, you can really talk some trash." Tommy had a thin mustache, like a charcoal line on his upper lip. It wasn't like the kid shaved it that way, that was just the best he could do in terms of facial-hair production. His mouth was set in a pout that went along with the slightly dour squint of his eyes. When he spoke, he bobbed his head, the range of movement widening with each syllable so that by the end of a sentence, his skull was bouncing like a panting dog's. "That company is diseased."

Laney shrugged. It seemed just like all the other companies they were recommending. "What's wrong with it? They're a taxi company. Have you ever tried getting a cab in Blok M on a Friday night?"

"I know what they do," Tommy said, "and I know they've floated a lot of debt. This firm was the lead Asian underwriter."

"So why shouldn't we recommend them?" Laney was getting a little annoyed. No one had ever questioned his analysis before. It was unsporting of Tommy to be changing the rules like this. If the analysts had to justify every call they made—or, even worse, were subject to this sort of grilling—they'd become too timid to answer the phones.

"Don't you ever wonder"—Tommy was leaning forward, his head bobbing above Laney's Bloomberg—"what's going to happen to all these companies and the funds that are buying all this shit you are shoveling?"

"It's not me," Laney said. "This comes from way up the ladder. The big guys are saying we're overweight Indonesia. This is the party line."

"I know, I know." Tommy shook his head. "But what are we going to do when something goes wrong?"

"Don't you think they've thought about everything that could go wrong?" Laney felt like he was lecturing an overly curious child, one for whom every answer would just bring forth another question. "Their models take into account what could go wrong. That's all part of the sigma."

"What about nonsigma events?" Tommy asked.

"What?" Laney was becoming impatient. "There are no such thing—that's why it's called a standard deviation."

"We are nonsigma events," Tommy told him. "You and me, all of us, the human race, the evolution of intelligent life, this planet being just this far from the sun. All nonsigma events. Yet they all happened. And here we are, living in this huge nonsigma event, and all you can do is tell me it's all been factored into the models?"

This was getting too philosophical for Laney. He sniffed his fingers reflexively to see if the smell was still there.

Tommy began to whisper. "Rupiah collapsing: nonsigma event. Jakarta Composite crashing: nonsigma event. President falling: nonsigma—"

"This isn't current-events class," Laney told him, "this is finance. We're talking about stuff in the real world."

Tommy nodded. "Okay. Real world. You know that taxi company you just recommended? My aunt owns it: she's already spent most of the cash she raised, and she hasn't bought one goddamn car. Did that show up on the report?"

Laney brought Tommy down to Club Olympus, the fitness club attached to the Grand Hyatt where the expat high rollers hung out after work. Club Olympus's lacquered wooden gym lockers and marble floors and gold-plated fixtures and white-jacketed serving staff and immaculate tennis courts all combined to become in Laney's mind's eye the heavenly city to which he'd ascended upon joining the moneyed classes. He reveled in the atmosphere of posh entitlement: if you were here, it was because you were somebody—at least in Jakarta. Even though he was only a local-hire analyst, his club dues were covered, and here he could mingle with big-money expats and powerful local business interests.

He'd become buddies with Tommy at work. Tommy was precisely the opposite of Laney; rather than being dazzled by the greed and money, he was bored. He'd been born into the sort of lifestyle to which Laney now aspired, so he didn't understand that desperate yearning. Rather, Tommy saw Jakarta's decadent carnival as being natural, as endemic as chicken porridge or sambal. He took for granted that he should drive a new Benz 320 and that his family should have a summer house in Puncak and even that he should be working in a financial-services firm. Tommy was part of the ruling elite of his country and was the beneficiary of the elaborate system of graft, greed and patronage upon which the whole economy seemed based.

So Laney found in Tommy a reassurance that there was somebody and someone actually connected to this spectacular, clanking machine of wealth creation, someone at the back end of the underwriting deals and public offerings. It was, somehow, all for Tommy. Laney liked just being around that sort of entitlement and easy-earned prestige. It was his way of feeling even more in the center of things.

But at Club Olympus, as Laney and Tommy sat beneath the Delonix trees drinking bottles of mineral water after tennis, their hungry gazes took different paths: Laney's toward the Chinese or Javanese girls in their tennis whites and Tommy's to the strapping expat wives and daughters in Nike and Adidas sports bras. While Laney was lost in a string of ever sluttier Asian hookers, Tommy was mesmerized by the big-boned, long-jawed sorts of Caucasian women Laney had had by the dozen back in L.A. For Tommy, this had been the primary obsession of his college years, the midwestern Maryannes and Jennys and Graces. These American girls who were just so *there.* In this area of most easily reached male consensus—this one's doable, that one's not—there was nearly perfect reverse correlation in Tommy's and Laney's preferences. Which meant their friendship was never put at risk by competitive pursuit of the same girl.

At work they had evolved into a sort of one-sided running commentary. Laney listened as Tommy told him the inside stories of the companies he was recommending. Laney was so used to not worrying about the level of foreign debt a company was carrying, about how companies were managing cash flow, or even whether or not the business models were sustainable, that he was captivated by Tommy's cutting descriptions of what these companies actually did. It was like Tommy was revealing the fecund guts behind the pristine, infallible flesh of numbers. The numbers, after all, had their own internal logic. Laney had never stepped back to question the basic assumptions. But for Tommy, all these companies were real, fallible people that he knew. His uncles, his friends, his cousins. They were real people running businesses that he could tell did not make sense. He would tell Laney stories of his uncle's construction companies and his friends' fathers' banks and how foreign banks were throwing money at them, $8 million to finance a $4 million project. The rest of the money was spent on Benzes and trips to Gstaad.

Which made Laney pause for a moment as he reflected that the buy-side pressure, for the first time since he'd started, seemed to be letting up.

Most weekends Tommy was busy with family obligations. Weddings, circumcisions, funerals, birthdays—he spent the weekend in elaborate jacalabas or dinner jackets, getting snookered with his Catholic relations or sipping tea with his father's Muslim business partners. Not that he minded it, he told Laney, he didn't even really think about it; his life passed in this succession of obligatory arrivals and reception lines. His day job was to sit behind a terminal, and his weekend job was to turn up and smile. That's why he had loved college, even if Michigan had been frigid. Those four years away from his family, the taste of freedom he'd gotten, had been delicious. It had all been fun: the off-campus apartment he'd shared with two other finance students, the girls from Detroit, Saginaw, Eau Claire.

"Why didn't you just stay there?" Laney asked.

Now was the time for Indonesians to be back in Jakarta, Tommy told Laney as he maneuvered the silver Benz through Menteng, past the monstrous, Dutch colonial houses crammed in next to one another like too many wedding cakes in a bakery window. He gestured at the gaudy real estate, as if to indicate that was the reason he was here.

What he meant, Laney knew, was the spectacle of the city. Tommy wouldn't miss it for the world. He wasn't stupid. What was Tommy in the States? Another Asiatic with a lot of money. A sidebar to the American story, which, despite the boilerplate about diversity, was a Caucasian narrative. Here he was a central character. A case in point was this party he was bringing Laney to, a shindig thrown by one of his friends, another American-educated Pribumi from a wealthy family.

They swung left as they exited the district, winding up a hilly lane that seemed to be carrying them up and out of Jakarta, above the humidity and the smog to a more ethereal environ where, Laney imagined, mere financial mortals didn't dwell. They passed between rows of posh apartment buildings before coming to a halt at a guard post where Tommy waved and was let through. Laney hadn't even known this district existed; it was an exclusive enclave in the middle of an enclave, an island of extreme wealth among the very richest Indonesians. The houses here were just as monstrous as those down in Menteng, only they were set farther back from the road on spacious plots and built with austere style rather than gaudy ostentation.

The party was held in a modern teak villa, designed by the same architect who did the Legian in Bali. The stained-wood foyer floor extended out past immense ten-foot-wide glass transoms that had been swung open onto a patio that was an unbroken continuation of the living room floor. The two wings of the house, in the same sublime combination of teak and glass, prowed out past the black stone swimming pool to a garden and carp pond.

There were only two other *bule* at the party: the American

ambassador and a youngish executive from Royal Dutch Petroleum. But Tommy introduced Laney to some of his friends: other young Indonesian boys and girls, most of whom had been educated in the U.S. Laney sipped his Scotch and soda and engaged in small talk about Jakarta and Los Angeles, little discussions about weekends in Bali versus Puncak, and how the new BMW Z3 compared with the old 325ic. One girl seemed to be the owner of an entire island, and not some rinky-dink one-palm place but a major resort Laney had heard of. Another fellow was, unless Laney had misunderstood, the minister of tourism. There were two actresses he recognized from television commercials—could one of them be the deodorant pitchwoman he had so admired?—and an older man whom Laney believed he had seen in a music video strumming a guitar.

Laney's job wasn't particularly impressive, nor was his lineage in any way comparable to these people's. But as far as the locals were concerned, if he worked with Tommy, then he couldn't be entirely bereft of status. As he made his way through the crowd, handing out his business card but really winning people over with that wide-toothed smile and hangdog expression, he felt like he was breaking through to yet another level of Jakarta. He stopped for a minute by the pool, catching a glimpse of Tommy in animated discussion with two other young men in jacalabas. Laney couldn't hear them, but he knew Tommy well enough to guess the gist of the conversation: he was probably relating something one of his uncles had said. It would either be Uncle General or Uncle Minister. Tommy was always well informed and was valued by his friends—and by Laney—as a great source of gossip.

But the other reason this party was inspiring was the women. He felt a million miles from Bryn and his LBFMs. These were refined Javanese princesses, with pearly skin and slender frames and couture gowns that cost as much as those Tanamur girls earned in a year. Laney, for all his getting around, hadn't been with rich girls. It had taken him a while to get here, but now that he had arrived, he knew what it was he wanted. As he lifted his drink to his lips, he checked for the stench of that bar girl on his fingers, but she was all gone.

Several of the women were eyeing Laney—he was, by a long stretch, the most attractive *bule* at the party—and Laney, shifting his weight and nursing a drink by the pool, couldn't help but seem approachable. Again, this was his talent, to be cinematically handsome and yet seem unaware of it. It was as if every girl at the party could imagine she was the only one who saw the sexual potential in this tall, rugged American. Laney didn't know it, but his slumping form, alone, quiet, shooting furtive glances at the girls, was at that moment in the sights of at least a half-dozen women at the party, one of whom was now making her way across the hardwood deck, alongside the pool and around a clump of mustachioed Javanese to see what was what with this fellow.

"You're friends with Dion?" the girl asked Laney.

Laney turned to take in a slender Asian girl with short, wide lips, a delicate, wide-nostriled nose and narrow brown eyes. For a local, she had protuberant cheekbones—two pronounced ridges beneath her eyes that gave her face a melancholy slant. It was the vaguely sad cast of her face that made her seem severely beautiful, like she had been damaged once before, so that her wariness now made her seem cruel.

Laney shook his head. "Do you know Tommy? I came with Tommy."

The girl turned her head sideways, as if to get a better look at Laney's answer. She wore a white gown of some sort of diaphanous material, cinched at the waist with a thin silver belt thrown over tight black pants. It was the kind of outfit that would be flagrantly sexy on some women and in some settings. But here, where everyone knew that this was what Biyan, a currently esteemed Jakarta designer, was doing this season, the getup came across as a badge or statement, the semiotics of which Laney couldn't yet comprehend. The girl mentioned Tommy's last name and then asked if Laney was Australian.

"Yank," Laney said. "I'm Laney." He held out his hand.

She took it. Her name was Quan Quan. She'd been to college in the States, at UCLA, where she'd studied biology for two years and had planned to go to medical school. Her father had been enthusiastic about this, she told Laney; he was very modern that way. However, she had not been an eager student, and she'd found myriad activities in Los Angeles more compelling than schoolwork, and after a few semesters she had taken to spending more time heading to nightclubs in her leased Toyota than cramming for finals, and then one semester she'd just stopped going to class and it took her father nearly nine months to figure that out. At the end of that run, she had no choice but to return to Jakarta.

"But I'm going to go back," she said, "I love it there. This place is nothing for me."

Laney shrugged. He wouldn't call it nothing. But then, any place with a girl like this—he was admiring the delicate tapering of her wrist, the platinum Chanel tank watch—was quite something.

"I'm having a blast here," Laney said. "It's exciting. Back home there isn't this much . . . growth."

Quan Quan squinted at him. "Growth?"

"I mean the pace of the place, like a current running through you, a surge coming up through the floor." Laney gestured with his drink, a sweep of his hand up his body. "You feel powerful."

Quan Quan laughed, covering her mouth with the back of her hand. "And you, Laney, you feel powerful?"

"I did." Laney grinned. "And then I met you."

Quan Quan began to walk along the pool, her heels making soft clicks against the patio. Laney fell in beside her. "You grew up here?"

"I went to Tarakanita." She looked at Laney as if this was supposed to mean something. "And then after, of course, the States."

Laney nodded.

"And you?"

Laney told her about Brentwood, about Palisades High School and then about Pepperdine. They talked about places they'd both been in Los Angeles, Tatou, Vertigo, Roxbury. They realized they'd probably been in some of the same clubs on the same nights. Laney mentioned his sisters: Trish, who was married to some fellow named Brett in San Diego, and Kate, who Laney believed was a lesbian.

"You must miss them," Quan Quan said, walking with her hands folded behind her back. Her hair, thick and slightly curled, swayed in a wiry curtain with each step. "Family is very important to me. My sister is married as well. She stays at home with our parents. My mother built her and her husband and my nephew another house on the compound."

Laney thought about his family's modest Brentwood split-level. Three bedrooms. A strip of backyard the size of this swimming pool. "Compound" was not the description he would use. They sat down at a table beneath a fishtail palm, where a few other couples made small talk and sipped cocktails. Quan Quan and Laney were locked in, both slightly drunk, the chat coming easily and their conversation comfortable in the way that new friendships can be when neither party feels they are working harder than the other. Laney even admitted to her that he didn't know what he was doing at the firm, and that he sometimes wondered why they kept him on there. But then again, the other guys at the desk were as clueless as he.

Quan Quan didn't work. She baby-sat for her sister once in a while. Or she helped her mother oversee the various family businesses: palm farming, orchid cultivating, arwana fish raising and false-teeth manufacturing.

She had a slight tan beneath her white top, and her skin showed the color of honey beneath a strand of pearls. What struck Laney was her insouciant elegance. Yet her frank ease was balanced by some sort of pathos that made her seem total, full, a real person. Otherwise she would have been just another rich girl, and Laney would have seen in her a potential sexual conquest, nothing more.

He walked her to her car, a waiting, idling chauffeured Lexus four-wheel drive. As she climbed in, she turned and extended her hand, which Laney took and held for a moment, gazing at the smooth flesh, the light glow of it in the night's blue light, and then he looked up at her, taking in that half-smile and half-frown, her confident entitlement and desperate longing. She was wonderful.

Later, as he stood with Tommy and a circle of his friends—an observer would have pegged them all as rich swells in good suits—Tommy asked him about Quan Quan. Laney raved.

Tommy took him aside. "I have to tell you something," he told him, nodding. "She's Chinese, you know."

"So what?"

"I just thought you should know," Tommy said.

Laney shrugged. This inter-Asian bullshit didn't concern him.

He had Tommy drop him off a few blocks from his apartment. As he walked between the edge of the road and the parked cars, skipping over the puddles, he was surprised that he didn't feel like heading to Tanamur to pick up a Kiku or Sisi. Not that he didn't feel a longing—he did—but now, rather than a nameless desire, his needs had been clearly defined. Quan Quan.

Calling her the next day, he hadn't felt anxious or unsure of himself but rather that this was all proceeding according to some plan. Their talk came easily, and even when Laney recognized it as juvenile chatter, it didn't seem constrained because they were not awkward with each other as fresh crushes usually are.

He visited her house, the vast compound out in South Jakarta where rows of orchids and palm trees extended in geometrically correct lines over a red earth hill, vanishing in the misty sun. There was a black-bottomed pool and, of course, several carp ponds that Quan Quan pointed to, explaining, "These are for good luck and getting rich." There was even a fashion shoot going on in a bamboo-shaded pagoda where slender Pribumi women were posing in what looked to Laney like saris. Laney and Quan Quan stopped for a while to watch as little brown boys adjusted reflective silvery circles and little brown girls touched up the makeup on these tiny models. They didn't seem like women at all to Laney; they looked like props, extras to provide a backdrop for Laney and Quan Quan's afternoon. As they strolled the grounds, she pointed out the concrete pillboxes that dotted the hillside next to the house, where her mother had hoped to raise swallows for bird's-nest soup. Quan Quan explained that another company had the government license, forcing the family to abandon that business. Laney shook his head. He felt like he was penetrating the innermost reaches of this society—hadn't he started with a misunderstanding about birds' nests? And now here he was, in a place where actual people were affected by the crooked licensings and corrupt cronyism.

When you're in houses like this, on properties this grand, you almost feel that you have become a member of some club. That just getting there as a guest requires a certain skill and talent that most of the world's impoverished billions will never have. If Laney had stayed in the States, in Malibu or even Los Angeles, would he have ever gotten this deep into his own native culture of capitalism? In twenty-three years of living in L.A., the goings-on of that town, the movie studios and record labels and Katzenbergs and Geffens, he had felt as if it were all happening on a planet other than the one inhabited by him and his buddies down at the beach. Perhaps he hadn't been ambitious enough? But he hadn't changed. He was no more ambitious in Jakarta, but here he felt connected. Even this girl whose arm he now took in the shade of a florid palm, whose tan flesh he stroked gingerly as he watched her chest rise and her breathing become more rapid—she represented the finest reaches of this society, of this great nation.

He pushed her gently against one of the abandoned aviaries, finding shade and cover under the low-slung eaves. It was still early afternoon, too early for this, Laney felt, but he also felt a stiff insistence that he pressed against Quan Quan, who pushed back, her own yearning warm and moist, though that was as far as they went that afternoon, feeling each other and pushing against each other and not yet consummating, for reasons Laney couldn't explain but that Quan Quan believed had to do with his being traditional and respectful and all those peculiar traits Westerners seemed to value and which she had never actually found in the West.

That night the cook prepared coconut rice and some sort of crispy chicken and a whole steamed fish, and they ate sitting on the *pendopo* by the swimming pool, their shoes off and their legs folded beneath them on the warm wood. A servant lit jasmine incense that kept mosquitoes away and then set paper lanterns adrift in the swimming pool, the current cast by the water filter making the lanterns bob and the shadows of the trees sway.

Quan Quan's sister, Ginnie, came in with her son, a three-year-old whose name Laney heard as Bam, and the boy climbed up onto the raised platform and stuck his hands in the rice before stomping loudly in his tiny Nikes around on the wooden platform, as if daring his mother to stop him. You could tell Bam was Quan Quan's nephew. He had her roundish, sleepy eyes and her angular cheekbones. Ginnie was shorter than Quan Quan, and perhaps it was the trials of motherhood or just age, but she was like a slightly smudged Quan Quan, her ass just a little wider and breasts seeming a little saggier. Quan Quan tried to take the boy in her arms, and he acquiesced for a moment but then shook his head, giggling, and resumed stomping.

Ginnie greeted Laney with a handshake, her slim arm protruding from beneath a rolled-up white shirtsleeve. "We've been shopping. Bam wanted Kentucky Fried Chicken." She spoke in a twangy English accent, almost a cross between Singaporean and Australian accents. "So the driver stopped, and when Amah was going in, Bam threw a hissy because he insisted we eat there." Suddenly aware she didn't know this *bule* friend of her sister's, she asked, "You wouldn't happen to be the owner of that restaurant?"

Laney shook his head. "Can't say that I am."

"Well, it's a wonderfully funny little place. Its patron saint is this man who looks like Santa Claus. At first I thought he was Santa Claus, but then I noticed he had no hat and the wrong type of glasses—Santa has those wire-rim, sort of Armani-ish glasses, and this man had glasses like Elvis Costello. Anyway, everything has this crust on it, not crispy but an actual sort of dough or second skin that crunches and tastes, well, tastes basically like salt. And that's all Bam would eat. Three pieces of chicken—what they call breasts, as if chickens were people—and Bam peeled off this second skin. He loves it. I think it's a quite popular place for students. And now Bam has to go to bed."

The boy stopped stamping around in circles and got down on his hands and knees, sliding down the far end of the platform, intending to slip from the conversation and thereby stay awake for a few more precious minutes. He looked up at Laney as he went over the side. Don't give me away, his eyes said.

Laney shrugged. He could be relied on when it came to kids against the adults. His allegiances still remained firmly with the more subversive and anarchic children's team. So as Ginnie began to look around—"Where's he gotten to?"—Laney kept quiet.

Quan Quan's father, mother and brother-in-law had all gone to central Java, where the family's false-teeth factory was in the midst of expansion—as Indonesia prospered, upward went the dental aspirations of its populace. So many men and women, teeth blackened from *kretek* smoking and reddened from betel-nut chewing, were being bombarded by Ciptadent and Colgate TV spots and feeling suddenly insecure about the inside of their mouths. The false-teeth business preyed on their insecurities, providing them with ill-fitting—but blindingly white—teeth that left some of the more remote and primitive villages practicing cannibalism with pristine plasticine chompers.

Before Laney left, Bam insisted on showing him the plastic dinosaurs he had received with his meals at Kentucky Fried Chicken. "These are animals from a hundred years ago," Bam explained, showing Laney the red and green T-rex and a grayish brontosaurus. "I'm going to get, oh, a thousand of these."

Laney took the T-rex. "They lived more like a hundred *million* years ago."

The boy started laughing at such a preposterous idea. "A

hundred *million million million*." He took the T-rex and tossed it in the air. "Million, million. My mother is two million years old. How old are you?"

"About that, give or take a million."

Bam sized Laney up, as though guessing his age, and then decided he had been on the level. "Well, can you get me some of these, oh, get me the triceratops. That's the yellow one who fights with the T-rex."

Quan Quan, who had been giving the driver instructions about taking Laney home, joined them in the foyer. "Laney is a busy man, he can't be hunting down your toys."

"Not a problem," Laney said.

"The triceratops." Bam nodded to Laney.

Quan Quan took Bam by the shoulders, bending over to kiss him on the ear and then turning him to face Laney. "Say good night, Bam."

Quan Quan's driver took Laney back to Blok M, the chauffeur-driven Lexus flying up the Merak toll road, past trucks overloaded with cotton bales and baskets of tea and bundled cords of lumber. It was a cloudy night in Jakarta, the equatorial sky obscured by low gray clouds that reflected the city's excessive neon back on itself. The driver wound between the trucks, slowing down for a roadblock before being waved through.

When they swung off the highway near Tomang Raya, they were immediately bogged down in traffic. Up ahead, Laney could see piles of smoke rising skyward and, here and there, a flickering tongue of flame. Drivers were trying to back their vehicles up or cut U-turns over the highway divider. And now individual men or groups of two or three were running back through the rows of cars, shouting something Laney couldn't understand and banging on the hoods.

This was a *demo*—demonstration—of some sort. They were written about almost weekly in the newspapers, *bonek* gatherings of soccer fans who fought with one another and destroyed some property before police drove them back to the provinces. The driver, shouting in Bahasa out his open window, was clearing the way between lumber trucks and was about to head back to the highway. "We go back," he said.

Laney nodded but then told the driver to wait. He'd get out here and have a look around. After all, he reasoned, he had no beef with these people.

The driver looked at him curiously. Then he saw his opening in the traffic, but still he hesitated. "Miss Quan Quan will be angry. We go back."

Laney opened the door. "You go. I'll be fine. Tell Quan Quan that: Laney is fine."

As he walked off between the rows of idling trucks, he saw that the drivers, used to such demonstrations, were flipping through gaudy colored sports magazines with their bare feet propped up on the steering wheels. A few of them were napping. How bad can this be, Laney wondered, if the drivers can sleep through it?

Up ahead, Laney knew, was a wide plaza to the north of the Democracy Monument. From what he could see as he cut over to the guardrail and then hopped to the sidewalk, that was where the demonstrators were gathering. He realized as he saw the young men rushing to join the demonstration that these were not soccer hooligans from the countryside in town for a match, these seemed to be students—and there were some girls in the crowd as well. The girls wore jeans, platform sneakers and colorful shirts; to them, this seemed almost a social event. Laney, this tall, brown-haired American wearing Cole Hahn loafers, Zegna chinos and a navy blue Pink's short-sleeve shirt, was clearly out of place, drawing curious glances from the students who were rushing in from the side streets to the square. Roadblocks had been set up by the kids, who were systematically redirecting the cars down side streets. Several bullhorns were blaring, eliciting occasional in-unison chants from the students.

Still, this was a small gathering. And when the police arrived in their black squad cars, the students began to disperse, chanting as they went. But the police moved into the crowd in dense phalanxes of ten and twelve, prodding at the students with rattan canes and striking out every few seconds as a student would stand up to them. There couldn't have been more than a thousand students, and this show of force by the police amounted to the sort of bullying tactic common among Asian police forces. Laney had never seen it firsthand. This little demo was hardly a threat to national security, Laney guessed, but the police and those they represented could truck no disobedience or criticism, even when it was coming from young girls in platform sneakers. So the response was to lash out. Laney thought of Tommy and his discourses on how Indonesia was all much more fragile than it seemed, held together, really, by the cruelty of the regime, the greed of the entrepreneurial classes and the ignorance of the peasantry—and, of course, the active participation of the armed forces and security services.

The students were fleeing now, their Trisakti and Tarumanegara University banners being trampled underfoot. He saw a girl rush by with blood pouring from a head wound, and then a kid who had lost his shoes and was limping, his toes apparently crushed in the melee. Laney stood by, tucked into the shadow of a loquat tree, not knowing if he should risk himself by going to help. He was, after all, just a bystander, and all these goings-on really had nothing to do with him. What Tommy hadn't said but Laney now suspected was that they too were complicit, part of the system that was corrupting and depleting this country. All the money for which Laney smoothed the path into the country was fuel for the problem, sustenance for a system of greed and corruption. And what about those girls? All those LBFMs, the whoring and using of these people? Laney wondered if he was actually part of the problem, if he was as complicit as these cops. Could the argument even be sustained that the cops were here, beating up college kids, to keep the brothels open and safe for men like Laney?

As he wondered about this, and fingered his mobile phone to call Tommy and pose the question, a policeman appeared before him in a gas mask, his eyes invisible behind tinted plastic goggles, his truncheon waving menacingly over his head. Laney ducked, shaking his head, *no, no.*

"PERS?" the cop shouted.

"No," Laney insisted. He was not a reporter.

And the cop looked him over and pointed back in the direction he had come from, toward police lines, showing Laney the safe way out.

For weeks now, they'd had virtually nothing to do. Currencies throughout Asia, the Thai baht, the Malaysian ringgit, the Philippine peso, had been imploding since the spring. And virtually every currency and central bank in Southeast Asia had been under intense pressure from speculators to float their currencies, while the banking systems had been squeezed by hard-currency investors who now wanted to repatriate assets. It was a regional economic crisis that was turning all the suppositions about the Asian miracle upside down. The historically high rates of growth, savings and exports were all being overlooked now because of—what? Asia was now seen by investors as a region with deep troubles, including overinflated property values, corporations burdened with foreign debt, banks with stinky balance sheets. But that had always been the case, Laney reasoned, what had changed? Sentiment. It boiled down to that. Just a few months ago, financing growth with foreign debt seemed like a good idea, and pegged currencies seemed sustainable. Now you had Barton Biggs, that lerpy bastard who looked like a rhinocerous, saying he believed a vicious circle was at work. *Bapak*—the Bahasa word for "father" used to denote Suharto—had no choice but to make the historic decision to let the rupiah float. The roop was already down 35 percent in just six months, while the Jakarta Stock Exchange was off by close to 50 percent from its high. Laney and the rest of the analysts and brokers would gather around the squawk box in the afternoons and listen to the firm's global economists from London and Hong Kong saying this was a correction and some reassuring of investors and fund managers would be required. From the ashes, the disembodied voices announced as Laney sat gazing at the skyline and the brown smoke from distant trash fires, a new miracle will arise. Also, they were told, start looking for good values in this depressed market. Clients would be buying again soon.

But the phones were dead. No one was looking to go skin-boat on anything Indonesian anymore. The markets were talking louder than the squawk boxes, and for the analysts and brokers that meant bonuses would be skeletal this year. And it wasn't likely to get any better anytime soon. Look at Thailand, where the baht had gone from twenty-five to the dollar to fifty virtually overnight, forcing the closure of hundreds of Thai banks and brokerages. The situation in Malaysia had also been tragic. The Philippines, worse. What was going to hold the Indonesian financial sector together, Suharto's blandishments and promises that he would rein in his own profligate family and cut off a few of his cronies? By the time the government really lifted the peg, it was a moot point, with no banks in Jakarta—or anywhere in the world, for that matter—willing to take roops for dollars. And Suharto's initial unwillingness to agree with the International Monetary Fund's terms for a $43-billion bailout package was only making the currency more unstable.

Tommy had been right all along. All the models and projections and calculations hadn't asked the right questions: What if the peg collapses? What if Suharto himself falls? What if the country dissolves? "This is the imperialism of numbers," Tommy told Laney. "We don't have valuation models for a revolution. Yet our numbers have their own internal logic, no one thinks to step back and question the basic assumptions." Laney, thinking of the riot he had seen and the five Versace boutiques and the legless and armless indigents who swarmed around his chauffeur-driven car on the way to work, was now questioning the basic assumptions.

The change around the office was unmistakable. Everybody had too much time on their hands. For the brokers and analysts, this meant sustained discussions about when to head over to Club Olympus or whether the best move was take a month off and head to Bali. Another subject had also popped up in the discussions: politics. When Laney had first arrived, no one had discussed politics; the attitude had been "Hey, that's politics, we're professionals." As long as there was growth, no one could see any problems.

But somehow, when plumbers and *bajaj* drivers can't afford to buy rice or cooking oil or gasoline, then the talk about politics takes on an edge that even jaded brokers can't resist. Because that's what was happening in the country. The collapsing currency didn't hurt Laney or his kind—they were paid in dollars deposited into foreign banks—but for the locals who saw their average income drop from $23 a week to about $4, this was a full-scale economic cataclysm. They had a name for it now, *krismon*, monetary crisis, and it was being blared from every radio and the lips of every TV newscaster. The riots and demos had become almost a daily occurrence, with one campus or another being shut down by police and, gradually, a blending of soccer rioting and political rioting happening that meant the *boneks* were now listening to the students, or vice versa. The protests could now take a high and low road, appealing to both patriotic intellectuals and xenophobic thugs. With nearly a million workers being laid off every month, there were more and more peasants ready to join the marches, singing along to the dangdat music, a sort of Javanese country-western, and taking every opportunity to loot or rob an unguarded store.

On the grounds of Club Olympus or Quan Quan's house in the suburbs, there was barely a murmur of this discontent. Once a tennis match with Bryn had to be postponed because of lingering tear-gas fumes the gardeners couldn't dislodge despite the wind machines rolled onto the court. And at Quan Quan's house, there was general concern about the increasing incidence of anti-Chinese violence throughout the archipelago, in particular a spate of attacks directed at Chinese merchants on Java and Sulawesi. Though the Chinese comprised just 3 percent of the population, they had historically made up the bulk of the merchant classes—so they were now the most immediate local target for hungry, angry peasants. The regime itself seemed to be using the Chinese as scapegoats for the troubles, withholding police protection and allowing looters to ransack Chinese shops. The Chinese had often been persecuted by the Pribumi majority, and before them the Dutch colonial authorities. They had even been forced by the colonial Dutch governor to live outside of Jakarta proper. In 1740, when Chinese bandits were blamed for attacking city outposts, the good citizens of what was then called Batavia rose up and murdered five thousand Chinese. In 1965 hundreds of thousands of Chinese had been murdered in the aftermath of Suharto's successful coup, in which he overthrew the Sukarno regime. The Chinese were rounded up as suspected communists—though most had not been in China for several generations—and murdered by army and militia troops. There had been periodic bouts of ethnic violence throughout the seventies, but in the eighties and nineties—with economic growth raising the tides of the middle class—anti-Chinese violence, at least in Jakarta, had been sporadic.

Still, Quan Quan's father, a taciturn man who wore thick glasses and read imported Cantonese newspapers while he drank beer and ate peanuts, had been grumbling that perhaps the whole family should move up to Singapore for a while. But Faugai, the matriarch of the clan, opposed any such maneuvers as being terrible for business. And here, behind the compound's broken-glass-topped stone walls, all was serene—the orchids bloomed, the palm trees swayed, the sparrows chirped and the carp swam.

As Laney sat down with the family for supper some evenings, it seemed his problems were really here in the house rather than out on the streets. He was tolerated by the clan—except for Ginnie and Bam, who truly seemed to like Laney. He won Bam over by presenting the boy with a prized tricerotops from KFC along with a few dinosaur coloring books. And Ginnie would have been won over by anyone with Laney's looks, even if he turned out to be a child molester.

It wasn't that the rest of the family was unpleasant or rude, they just seemed totally indifferent to Laney's presence. At supper, bent over his plate of rice and steamed fish and ginger sauce and sambal, he interacted more with Bam than with the other adults. Perhaps that's how they saw him, Laney suspected, as a sort of novelty, a useful entertainment for the child—it certainly would improve the boy's English—but unfit for general conversation.

Once in a while, Faugai, who didn't speak English, would say something to Quan Quan in Cantonese or Bahasa, which Quan Quan would translate.

"She wants to know how much that jacket cost," Quan Quan would say.

"Tell her, I don't know, tell her it was a gift," Laney would say, shrugging.

Quan Quan and the mother would then talk for a while before Quan Quan would turn back to Laney. "She says if you paid anything more than seven hundred Hong Kong, you're a fool. I told her it's rude to talk this way."

Laney smiled. He'd paid fifteen times that. "Tell her I'm a fool."

And this comment, untranslated, elicited great laughter around the table.

After supper, Quan Quan would ride back to Blok M with him and then go upstairs to his residential hotel to steal twenty minutes or so of passion while the driver waited in the idling, air-conditioned Lexus outside. They usually wouldn't get further than his entry hall before they were pulling each other's clothes off. She usually wore these black one-piece numbers she could just pop out of with little struggle, and then Laney would get down on his knees—right there in the foyer, on the steps that led to the living room—and he would lick into her and she would already be wet and she would reach down with her fingers and spread her lips apart and pull herself back so that he could lay his tongue on her.

There was a heaviness to Quan Quan's lovemaking, she moved slowly but with great purpose, gyrating her hips to some internal rhythm that Laney found mesmerizing. She had so many levels. She could be this quiet Chinese girl, listening attentively, pouring him tea, studying an Australian *Vogue* or *Dewi* magazine, but with a sniff or a look she could tell him she wanted to leave a restaurant or that he should change the channel. Yet in bed she surprised him, becoming brooding and determined, almost hypnotically fucking her way to orgasm, losing herself in these moments they had together but always making Laney feel included rather than excluded. (That was so unlike inducing a whore's orgasm. The whore's orgasm was entirely personal—you became her tool.) And afterward she would prop herself on her elbow and play with his brown chest hair, or sometimes distractedly keep on playing with herself, her hand working down below her straight and sparse pubic hair, keeping herself moist until Laney was ready again. Surprisingly comfortable with her body, she would walk around the bed naked to get a glass of iced tea, making an awkward bowlegged step when some of Laney's semen would drip out of her.

For Laney she was a marvel, not because of the sex but because of what she was letting him discover about himself. He saw through the tangle of limbs and the arching of her back and the way her eyes rolled and pupils dilated as she came, he saw through their humanity like it was a thin veil through which he could make out this idea: love did matter. He needed to unload himself of his own history. Like a sinner at confession, he wanted to reveal that he had doubted that simple idea, had been on a mission to destroy the notion that it mattered. Pussy and money, he told her, were what he had embraced. Nothing else had applied. It was all irrelevant. The country could collapse in riots and looting and mass murders, but the Laneys of the world would thrive on the chaos—the hookers had already been lowering their rates. That's how he had been remaking himself until now. He told her about the hookers, about the strippers in Tokyo and even about the freckled blondes back in Malibu—God, that seemed like forever ago—and she pouted a few moments about the girls he'd had. She even asked how many women there had been, and he honestly had no idea.

One evening, as she was slipping into this green and black Richard Tyler number, she stopped suddenly, holding her pumps in one hand and lifting her hair with the other.

"Let's tell the truth," she said, turning in the direction of the lamp on the night table beside Laney.

"I've been," Laney said, "I mean—"

"No, me. It's quite disgusting, actually," she said. "I have a son."

"Wha—?"

"I became preggers while I was in school. That's the real reason I came back to Jakarta. We've kept the boy. My sister raises him."

"Bam is yours?"

She nodded. "He doesn't know it. He thinks Ginnie is his mum."

Laney sat up in the bed.

"It hurts," she said, but shrugged. "Now you can blackmail me if you like. My family, our reputation, you could destroy it in Jakarta. You see, I'm damaged goods, unfit for a proper marriage. Do I disgust you?"

"Hardly," Laney said, hugging her. "But now you're stuck with me."

I was in Jakarta doing a story when I caught up with Laney and Bryn at Club Olympus. Bryn told us he was leaving Jakarta. His firm was recommending that all its non-Indonesian nationals pull out. They had chartered a few jets. Pulling back to Hong Kong, Hawaii if necessary. (What was this, Laney wondered, a war?) There was no reason to stay anyway. No one was making any money.

"But we have friends here," Laney was saying.

Bryn just waved that off. "All the Yanks and Pommies and Aussies are going, leave this place to the locals to squabble over. We'll be back to underwrite the bonds when they need to rebuild the whole mess."

Bryn admitted he would miss the LBFMs, but frankly, he was getting sick of Asian pussy. What he wanted now was an American girl, something white and pink and smelling of soap and deodorant. These girls, my God, the smell. It was fun for a while, a novelty, but come on—a chick as pungent as an NFL linebacker's game-day crotch? At some point you missed that floral and baby-powder scent of a girl from back home.

"Don't you?" asked Bryn.

Laney nodded. He didn't, really. He told me he was now worried that Falcon would pull everybody out. It was probably cheaper to charter jets and send everyone home than to keep the office running and the systems going. He wouldn't go. He couldn't.

Laney wondered if it was as bad as all that. The riots had become a daily occurance by now, a regular nuisance, a part of life. Just like the increasing number of stores that were marked *Milik Pribumi*—native-owned—so that no one would mistakenly assume they were Chinese-run and therefore fair game for looting. And while it had become harder to procure some basic supplies—toilet paper, new CDs—because so many shops were always shut down, at the Kronus, his residential hotel, his fridge had remained stocked with Grolsch and Bintang, and you could always buy pirated CDs on the streets. Tommy had told him that most Indonesians could no longer afford to eat chicken, the protein staple of their diet. The price of fuel had doubled. And to worsen matters further, a drought had depleted rice harvests. The economy, in the words of one government official, "had a stroke." And now they were talking about the roop going to twenty-five thousand to the dollar. Savings were being wiped out overnight—and that was if you could withdraw from a bank, if you could find an open bank.

Laney looked around Club Olympus. Here were two Western wives walking back from the pool in thick, cottony bathrobes. An older couple was walking along the botanical path amid the snake plants and nut palms. Perhaps he and Quan Quan could just stay here at the club, taking refuge in the lanai and living on Pimms and melon juice.

"You should go," Bryn said. "Don't wait till the last minute. There's nothing here anymore. Falcon will put you somewhere else. Even as we speak, another market is emerging somewhere. Growth is happening. I hear Mozambique is blowing up— proximity to South Africa, decent highway system and they've got their civil war all squared away. Next thing you know, they'll be funding huge infrastructure projects that require foreign investment. Plus, they've got great dope that goes for like a dollar a pound."

"I'm not going anywhere," Laney told Bryn. "It's not like I have anywhere to go. And there's this girl—"

"Oh God," Bryn said. "Not some LBFM from Tanamur?"

"No, no, Jesus." Laney shook his head. "No, she's Chinese."

"Then she should be getting the fuck out of here as well. Before the Pribumi start machete-ing everyone who's not as brown as them." Bryn looked over his bill. "Hey, get her a ticket. To Mozambique, baby, the Bique."

To get to the tennis court, they had to follow a trail up over the hill, past the abandoned aviaries, to a wide, shallow canyon that was in the shade of some eucalyptus trees. The grass court was well kept but buckled in one corner from a tree root pushing up the chalk lines. Laney and Quan Quan would volley for a while and then play singles—Laney's harder service usually allowed him to prevail, but Quan Quan had superb racquet control and was able to give Laney a good sweat. She was by far the more stylish player, her backhand more level and her follow-through more complete. It took all of Laney's strength and speed to beat her, although he let her believe he was going easy for the sake of more competitive matches.

They both loved tennis—no one else in the family played besides Ginnie's husband, Ray-ray, and he was always off somewhere worrying about the family's businesses. This was one of the few places on the property they could be assured of being totally alone. No one else bothered to come out here. Faugai had actually proposed using the flat and relatively fertile land as a small pen for raising Kobe beef—much prized by the Japanese businessmen posted in Jakarta.

But in the meantime, Quan Quan and Laney hit balls back and forth, then made love in the little clubhouse just up the hill from the court, squirming out of their skimpy tennis whites on the rattan furniture. That was also where they talked about their plans. Laney asked Quan Quan if she was thinking about leaving. "A lot of firms are pulling out," Laney was saying, "and if Suharto goes and all that, you know—the government falls. Then it could be bad, especially for you—"

"Because we're Chinese," she said.

"Right. So we should just go. The two of us." Laney told her he had some money saved. He proposed Thailand. Or Spain. Or Los Angeles.

Her family even had apartments in Vancouver and Hong Kong. But Quan Quan wouldn't budge, not without Bam, and that meant she had to go wherever Ginnie and Ray-ray went, because they were Bam's family now. Ray-ray wouldn't go anywhere as long as Faugai and the father were staying—he was a good son-in-law and had to help with the businesses.

"But the businesses—who cares about the businesses?" Laney insisted. "You might get killed."

Quan Quan told him not to get so excited. It was politics, a minor flap, a few drunken *boneks* smashing in windows. It has been like this for decades in Indonesia. Her family knew, they had been here seventy-five years and would be here a hundred more.

"Now," she told Laney, "hug me."

And by that she meant fuck me. When he was deep inside her, that idea, of going away, of leaving, seemed absurd. He would be here. As long as she was.

Later, Quan Quan told Laney about Bam's father, a tall Filipino-American with long hair and a narrow mustache. His name was Ferdinand but everyone called him Ferdi. He was a lead singer of a salsa band that played around in Los Angeles—at the Arroyo, the Bell Ballroom, even the Tropicana. And they toured the Southwest and played once in New York. He had a soft, smooth voice—like a Latin-Asian George Michael—and to make money he sang on commercial jingles. Had Laney ever seen that commercial for Del Taco, the whole "Mexican with a Twist" campaign? Laney didn't remember it.

"Well, he was the voice," she told him.

And he was a wonderful dancer—a gentle but confident lead, whether they were dancing ballroom or merengue or salsa. Quan Quan had hardly needed to know a step and they still looked great on the dance floor. That was where they'd met, dancing at Flaming Colossus, they bumped into each other on the floor and she had refused to give him her number. She was there with a few of her friends, one of whom was Mexican and knew the name of Ferdi's band. They went to see his band—the New Swing Army—and during a break between sets, she found him and they talked. God, she was just a kid then, a sophomore living in one of those Westwood apartments off Veteran. She was sharing a one-bedroom with another girl, a blonde from Newport Beach who would vanish into drug rehabs and halfway houses before the semester was over. Quan Quan didn't miss her—the girl had paid her rent for the whole academic year in advance. Quan Quan's world had been econ and stats and cooking her own nasi goreng and using sambal she had brought over from Jakarta and going out with a few other underclassmen to frat parties and the occasional club—and then there was this guy. He was gorgeous and sweet and he was in a band. What he looked like, really, was this sort of taller, slightly thinner Johnny Depp, only with a hint of menace in his eyes. He was tough and sexual, in these shiny black suits and Italian ankle boots.

Well, when he went back onstage that night, he sang a song to Quan Quan, called her his *Bagong bahilan para mabuhay*—his new reason to live—and she felt like she was fifteen years old and listening to Bros again. Only she was twenty and would be bonking this guy within two days. He introduced her to a whole new way of life. He lived in a converted storefront way out in Hollywood, past Vermont. He had tattoos up and down his arms and his chest: a sunglassed, Rolex-wearing Christ and a Virgin Mary in Louis Vuitton and another one, of the Filipino flag, and underneath it, in Tagalog, it said, "For My Country, For My People."

"God, do you know what it's like to fall in love that hard?" Quan Quan asked Laney. He did.

Ferdi lived in this hypermasculine music scene where the guys—mostly Filipinos and Mexicans with a few Peruvians and Colombians—dressed in these sort of updated *Miami Vice* outfits, but never in those stupid pastels, always in black or gray with white tank tops underneath. Ferdi drove a Corvette from the early eighties, a ridiculous muscle car with a T-top. And when he and his friends talked, in Tagalog or Spanish or English, it was like they had marbles in their mouths, they had this sort of Mickey Rourke monotone, the words stumbling out around their Camel Filters. They fixed cars. They were always buying and selling guitars, trumpets, motorcycles, drugs. Other girls came and went, young Chicanas with names like Lorainna or Louissa or, God, how many Marias were there? Quan Quan couldn't stand the way the girls dressed, in tight jeans with flared cuffs and chunky black shoes or red pumps or those skateboarding sneakers. When they went out, they would wear floral print dresses or tight blue and red minis, sometimes leather, stuff that was easy to dance in. And they went out together all the time, to Tatou or Roxbury or even to Slim's, and it was like they were a gang or something—when they walked in, it was like they owned these places. They would get pitchers of margaritas on the rocks, no salt, or Cosmos, or the guys would pay a bottle charge and mix tequila and ginger ale and bitters at the table.

"But Ferdi, he made me feel like a princess. You know where I come from? Look at this place. What he was showing me was a completely different society of, like, tough men who just reached out and took things. And Ferdi took me. I was drunk with him, intoxicated, in Bahasa the expression is *cinta itu buta*, you say—what?—struck by Cupid's arrow? Love is blind?

"I got pregnant—and it wasn't like I even thought about whether I wanted to have the baby or not. And Ferdi, when he noticed and asked me, he just shrugged, like of course I was pregnant—but secretly, I thought he was happy. You know, like this was the macho thing to do, to have kids when he was twenty-five. He was so proud of himself, I thought he would be proud of a child, and even prouder of a son. So I kept meaning to have a talk with him, to discuss what we should do, to really hear from him a commitment—but between school, which I was failing at, and the clubs and Ferdi, well, it didn't come up on its own, and I didn't know how to start that conversation. I know it sounds un-believable, that you could have this child growing inside you and not talk about it—but it happens. Or maybe I just wanted to have a baby, maybe I knew that Ferdi would be gone and that would be the only thing I would have of his.

"Well, I was five months pregnant, and finally starting to show a little, and Ferdi and the group were going on tour, to Florida, Miami, South Beach, and he didn't want me to go. But he'd gone on tours before, to Arizona, New Mexico, up to San Francisco, so I didn't think much about it. The day they were leaving—they were taking a night flight east—Ferdi told me to keep the baby, whatever I did, I should keep the baby. He told me we would live together. He said I would still be hot after the baby was born, right? I would still be all sexy and stuff. I didn't know, but I told him I would.

"Well, that settled things, right? I was preggers, but I was keeping this kid, and then—who knows?—maybe in a few months, after the baby was born, we'd be flying to Jakarta to meet my family, and I bet they would have liked Ferdi. He was great with men; he and my father would have hit it off.

"He went down there and he didn't call me for the first few days, and then he said they were going to stay down there for a few more weeks—that the gigs were going really well and this place down in Key West wanted them and they might even be opening for Gloria Estefan and how this was it, it was all finally happening for Ferdi and for NSA and I felt, like, I felt how could I say I needed him here, that I was pregnant with a child and felt alone and frightened when he was gone. I asked if I could come down and he said no, there was no reason to.

"So you know what's coming now, don't you? Well, he did

come back after three weeks, and by then I was six months along. And he didn't call me or anything, didn't come by to see me. The only reason I even knew he was back in town was because a friend of mine saw his car in the lot at Small's, and then ran into him inside, where he was with this skinny girl he had met in Miami.

"That was it, I mean, how dumb was I? A kid, totally in love with this guy, this singer, who, when I finally called him on the phone, told me he would like to see me after I had the baby, after I got back in shape, when my titties and pussy were ready for him again. I never even went and picked up my stuff—I left some great outfits there, Helmut Lang, a few pairs of Prada shoes—but I was getting big, I needed maternity clothes, I wanted, like, a pair of overalls or something. He went back to South Beach, I think he lives there now. Some other girl is probably wearing my Prada shoes.

"I called my father and told him everything, that I was pregnant, and he told me to come home. I came and stayed here in the compound, never leaving for those three months, and when the baby was born, my mother handed him to Ginnie straightaway— Ginnie was the first person he saw when he opened his eyes.

"But I still think about Ferdi. I still think there's, like, this other life that's going on out there, and in that life I'm living with him and Bam and we're a family. At night sometimes, in those moments before I sleep, I imagine myself floating up over all of this, the compound, Jakarta, Indonesia, the whole ocean, and somehow in Miami, I can see the three of us, all together, a family."

Even Tommy was surprised by the pace of change now. Just six months ago no one had talked about politics, and a month ago no one had talked about Suharto resigning—now all the speculation centered on that. Tommy had said the transformation would be like in Thailand, where the middle class suddenly found its political voice and forced the regime to become more transparent and democratic. Here, where Suharto had ruthlessly depoliticized the college campuses during the last three decades, it seemed the only group that could create change was the middle class. Yet it was the alliance of students and thugs that was making change happen. And the younger members of the elite classes—guys and girls like Tommy, educated in the West—knew that change was inevitable, that only a new regime could save Indonesia. "It's not about whether the index is at seven-fifty," Tommy told a fellow Pribumi while Laney sat in front of his terminal, reading the Bloomberg feed. "It's about what kind of country we're going to have, what kind of society we're living in."

Then, all of a sudden, the question became whether there would be a country at all. On a Tuesday afternoon, stories began crossing the wires that up to a dozen students had been shot by security forces at Trisakti University. For three months, the students had been demonstrating virtually daily against rising prices and the corruption of Suharto's regime. It wasn't clear who began firing on the students, if it was the army or special security forces or the police, but no one was disputing that live ammunition had been used and students had been killed. And now, as Tommy had predicted, the middle classes were enraged—by the murder of the four students and a new gasoline-tax increase ordered by Suharto. For the first time they joined the students in the streets.

Laney, Tommy and a few of the other brokers stayed in the office that night, watching from the darkened windows as Chinatown went up in flames. The wave of rioting and looting set off by the shootings swept through the city. "Amok" in Bahasa means to go berserk, and Jakarta's mobs were doing just that. Within hours, Laney counted almost a hundred fires throughout the city. And over the Bloomberg, he was reading that maybe a million Javanese had taken to the streets, and that the major roadways had been cut between here and the airport and, even more important, here and Quan Quan's compound. Tommy was pointing out to him the fires gradually moving up toward Suharto's Cendana residence in the Menteng district. This showed that even the good areas were being hit—that the army did not have control of the situation.

When Tommy got in touch with his family, he learned they had bivouacked in the Regent Hotel and were dining at the buffet. His uncle, a general in the Kopassus—special forces—had assured the rest of his family the hotels would be safe. Laney got through to Quan Quan's house, but the housekeeper was unable to find Ginnie or Quan Quan. He kept trying, but circuits became busy.

He had to admit, it was exhilarating, watching this piece of history unfold, the end of the line for one of the longest ruling autocrats in the world and the possible dissolution of one of the world's largest countries. As Tommy and the other brokers kept up a running commentary—and observed that the DPR building, visible from their window, seemed to be deserted—Laney couldn't help but feel intoxicated: he was in the middle of something, for the first time in his life, he was sure he was dead center of the action. And then, amazingly, between the Bloomberg reports on looting, fires, rioting and the announced return of Suharto, who had been on a state visit to Egypt, up popped the closing number of the JSX Index. Laney and Tommy blinked at that for a moment and then began cracking up.

More sobering were the eyewitness accounts of murder and mayhem that began appearing on the wires—a Chinese shopkeeper stabbed to death, his daughter raped. Glodok Plaza was being burned down. Drivers were being pulled from their cars and beaten. "Now it is revenge time," one protestor told a reporter. Police were demanding bribes to protect shops and residences and then vanishing with the cash. The Rapid Reaction Force was protecting certain families and areas—Menteng would be safe, as would Suharto's residence and his family. And they were sending out units to protect selected properties and residences around the city. Jeeps, armored cars and helicopters were taking control of certain blocks and areas; no one knew who was deciding what to let burn and what to save. It had a schizophrenic quality, but the general feeling was that the army had decided not to stand in the way of the rioting. The city was burning. The squawk boxes crackled to life, telling Falcon employees that a chartered 757 would be standing by at Soekarno-Hatta to remove foreign nationals and families. A bus with armed escort would be leaving from the Falcon offices at ten A.M. Employees and families were encouraged to spend the night at the office. Laney was determined not to go without Quan Quan.

By the time Laney and Tommy left, riding a motor scooter and staying on side streets, the air was bitter and the streets were virtually deserted, save the occasional tank-topped figure pushing a bicycle with a sack of stolen rice in the basket, or a couple of boys rushing down the street, hauling a VCD player still in its box. Laney wore a pair of sunglasses and a helmet obscuring his brown hair. Both he and Tommy had taken off their dress shirts and now wore only their T-shirts and slacks. They rode past crowds barricading residential streets and wary shopkeepers armed with cricket bats and rattan poles standing in front of stores with *Milik Pribumi* painted all over the glass windows and steel grating. Nearly every automobile dealership had been looted and burned down. The roads down to Blok M were relatively secure, and they got to Laney's home without serious incident. Tommy let him off and then swung around, heading back up to the DPR building to meet his family for a late-night supper.

A gang of local thugs the Chinese owner had hired stood around the Kronus, ostensibly protecting the building. Laney was one of only three guests remaining. In the muggy, dark lobby, he asked if there were any drivers available. The desk clerk shook his head and pointed across the room to the row of sofas and upholstered chairs that ran along one wall. Six Pribumi drivers were sitting there smoking *kreteks*. "But no one will drive today."

Laney stumbled upstairs. The elevators weren't working. The power and telephones had been shut off. He tried Quan Quan's mobile again but heard the same impassive all-circuits-busy bleating. He fell asleep. At some point early in the morning the power came back on and he woke up sniffling from the air conditioner. He fumbled for his cell phone and hit Quan Quan's preset.

Ringing. Ringing. He got through.

"Oh, it's you," Quan Quan said, sounding almost surprised. "Where are you?"

"I made it home."

"Be careful," Quan Quan said. "They're pulling *bules* from their cars on the way to the airport. They're beating people up. It's on CNN. Oh, and did you know Frank Sinatra died?"

Sinatra? Laney thought he had died a decade ago. Propping his cell phone in the crook of his neck, he poured himself a glass of water from the pitcher by his bed and then dug a pair of tennis shoes from the closet. "I'm going to come and get you."

"No," Quan Quan said, "don't. This area is bad. They've been burning down houses and smashing cars all night. I don't know who these people are. They're not from around here. They just moved in and set up roadblocks. They're right outside on our street. They made my cousins pay a thousand Hong Kong just to turn down our driveway."

"But you're okay?" Laney asked. "Your family's okay?"

"So far."

"I'm going to try to make it through," Laney said. "My company has a plane leaving in a few hours. I'm gonna get you and then we'll get on it."

"Not without Bam."

"We'll take Bam," Laney said.

Quan Quan was quiet for a moment. "Then we have to take my sister and Ray-ray and my parents. You see? We can't all go. It's too late to go."

"Wait for me, then," Laney said, "I'll get through. Keep your mobile with you."

"Go—" Her voice became garbled. "Get on—" And the connection dropped. When Laney tried again, circuits were busy.

His cell phone chirped. It was Tommy, telling him he could send a car down to get Laney back to the Falcon offices.

"Take that plane out," Tommy told him. "You don't want to

be here. My uncle is saying Blok M is next. They can't protect it. Pull back to the offices. And then get on that plane."

Tommy could send a Toyota Kijang and a driver and armed guard who could get Laney out of there. Otherwise, the roads between Blok M and downtown were closed. He was sending the car, Tommy told him, just wait. Tommy hung up.

Laney walked around his bedroom, drinking more water while wishing he had a cup of coffee. He looked out his window at the little bougainvillea-covered courtyard and murky, carpless pond. Bad luck. But the women who worked in the kitchen were still there, sitting in the shade of a trellis, fanning themselves and chattering in their nasal voices. He picked up the phone to see if he could reach the concierge. The line was dead.

He opened his window and shouted down: "Hello. *Selamat pagi. Bolch minta kopi*—and—" He looked around. He needed toilet paper. *"Tissue. Terima kasih."*

The women looked up at him like he was crazy. *"Maaf, lagi krismon. Tisu habis. Kopinya habis."* And they giggled. Because of the crisis, the hotel's services had been shut down.

There must be some Nescafé about. Oh, fuck it. Laney had never realized how dependent he had been on native services for everything. It turns out that one of the first things to go in a revolution is basic services. There was simply no reason for anyone to do any of the scut work, since they weren't sure if their currency would be worth anything tomorrow. He leaned back out the window, this time waving U.S. dollars. Two of the women jumped up. Within minutes he had a pot of lukewarm instant coffee, an old apricot Danish and two rolls of toilet paper, all acquired for less than $20 U.S.

One of the peculiarities of watching the country fall apart, Laney noticed, was that he couldn't stop thinking of his own rotten situation. He should have been striving to somehow document or analyze the situation, to divine from all this what was going to happen, who would be running the country tomorrow and, more important to his company, who that person's cronies would be. But how was he supposed to be thinking as his world

fell apart around him? Was it selfish to be worrying about feeding himself and cleaning his ass and—really, only—about Quan
Quan. And not just about Quan Quan's well-being. It wasn't
enough that she was out of danger or healthy; he needed to be
with her. If she was living but not with him, then as far as Laney
was concerned, she might as well be dead.

That's what it felt like to be separated from her. The feeling
was not a yearning or a longing but a desperation, an intense
awareness of his futility and hopelessness. What could he do?
The gap between them, about twenty miles of Jakarta, was as
wide and vast as any that existed on this earth right now. Twenty
miles of rioting Preman and burning shopping malls and murdered Chinese. Quan Quan on one side and Laney on the other.
But if he had chosen this path—of throwing in his lot with one
woman instead of paying to have his way with many women—
then he could not abandon it now.

What could he do? He needed perspective. Perhaps if he
understood the global significance, he wouldn't dwell so relentlessly on his own problems. He switched on CNN. They were
showing a Frank Sinatra tribute.

A man in a khaki shirt with epaulettes was waiting for Laney
downstairs. He wore a pistol in a holster on his hip. Outside, the
Kijang stood idling, the driver in mirrored shades smoking a
kretek as he surveyed the street behind him.

"Airport," the man with the pistol said.

Laney nodded. He had put on an old Hanshin Tigers baseball cap with the logo taped over, and a pair of mirrored aviators.
He didn't want to stick out as a foreigner in a chauffeur-driven vehicle. He had spoken to Quan Quan a moment ago. Her voice
had been trembling. In the background, Laney had heard shouting. The compound was effectively under siege now, Quan Quan
told him. They were demanding her father pay $10,000 U.S.
The compound's staff had gathered garden tools and machetes,
and Ray-ray was organizing the defense. So far, with the high

walls and the large staff, no one was daring to come in. But at the same time, no one could go out. They were trapped. Quan Quan kept telling Laney to get out while he could. To take that plane.

But once he was in the backseat of the car, he gave the driver the Lenteng Agung address and told him he had to pick up his wife. The driver and the guard argued for a few minutes.

"Airport." The guard turned to him.

Laney shook his head. He gave the address again. "Yes airport. But first my wife. We go. *Jalan terus. Saya mau pergi ke Lenteng Agung.*"

They wound their way out of the eerily deserted Blok M. The action was shifting toward the center of the city now, the students and rioters and angry citizens converging nearer the seats of power. According to the Chinese owner of the Kronus, Liem Sioe Liong, one of Suharto's chief cronies and among the richest men in the world, had had his residence in South Jakarta set on fire and his fleet of five cars destroyed. Here on these empty Blok M streets, it seemed as if the revolution was over. Laney knew, however, that this was just the daylight lull—armed police prowled the streets by day. The rioting and looting moved about like a winter squall, now in Blok M, now in Pasar Baru, now in Slipi, sprinkling destruction and flame, spitting out corpses and ash. All in the name of—what? A better life.

This whole calamity or uprising or demonstration—this whole turning upside down of an old order—was only an obstacle for Laney. The old Laney would have been on that plane—there would have been nothing keeping him here. When he'd left Tokyo, he'd gone straight from the bar, his two nylon duffel bags slung over his shoulder as he walked down to the subway at dawn. That seemed like such a long time ago now. He hardly knew that guy who could carry all his possessions, his cares and loves and wants, in a bag, who could walk off down Gaien Higashi Dori without saying good-bye to a soul.

Now he couldn't bring himself to leave. This journey, this pilgrimage across a riotous city to save an imperiled Chinese princess—this was how he defined himself now. He was the sort of guy who stayed, who fought through a tough patch for the girl he loved. Come on, he thought to himself as he squinted in the morning haze, isn't this the guy I've always wanted to be? Isn't it better to care than not care, to feel than not feel? I am alive now, fully and completely, and with this feeling for another person I suddenly understand every TV movie and cologne ad and flower shop and romantic candlelit dinner. The move was obvious. Let that plane go.

He called Tommy. "Listen," Laney said, "I'll be up at the office in a few. Can you do me a favor?"

Laney wanted Tommy to ask his uncle to send a squad or platoon or, he didn't know, task force, to Quan Quan's house. Tommy's family had the power to reach down, with helicopters if necessary, and pluck survivors from Jakarta. Tommy had already been ensuring the safety of his family, friends and coworkers, he could do the same for Quan Quan's family.

Tommy listened to Laney's plea. When Laney finished, there was silence on the line.

"I told you she was Chinese," Tommy said.

"So what?" Laney asked.

"I can't ask my uncle to send Pribumi soldiers to guard a Chinese family," Tommy explained. "That's just not done."

"Come on, Tommy," Laney implored him. "Do it for me, then."

"Didn't I send a car for you? Didn't I send you an armed escort?" Tommy said. "I've done everything I can for you. I am risking Pribumi lives for you. But we can't do that for some Chinese dog. Get on the plane, Laney. The time for *bules* is over. Now is the time for Pribumi in Indonesia. Not Chinese. Right now, Laney, it would be best for you to get on that fucking plane. I'm telling you this as a friend." He hung up.

The Kijang had managed to reach the Jalan Tol, and they were now driving north, amid stalled and abandoned cars. As the highway rose up above the cluttered shanties and abandoned buildings, Laney could make out the hundreds of fires smoldering throughout the city. Downtown looked the same as it ever did, the glass and steel office complexes shimmering in the haze, only now the cranes atop the unfinished towers were frozen. The race to the heavens was over, for now. The financing dried up, even the will to build expired. He'd seen that sight before. Idle construction cranes, like huge gallows set up and waiting for some race of condemned giants who would never arrive. It reminded him of Tokyo, Laney realized, of the real estate projects and twenty-story residential mansions that he used to marvel at when he was walking around Shinjuku or Maranouchi. Booms end suddenly, no one knows why or how because it has as much to do with sentiment as it does with economics. It could just be simple gravity, or the inevitable result of too much greedy panting in too small a space. Something had to burst. You just hoped that when it happened, like in Tokyo in the early nineties, the fallout was lost second homes and cratered portfolios rather than starving families and dead bodies.

The traffic halted as the expressway merged into one lane. Pedestrians wandered around on the macadam. The cars jockeying for position, mostly Ford Lasers and Mazda 323s, were packed to the ceilings with household goods and baggage. Everyone was on the move. Worried brown and yellow faces, black eyebrows and pursed lips bobbing over black steering wheels as the drivers surveyed the traffic and the wandering, seemingly drunken crowds who had gathered on the highway. Even more disconcerting, a few burned-out hulks had been abandoned alongside the highway, the drivers nowhere to be seen.

Laney's driver leaned out his window, shouting to a group of boys who were selling newspapers and had apparently started a business selling stolen mobile phones. They were saying the road was closed. That every car to get through was being searched and ransacked by other gangs farther up ahead. The driver shouted some more and then turned to Laney. "We go back."

As Laney watched, a white man two cars in front of him was violently ripped from the back of an Isuzu Panther. Three Preman with long hair and bandanas began shouting at him. One grabbed his mobile phone and used it to gesticulate. They were scolding him for something, Laney guessed, maybe simply for being foreign, for not suffering along with the natives. Laney realized he had been living in a bubble, a safe, proscribed, protected area in which he'd lived at the sufferance of the natives—those in power as well as those impoverished—and now that privilege had been violently revoked. He wondered now if all over Asia this *krismon* was really somehow an emotional reaction to the supercilious, postcolonial economic and sexual imperialism of white men with hard currency. And hadn't he been complicit, crossed all those unspoken and invisible lines? He'd plainly gotten into too many native girls. And what if he could somehow tell them— these guys who were now shaking down this tall foreigner, obviously demanding payment, a bribe of some kind, as they ransacked his luggage, pulling out polo shirts and khakis and then grabbing a few manila folders and throwing the contents in the air? The man was waving an index finger violently, but he was clearly frightened. The Isuzu's driver sat behind the wheel, staring forward, wanting nothing to do with this—

What if he told these *boneks* he was in love? Would it make a difference to starving, entitled thugs? He had seen the error of his ways, was on his way, actually to make things right by picking up with a native girl. Ah, but that was the rub. Even Quan Quan was a symbol of the order they now wished to overthrow. The dreaded, hated, despised Chinese. Poisoners of water. Eaters of babies. They were the Jews of Asia. And Quan Quan, she was a symbol, a prized curio of this cloven-hoofed species, exhibiting the markings and characteristics of her inferior, but sinister, race. And Laney, he was suspect just for liking her.

"Go back," Laney ordered. The cars behind them had already started pulling away, but the mob up ahead was working their way back to the Kijang, eager to find another dollar-carrying foreigner. They would take his money—who cared about that?— but they would also take his phone. And how would he call Quan Quan?

He slid the door open, stepped out and began trotting away

between the lines of cars. The driver and the guard turned and saw him go but didn't chase him. It was better to be rid of him at this point.

Laney ran about two hundred meters, sweating through his T-shirt. His lungs burned from the smoke and cinders. He found a ladder down from the highway—it had been built as an emergency exit of some sort—and scampered down it, almost slipping on the oily, sooty handrails. When he was back down at street level, he found himself on a quiet residential block. The difference between the mayhem up on the highway and this deserted—for Jakarta, anyway—suburban street left him bewildered and anxious, as if at any moment a mob of pitchfork-wielding peasants would be charging from around the corner. Instead, around the corner came a teenage kid with a buzz cut, wearing a Metallica T-shirt and riding a rusted lady's bicycle with a squeaky chain. He seemed surprised to see Laney standing there—this tall, sweating, nervous-looking *bule* in a shirt blackened by soot—but then, stranger things had been happening the last few days.

Laney waved him to a stop and tapped the handlebars of the bike. *"Berapa?"* How much? Before the kid could answer, Laney pulled a gob of bills from his wallet—about $400 U.S. He stuffed the money into the kid's hands. The kid nodded. This was a fortune. He got off the bike, holding it up for Laney. Strange things had been happening.

Laney pedaled north and west, sticking to side streets and avoiding major thoroughfares. When was the last time he had been on a bicycle? High school, he guessed. With his rusty chain, he squeaked past angry mobs and groups of drunken looters, but they were out looking for Chinese shops or rich foreigners in chauffeured vehicles. Laney, sweating and dirty and riding on a bicycle, suddenly didn't seem like the enemy.

He tried calling Quan Quan on her mobile. Someone answered, but then all Laney could hear was what sounded like a struggle—feet skidding, engines starting, or was he imagining things?—and then the line went dead. He would be there in a few minutes, anyway. He was already climbing up the hill toward the University of Indonesia, just a mile or so from Quan Quan's house. Students had set up barricades in front of the campus, with signs imploring Bapak to resign. Demanding that he and his family be prosecuted for corruption. But only a dozen or so were milling about. At the end of the road, preventing the students from leaving or prevented by the students from gaining the campus, a boxy armored personnel carrier straddled the lane divider. Four helmeted troops in crisp uniforms were seated in its shade with their automatic rifles leaning against the armor, picking through bowls of rice and chilis. The atmosphere here wasn't confrontational. It seemed the students and soldiers had reached a mutually agreed-upon standoff. Until further notice, the revolution was postponed.

But when Laney made the turn onto Quan Quan's block, he saw that a mob of a few dozen had blocked off the road. They seemed tired now, exhausted after a few days of rioting or looting or whatever they had been doing. They were preposterously equipped, some with stolen flashlights and cassette players, others wearing new T-shirts. One man wore a life jacket and carried a tennis racket, of all things. They sized Laney up as he got closer, ordering him to slow down.

Once he stopped, an older, drunken man with a thin mustache began pushing Laney around, calling him a stinking *bule*. A few of the others were pushing at him as well, accusing him of being a sorcerer, a foreign-devil magician seeking to destroy the rice harvest, and Laney felt someone punch him in the shoulder blade. He wasn't frightened; nor did he have any great welling of courage. Whatever they wanted, they could have, Laney reasoned. He slipped off his Tag Heuer watch and handed it to the old man; he gave his phone over and pulled open his wallet to show them it was empty. "Nothing."

The old man sized up the watch, clearly disappointed. He had no way of knowing it was worth about $1,000 U.S. Another man, a boy really, dressed in a khaki shirt with what looked like a dirty pink towel wrapped around his head, stepped forward and socked Laney in the side of the head. The boy was too light for the punch to do much damage. But it did cause Laney to leap from the bike, holding his hands up to protect himself.

"I am Super King," the boy shouted in English, holding his hands up like a boxing champion. The boy grabbed the bicycle and rolled it away, leaving Laney standing with his arms folded.

All he had now was this greasy shirt, his pants, his tennis shoes. Before the gang moved on, a chubby man in sandals pointed to Laney's sneakers with his rattan pole and began nodding. "Ya, ya."

Before Laney could object, the man swung the stick down hard, catching Laney in the ribs and doubling him over. Laney coughed. He quickly untied his sneakers, handing them to the man, who held them up, apparently satisfied. Looping them together, he slung them over his shoulders.

Laney stood up, still coughing, gathering himself. He could see the gated entrance to Quan Quan's compound from here. Walking the last few hundred meters barefooted, the uneven pavement cutting into his arches, he wondered how he would alert Quan Quan without his mobile phone. He would just have to shout over the gate.

The large tan-painted metal gates to the compound had a barbwire crown that wound up over the side walls before giving way to the broken glass embedded into the concrete. It was a sinister-looking gate, and apparently effective, as Laney approached the compound and everything seemed quiet inside. He banged on the gate, shouting Quan Quan's name, calling in English for one of the family members or a servant to come and let him in. He clutched his side as the sharp ache from his rib cage seemed to expand when he yelled. He heard the heavy latch of the gate being lifted, then the loud creaking of the gate swinging inward.

He had made it.

The servant looked down at Laney. This *bule* friend of Quan Quan's. Bruised. Barefoot. In a greasy shirt. She would help him down the driveway and into the kitchen, where she would give him coffee and water and a cold towel to clean himself off with, and she would try to explain to him, in a mixture of Bahasa and English, that the family had left for the airport hours ago. Flown to Hong Kong. That Quan Quan was gone. "She say, she say," the servant mumbled, "she say she go to Miami. She say she go see Bam-bam daddy."

Every year the Pacific Palisades holds a Fourth of July parade that winds down Sunset Boulevard past the banks and Starbucks and gas stations. I saw Laney at a party given by a mutual acquaintance who lives along the parade route. Laney was shirtless, his arms and torso deeply tanned, and he wore a plain white visor with Oakley sunglasses. He told me he had joined the Merrill Lynch broker training program and that was keeping him busy twelve hours a day.

Miami hadn't worked out well for him. There had been the other guy, Bam's dad, and there had been Quan Quan pregnant with another baby. But that was all ancient history, Laney explained as he pulled another Budweiser from the plastic six-pack ring. Whatever; she was just another LBFM, he said.

He was still Laney, and girls were still checking him out, but he didn't seem that cool anymore.

GAL

The crowds of turbaned and dhoti-clad
Bombayans along the dusty Colaba street parted for her;
something about her stride, her loping, angry steps and the way
her curtain of curly brown hair swung as she stomped up the
street caused this otherwise unflappable, immovable mass of
pedestrians to veer to the side of the uneven sidewalk and press
against the racks of cheap silver jewelry and cases of cigarettes to
let her pass. She was a startling sight on that Bombay street, a tall
brunette of Amazonian proportions whose surly, downcast expression failed to disguise lovely, da Vinci–esque features. She
wore an olive tank top in which her tennis-ball-size breasts
bounced in accompaniment to her swaying hair, and a pair of
faded, dusty Levi's tucked into tan desert boots. When she
walked by, she gave off a musky, spicy scent coupled with a mysterious whiff of wherever she had been in those boots and jeans,
somewhere muddy and dark and forbidding. She was one of
those visions, a beautiful Occidental woman striding through a

bustling subcontinental street, that you assume is fleeting. She will bull her way through the crowd, you think, and then turn the corner and be gone, out of your life, and you will go back to haggling with the merchant for your rolls of film or the carved teak Ganesha and she will have been an ephemeral titillation, a vision exquisite yet so jarring that no pickup line was ever conceived, no maneuvers to position oneself to speak to her ever executed.

I know that she roused the interest of every male on the block, the brown-skinned faces turned toward her in mute appreciation—the street vendors, *dabbawallahs,* dope dealers, hustlers, pickpockets and pimps who could usually be counted on to make threatening, though meaningless, propositions were momentarily silenced by her swaggering physical sexuality. One reason they may have kept their prurient ideas private was the fact that she probably could have kicked any one of their asses.

My friend Trey and I were making our way down this crowded lane hoping to find Easy-E, the Indian "guide" who had joined himself to our peripatetic, rambling mission. Easy-E, when he wasn't crashed on the floor of our hotel room smoking sour-smelling mixtures of hashish and black tobacco and watching Mahabharata cartoons, hung around the Mighty International Center for Industry and Commerce, a small glass storefront down a muddy Colaba alley that advertised international fax and telephone as well as taxi services. (Easy-E had confided to us that the fax machine was connected to a local line that rang a telephone answering machine playing a tape of a fax machine's peeps and bleats. The fax machine was programmed to send automatically. In other words, the tourists who wandered in to send a fax were actually paying for the privilege of watching their paper go through a fax machine, with no concurrent emergence of a fax document on the other side of the world.) Easy-E, when he was in the Mighty, as it was called, sat hunched over the shop's one broken-down knockoff Selectric typewriter and tapped out a meaningless series of letters and numbers, sometimes typing birds or snakes from A's and Y's, sometimes elaborate mandalas of the home keys. Easy-E was illiterate.

Most evenings he stayed in our suite until the Bombay television stations signed off with a tinny-sounding series of state and national songs. He then rode the elevators back down to the lobby, where the bell captains and porters gave him nasty looks as he padded out into the street, down the alley to the stretch of pavement that he slept on during the warm premonsoon season. The staff of the Mighty slept en masse on the street in front of their narrow shop; only the owner, the trim, hawk-eyed, beak-nosed Mr. Nawab kept a proper home. The rest of the crew who hung around the Mighty passed the night beside a fire of paper and crates, smoking from chillums and trotting away periodically on errands and bits and pieces of small business.

In the early afternoons, we would find Easy-E waiting for us in front of the horseshoe drive to our hotel. The bell captain would not let him into the lobby unaccompanied, and the first day we had brought him upstairs with us, Easy-E confided to us that he'd never been inside the hotel before.

He had looked around the lush brass and mirrored lobby, with its ornate patinaed copper chandeliers and marble floors, and nodded several times, as if he approved of our choice of hotel. "It's a fine, fine place, I think."

We had originally bivouacked at a seedy dive down the block, the Diplomat, but after an editor at *Condé Nast Traveler* had called me at four one morning from New York giving me an assignment—and an expense account—I decided to move down the street to a more storied venue. That call from New York had been an amazing stroke of good fortune. Before, it had seemed likely we would have had to wend our way down to Goa by train and then find some economical accommodation for me to conduct my personal missions from.

Now, instead of opening onto a noisy interior courtyard that forever stank of something sour being roasted or charred or baked, our intricately shuttered window offered a view of the Gate of India and the Arabian Sea beyond. Our first night there, we took turns throwing oranges out over the bobbing yawls into the shimmering black sea, where they made barely perceptible splashes.

Easy-E was a short, curly-haired, maple-colored teenager with round brown eyes as large and innocent and full of promise as mint rupee coins. He had grown up in one of the shantytowns that lined the main roads into Bombay; he had attended school for two years—"Pratchanburi Elementary School Number Six, where the teachers beated me and no one gave me nothing to eat"—then dropped out and learned English from an older cousin who worked as an amateur tour guide, taking Westerners to visit the Elephanta Caves or arranging for them the purchase of Nepalese hashish. Easy-E was popular with the foreign women, his cousin had noticed, and when he came along, the tips doubled. When his cousin was arrested for selling hashish and sent to Ramsajit Detention Center, Easy-E took over the guide business, eventually shedding the Elephanta Caves and the dull walks through the Prince of Wales Museum in favor of more lucrative work satisfying the illegal needs of the many foreigners who came through Bombay.

We had retained him as a runner and procurer. We never paid him a salary; it was understood that he was skimming enough off the top.

Now, however, it was late afternoon, and Easy-E hadn't been outside the hotel and was missing from his usual post at the Mighty. Mr. Nawab, a portly man who sat behind a white counter ready to exchange currency or proffer the telephone to paying customers, shook his head when I inquired as to Easy-E's whereabouts. "Not here. Not here. Call your parents? Call your friends? Fax a letter? I'll arrange for you agreeable terms."

We walked back around the corner to the American Express office, where a wire transfer from the magazine was supposed to be waiting for me. As I stood at the counter, cashing in part of the money order with the helpful, grinning woman behind the counter and taking the rest in traveler's checks—it was a surprisingly ample amount of money, and it promised to provide for a fine few weeks—I heard Trey strike up a conversation with someone behind me. Turning around as I shoved wads of local currency into my cutoff cargo pants, I saw the girl who had cut a broad swath through the Colaba street now seated next to a dusty, olive-drab backpack. Her legs akimbo, she leaned against the tan stone steps to the second floor. She appeared to be impatient, vaguely angry at the women behind the American Express counter, and I could tell that by joining her conversation, I had lost whatever status I had earned with the American Express staff.

Something was fucked up, she kept saying loud enough for the staff to hear, fucked up, fucked up.

Trey, his shoulder against the wall, leaned toward her in a posture that indicated he was concerned and empathetic. He kept nodding.

She had been waiting for some money, a large amount, that she desperately needed. For a place to stay? For food? For a plane ticket home? Why exactly did she need the money?

She couldn't say, she could only repeat that it was imperative, was "terrible, terrible important" and "fucked up." Galit was Israeli, from the suburbs of Tel Aviv, a regular traveler to and through India. Judging from her looks, the sturdy physique, the drawn, unflinching features, her sheer physicality, she was a tough woman. But within minutes of meeting in that American Express, her anger had turned to tears, narrow rivulets that cut deltas down her beautiful tanned visage.

"Come with us," I told her as the American Express was shutting down for its midafternoon break. "You need to eat, regain your composure."

She shook her head, as if too proud to accept a free meal.

"It's not like you have anything better to do," I pointed out.

The Grimaldi Bar & Restaurant was supposedly popular with backpackers, bohemians, expats and billionaires alike. The food was good, the beer was cold—very important in India—and the service consistent. We sat beneath a stalled ceiling fan next to a dingy mirror with a menu written on it in what looked like lipstick. Trey and I ordered beer, samosas, french fries, vindaloo and a bowl of cornflakes; Gal, as she was called, asked for only a cup of tea.

"I'm so sick of Indian food," she said, wrinkling her nose as I tucked into my cornflakes and Trey dipped his french fries in chutney. I shrugged.

She had been here six months, crisscrossing the country with an Englishman named Andrew who had returned to London just a few days before. It was this very same Andrew who was to have wired her money at the American Express—and here her story became vague. What the money was for, she would not disclose. She had no intention of returning to Israel, and when I asked if she was supposed to meet this Andrew in England, she shook her head. "I do not want to go there. It's too cold."

"Then what do you need money for?" Trey asked.

"Plane ticket?" I asked.

She shook her head. "We had a plan, Andrew and I. Obviously it's shit. It's fucked now."

"What plan?"

She gestured vaguely toward the door, as if to indicate the plan had flown the coop, was gone, wandering up some Bombay alley. As Gal waved her arms, the tanned flesh of her upper arms taut against the straps of her too tight tank top, I stopped listening to her and took a mental step back to admire what a prodigious, well-proportioned creature she was. I know it sounds horribly sexist, but there was something so noble about her physical carriage that one assumed the same excellence must permeate her intellect and her soul. From a human being this well designed, you could not imagine deceit or lies emanating.

She resembled some writ-large version of an Italian starlet; she possessed that same Mediterranean sultriness. And there was nothing shy about her, no humility, no wonderment about whether or not she was good enough or beautiful enough or tough enough—she was, plainly, all those things.

Trey and I were already fascinated with her, and we spent the entire lunch doing our best to cajole her to join us in our journey.

We were here to find God.

The week I turned thirty, my photograph appeared in *Time* magazine. The picture was the visual accompaniment to a review of my first book. The content and nature of that book are irrelevant to this story. What matters is this: for seven years, give or take soporific summers in Ibiza and narcoleptic months in Koh Phangang, languorous winters in Goa and lost weeks in Kathmandu, I had been working—writing, to be precise—toward a goal: I wanted to be a writer. That photograph, run across two columns, somehow helped define me. For the first time in my life, I was no longer seeking, climbing or working my way toward some imaginary title, office or laminated sign that said "writer." I was there.

And "there" was nothing. Like so many of my generation—okay, here is that hackneyed label: Generation X—I had reached this stage in my career and life without pondering the spiritual, mystical and religious components that comprise being. I had spent my twenties busy with "meat," as William Gibson calls matters of bodily and secular existence. And where Gibson invented cyberspace as the alternative to meat, I guessed that spiritualism, or God, or karma, or something must have more gigabytes than all the circuit boards, mainframes and hardware in the universe.

It was now time to search for my soul, to look for my god, to greet—not meet—my maker, if indeed the whole universe is hardwired by some superguru. Besides, I had a book contract, a modest advance, and this trip would be research. When the magazine came through with an assignment, that was a lucrative perk that extended the trip and provided additional resources.

Trey and I had worked together on and off for years after meeting during junior year abroad in Paris, first as freelance writers hoping for a break in New York, then as editors of a Tokyo magazine and then, in our late twenties, as magazine writers bouncing around the Far East, filing stories for a wide array of American and British magazines. We had worked and partied in

Asian capitals, from Tokyo to Seoul to Hong Kong to Bangkok; we had been fiercely competitive with each other and supportive of each other and protective of each other. When I was fired from my position as managing editor in Tokyo, Trey had shown solidarity by resigning his own post as articles editor.

When I phoned him in Tokyo and told him I was venturing to India, he said he would meet me there.

"India," Pico Iyer wrote in *Video Nights in Kathmandu,* "was humanity itself, an inflation of humanity, an intensification of humanity. The very scale of the place was fantastic: . . . at least five major religions and 500 former kingdoms and thousands upon thousands of gods (many of them like humans, only more so)."

Gods like humans. Human beings as gods. The god-man. "Humanity has never been without them," wrote Swami Muktananda, a guru of Siddha yoga. India excelled at producing gurus. Remember the Beatles and Maharishi? Transcendental Meditation? Hare Krishnas? Rajneesh and his Rolls-Royces? India is a spiritual supermarket. And that season we were there to go shopping, to test-drive several gurus, then see which model worked for our spiritual demographics.

I flew into an India aflame with fervor. As the seasonable winter months came to a close, there seemed to be a procession of emaciated yogis and incense-wielding holy men, flute-playing *sanyassins* and drum-beating barefoot sadhus making their way down every dusty track; another teleguru on television promising to bring riches, fame, good fortune and cures for all our ills if we would just venture to his ashram; and another fresh-faced, soft-featured swami on the cover of *India Today* and *Sunday* whose millions of followers vowed was the incarnation of the godhead. The prime minister and his opposition candidates were photographed at every opportunity with Sai Baba or Swami Niket or the Maharishi Mahesh Yogi. It was an auspicious time to find God, for there were so many to choose from. In every storefront there were pictures of Brahma, Shiva, Vishnu, Buddha, Jesus, the Dalai Lama, Mohammed, Sai Baba and Elvis. There were gods around every corner, on every dashboard, dangling from malas around every gaunt neck. The nation was in a perpetual state of apoplectic thrall at every conceivable deity; Bombay stank as much of fervor as it did of fumes.

This atmosphere of fragrant spirituality coincided with what in London had been yet another Summer of Love—if it seems to you like all this happened decades before, and that all our experiences are mere epigones of someone else's Summer of Love and another era's search for God, then you are perhaps right, and in the same way that previous Summer of Love ground to a bloody halt with the introduction of amphetamines and heroin into an otherwise groovy scene, so too did this Summer of Love, at least here in Asia, succumb to a chemical-induced demise. But that autumn after the Summer of Love, there was still a sense of possibility in the air, that the good E-driven vibes of Manchester and London's glorious rave scene could make their way east with the kids who rode the circuit, and somehow the party could continue out here, in the Asian hot spots, positive energy spilling from cargo holds at the Sahar airport and then spreading north, south and east, to Pune, Puttaparthi, Ganeshpuri and Goa. Thousands of kids from England, Germany, Holland, Sweden, the United States, Israel and Japan, and a few hundred thousand hits of White Dove, Elephant, Pink Lady and Bubblegum, converged on the bungalows and retreats of Goa. This was to be our search for God, a chemical-induced god, perhaps, but a god of our understanding.

So we were here, I suppose, for the same reason so many other riders of the circuit were here that year: to seek some kind of release, to find the blissed, postcoital autumn that inevitably follows a Summer of Love, to shake off the effects of too many hits of snidey E and find a truly higher power.

Everybody was looking for something.

As soon as Easy-E turned up, we sent him out to procure the necessary supplies, and upon his return we set out in a chartered black Ambassador complete with Sikh driver who stolidly maneuvered us out of town along the cluttered, narrow Colaba streets and then the wider Reay Road and finally the half-paved, half-rubble interprovince trunk road that connected Bombay with points south. After what seemed like hours of stop-and-go maneuvering through Bombay's afternoon rush hour, we found ourselves by sunset driving along haphazardly subdivided stretches of farmland where hunched-over women in brightly colored saris with children in bundles on their backs worked behind plow-burdened oxen to till the soil. Each tiny, basketball-court-size field was to be planted with its rows of grain arrayed in different directions, so that the patches of earth visible between green acacia trees appeared to be a series of randomly dropped sheets of dirty notebook paper, extending to the distant rolling hills into which the sun was now descending. Alongside the road, women in bare feet carried sacks of flour and plastic jerry cans of water while their children scurried behind them. Occasionally we passed contraptions of tires, motors and bicycle seats that I assumed were tractors. These primitive mechanized vehicles puttered along at five miles an hour, their mustachioed operators seated at the back end holding on to tiny steering wheels attached to long, drooping steering columns.

Easy-E had taken a seat in the front next to the driver, who had become plainly annoyed by Easy-E's habit of tuning and retuning the radio to various raga stations. But Easy-E, apparently emboldened by his status as part of the chartering party of foreigners, ignored the Sikh's scolding and continued fiddling with the radio every thirty seconds.

At the time it seemed reasonable that Gal would choose to attach herself to our party. During the drive down to Pune, she sat between us in the capacious backseat of the Ambassador while Trey and I attempted to win her over, engaging in good-spirited, self-deprecating commentary about our lack of sexual prowess, how inept we were at satisfying women and how proud we were of our brevity when it came to lovemaking.

"I believe in quickness when it comes to making love," joked Trey at one point. "I believe in getting the act on with and over with as quickly as possible, on not wasting time on foreplay, but rather on cutting to the quick and completing the act with no unnecessary delays and with absolutely zero pleasure for the woman."

I don't know if Gal understood what we were saying or if she appreciated our spin on the usual sexual one-upmanship and competitiveness between males. But already, in the car, a new tension was perceptible to me: a beautiful woman had entered the picture, and what had previously been a compact, harmonious duo became a potentially divisive trio.

But Trey and I had competed for women before. Our friendship had been forged and built upon a mutual interest in skirt chasing, though he had always been far more successful than me. Prior to our meeting in Paris, I had been largely inept with females, and it was Trey who had shown me, by his sheer force of will and relentless efforts, how to pick up women. In New York, in Tokyo, in Thailand, everywhere we had been together, he had succeeded with the opposite sex. Though he was handsome, it was Trey's energy and charm, rather than his looks, that won over women.

But if he was more successful in seducing women, I had enjoyed some success, albeit very limited, as a writer and journalist. I had published more articles and essays, and a book, while Trey had struggled to earn a living as a writer. He had barely scraped by, often having to live off the women he so easily seduced. He had even had to borrow the money for this trip to India.

In the late-afternoon sun, with the banyan and bodhi trees suffused with glowing orange light and the cooing of doves audible over the trickle of water, the walk toward the wrought-iron main gate of Osho Commune International (OCI) felt like we had arrived at the end of all our searches. Where the city of Pune is a smoggy, choked metropolis of more than a million, this gate opens onto a lush, verdant oasis; where other ashrams are in grubby, desolate wastelands, beyond this gate is a tropical, prosperous wonderland; where the rest of India is dirty, this ashram is pristine.

As we entered the sprawling, thirty-one-acre garden of palms, ferns and exotic fauna and flora, we felt we had entered a New Age San Simeon.

OCI had created a stunning landscape, a vista of gurgling streams, curving paths and quiet, shady corners ideal for meditating. It was an admirable attempt to fashion a self-sufficient ecosystem, and it may have been the only community in India where the tapwater was totally safe for foreigners to drink. The grounds were immaculate—groundskeeping, in fact, was one of the forms of meditation recommended for those less well-heeled seekers of the light. (Other forms of bargain meditation: vegetable chopping and dishwashing.)

This was to be the place where my search would begin. That season, hundreds of Brits and Americans had made the pilgrimage to Pune seeking enlightenment, hoping to chill out after emotionally profligate nights and days on the circuit. OCI promised salvation. "This is a great experiment in Buddhahood," proclaimed a brochure. "Energies have been made available to you. Possibilities have to be made clear to you. You have to be made aware of your potential."

And all that was required to gain entrance was fifty rupees—about two bucks—and a negative HIV test. HIV test? "Yes," said Swami Nura, the magenta-robed representative who greeted us at the ashram's welcome center. "The master is very concerned about who is close to him."

The blood test cost $5. And we were all negative. When I asked what happened to those who tested positive, Swami Nura told me they were taken to a secluded corner of the welcome center and given a special talk. I wondered if eavesdropping on that conversation would somehow bring the real revelation.

While Easy-E arranged accommodations for us—he had no interest in the pursuit of some *angrezi* religion—we were ushered through a boutique that sold the required magenta robes and outfits, plus white robes for nighttime meditation sessions. We purchased a few hundred bucks' worth of magenta pajamas, G-strings, bathrobes and baseball caps. Gal sullenly went along with the orientation, trying on a magenta robe that showed off her youthful, bountiful cleavage.

In our new magenta outfits, while we sat in a duck-duck-goose circle under a massive portrait of Osho (actually, there were portraits of Osho everywhere in the commune—Big Buddha was always watching), two attractive and, I assumed, enlightened, women explained the ways of finding the Way.

"Take it slow," suggested Prem Shunyo, a tall American brunette, speaking through a microphone. "We wear magenta because the master feels it is good for spirituality and because of its calming nature. This has all been scientifically tested. And remember, we have magenta condoms, dental dams and rubber gloves available."

Around the commune, at the restaurants that catered to the *sanyassins,* or devotees, we ran into numerous other potential devotees our age who were having trouble finding God, getting into the flow of the ashram, staying connected to any spirituality other than that which could be smoked off a sheet of tinfoil, swallowed in a tablet or shot into veins. I would look around at a table of tattooed and pierced boys and girls, who, though lean and tan and in their twenties, were redolent of a used-up quality, a jadedness that stemmed from knowing that you could get whatever you needed by popping an E or taking a shot or smoking a spliff—why bother with all this laborious meditating and tedious mantra repeating? God was in a bindle of this or that, a tab, a hit, a glassine baggy. He had shown up when you were peaking on an E back at the hacienda in Manchester, and he would show up when you were nodding from some good Henry here in India.

Before leaving Bombay, Easy-E had scored for us a generous two grams of Number 3 *chandu,* or heroin, which Trey and I sniffed in copious quantities throughout the journey. None of our fellow travelers flinched when I laid out lines of heroin on a bakery tabletop to have along with my breakfast coffee and chapatis.

The frenetic, half-cocked search for God—I would have settled for a sense of purpose or some simple spiritual guidance—amid the abundance of casual, risk-free sex (we had, after all, passed AIDS tests) and hard drugs resulted in a superficial era of good feeling among perpetually titillated, terminally stoned kids. Other visitors to OCI have commented on the hint of sexuality that permeates the rich oxygen of the ashram, on the beautiful women's diaphanous silks clinging to their swaying breasts. The women outnumbered men two to one—a ratio that Osho had maintained to keep his workforce satisfied. The girls were stunning, originally handpicked by Osho himself because of their beauty or sexuality: sensual, dark-haired Italians, lusty and thick-browed Jewesses, sultry Frenchwomen, icy Scandinavians, musky Brazilians. It was a bizarre, Flintian apotheosis of all those Mountain Dew and "Generation Next" Pepsi commercials—except instead of those dour, hip, wild-looking models bungee-jumping or snowboarding, they were taking drugs and engaging in rampant fornication. I remember one young blond Kiwi woman with spiky hair and a pierced eyebrow yanking up her magenta panties upon reaching an essentially masturbatory orgasm atop her partner, popping ten milligrams of nitrazepam and then setting off for her morning massage appointment; her life was a series of easily achieved tactile pleasures. It was pointless searching for meaning in this constant state of instant gratification. Why would you look for God when you had everything you needed right here?

Instead of navigating toward an essential meaning of life, we were drifting dangerously into an emotional and moral Sargasso Sea. The only person who remained thoroughly centered was Gal. She wasn't interested in ingesting any of the opiates that were so prevalent or in joining the ashram and studying at any of the multiversity courses; she remained steadfastly aloof from the aimless searching that was afoot, instead swimming disciplined laps in the long pool beside our bungalow and smoking the occasional bangh-laced cigarette.

Sunlight broke through the trees in blinding shafts of yellow that mingled with the tints of green from the lush, dewy tropical canopy suspended above the ashram. The morning air was cool, crisp and fresh. Mornings at Club Meditation were delicious, especially after early dynamic-meditation sessions in Buddha Hall, though meditating while under heavy doses of very strong opiates was an exercise in redundancy.

The participants in New Humanity–New Art were gathered on a roof amid the verdant treetops beneath a slung tarp that shaded us from the sun. Our dark-haired, muscular Finnish instructor recounted his moment of self-realization for us: "I told my friend who was driving me to let me out in the middle of nowhere, a forest, miles from Helsinki; I was left for a week. I stripped off my clothes, I ate tree bark, I lived like an animal, I fucked the leaves. I learned that I was an animal, not a person. I was overcoming the mind—I was my body, a oneness. I didn't eat or drink for a week. . . ."

A German visitor raised his hand. "Did you use a condom when you fucked the leaves?"

The instructor shook his head. "I was beyond that. I was wild, like a caveman, even further back, back into the cosmic mire and muck that we all came from and still are. Now, in this course we will regain that consciousness. We will become a primitive tribe, a tribe of savages, and then surge toward a oneness. I want you all to take a paintbrush, take two, and begin moving the brushes around your partner's body, make him jump, make her squirm, make her cry out, make her collapse. BE A SAVAGE."

He then demonstrated the brushwork with Meera, his fellow instructor, a beautiful Japanese woman in black who hugged everybody at the start of the class. (Instructors and the ashram elite seemed to have some special dispensation to wear nonmagenta clothing.) Meera and the Finn were so in sync—her head moving with his right hand, her right thigh bending outward with his left hand—that their routine looked choreographed.

When my partner, a balding forty-year-old textile trader from Stuttgart, and I tried it out, we didn't achieve such synchronicity. I moved my brush up, he sagged; I waved my brush furiously, he wiggled a bit. Switching roles didn't help much; we just weren't savages. I noticed some classmates writhing in ecstasy as their partners whirled brushes over what were called in the ashram "the sex centers." One woman was whooping and shouting. Then Meera encouraged us all to scream, chant, "Let it all go."

"Osho! Osho!"

"Shout anything, whatever comes to mind."

I began shouting: "Go, blue! Roll, tide! Hi, ho, go with the flow! Osho! Osho!"

My German partner stuck with "Osho."

After that we painted. We were to paint like savages, whatever came to mind; with our fingers, our faces, our fists; slash the canvas; walk on it; throw it out the window.

I painted, in neat, even letters, SOUP IS GOOD FOOD.

Meera came up behind me and shouted, "No, we are a wild tribe, we are prelinguistic! Paint your emotion, not your thoughts. You have to get past your mind, to yourself."

I threw some red paint on the canvas. I splattered some blue. Then, in an effort to purge my head of negativity, I wrote, in black on white: Goallll!!!

And that got me in big spiritual trouble. While the others were finger-painting and scrawling and dribbling, I insisted on structure; where they were wild and savage, I was restrained and results-oriented. That was my problem.

"Your attitude," Meera explained calmly at the end of our session, "is not quite right. But I can see that you need this class."

I rode in the Ambassador back to our bungalow, where I disembarked in my magenta robes and sandals to sit on a chaise longue beside the pool, next to where Gal lay on a towel, reading through a Hebrew copy of *Serpentine*.

Trey had taken to riding in taxis across town to a four-star hotel with a business center, where he would dictate letters to a frazzled, blue-sari-clad secretary who tapped out Trey's queries and letters on an old Olivetti typewriter. Since my stroke of good fortune in receiving a magazine assignment, Trey had feverishly been trying to promote an India story of his own, faxing the poorly spelled, typed-up queries to numerous American magazines in between ducking into the bathroom for quick bumps of whatever pharmaceutical amphetamines Easy-E had procured for him. Trey had disappeared for the last few days into this haze of obsessive magazine querying; his latest idea: a profile of India's top starlet. When I pointed out that no one in the United States had ever heard of any Indian actresses, he accused me of being negative.

I had come to see Gal as my reward for putting in long days searching for an elusive spirituality. When I watched her swim in easy laps across the pool, or lying in her black bikini on a lounge chair, sipping vodka and Fanta orange, I came to believe that perhaps my search had been not for God but for Gal, for an idealization of a type of woman. I was afraid to even elucidate the thought, but if God was love, then maybe I had completed my search. This absurd lifestyle, of rising at dawn, slipping on robes and malas and heading off to the ashram to meditate and seek a oneness with the universe and then returning in the late afternoon like some sort of spiritual salaryman was leading nowhere. But right here, in my bungalow, was something real, something I could believe in.

The sagging trellises of wisteria around the pool rustled in the faint breeze. The air here smelled of a mixture of sour earth and the omnipresent smoke of garbage-fueled cooking fires that hung over every part of the city except the ashram. I had loaned Easy-E my Walkman and a few dance-music cassettes that he found hysterical; as far as he was concerned, what we listened to was plainly not music.

Gal and I swam in the pool together, the white-clad waiters

walking past on the patio sneaking discreet glances at us as we cuddled in the shallow end, my legs wrapped around her sunscreen-slicked body. She was muscular and sinewy yet with a layer of softness that made her powerfully feminine. I began to admire her for having no part in this tedious search for God, for having the common sense to see it as the nonsense it was, at least when it was conducted amid a plethora of narcotics.

"I had enough of religion and God in Israel," she told me as she broke away from me. "That's what we have: God. God. God. Everything is in the name of somebody's god. All our problems are because of somebody's god."

Her father was a baker and her mother a housewife. Gal had completed high school, fulfilled her military obligation by serving as a nurse, then taken off to see the world. She felt there was nothing for her back home, save a sixteen-year-old younger brother who she hoped would get the chance to travel as she had.

Gal was deeply cynical without being condescending, skeptical about the future without being negative. She knew, for example, that Trey and I were involved in pointless and essentially meaningless endeavors: my search for God and his search for a magazine assignment. It didn't interest her in the least that we had aspirations to write great stories and books, or that this was all somehow a part of that process. But she managed to dismiss our activities without belittling us.

However, because Gal was the only one of us—besides Easy-E—who had no stake in what was going on, more power gradually accrued to her. She was here on a temporary basis; she had deigned to accompany us. The implication was she could leave at any time, just as easily as she had shown up. And therefore it was up to us to please her. I felt responsible for making sure she was satisfied and happy, and on those occasions when I caught glimpses of her unaware, I could see she was turning something over in her mind, was weighing options, was trying to come to a decision.

But that afternoon in the pool, and then later in the starched sheets of the bungalow, where she lay naked flipping through the pages of her diary and I nodded, spent, beside her, I realized that Gal had become the one thing I was holding on to. Through the Vaseline-smeared lens of dusty India and strong narcotics and promiscuous, hard-bodied boys and girls and aggressively proselytizing swamis, there was very little that seemed real. But Gal seemed real.

Trey came back and pretended not to notice us sprawled on the bed. He babbled about an editor at a fashion magazine in New York who was terribly interested in his work, about an impending assignment to write about the Indian film industry.

It was like he was talking about another world. All that stuff: book contracts, magazine articles, agents, fees; and even everything else: stock markets, careers, apartments, bank accounts; none of it seemed to matter to what was going on here and now. But it was hard to figure out what about here and now mattered: the decadence of this whole karmic bum's rush seemed to negate any value it might have had.

There was a wildness about Trey's eyes as he related possibilities on the magazine front, a fervor in his voice. Of all of us, he seemed like the one who had glimpsed the godhead.

Easy-E entered toting a black athletic bag, which he opened to withdraw glass ampoules and hypodermic needles. Apparently this was what had fueled Trey's rabid optimism.

"Special medicine," Easy-E explained. "Special Indian medicine. It's good, I think. Only in India, I think."

Trey nodded, sitting down on the bed. "Ketamine."

I watched as Easy-E dipped a bezel into an ampoule of Ketamine and then turned the bottle upside down, filling the syringe with clear liquid. Trey pulled his loose linen pants down to his ankles, proffering the inside of his right thigh to Easy-E, who sized up the soft flesh flecked with strands of Trey's brown hair. Easy-E seemed to lunge forward to stick the needle into Trey's thigh. Trey let out a soft hum and sat back. "You gotta try this."

My dose, which Easy-E shot into my buttock, served as a

catalyst for a euphoric flight of soaring rhetoric about my long-term plans: to find God, to finish another book, to complete a magazine article, to marry Gal, to take her back to live in Tokyo, no, even better, New York, no, to travel with Gal around the world, to show her the wonders of this universe, to lavish jewels upon her, to dress her in the finest silks, to sire a vast family with her, to grow aged with her and then to rise together to the heavens aboard a white chariot pulled by a dozen swans. It would all cost money, I knew, but that could be arranged.

I found myself standing on the bed, a thick, multithousand-rupee wad of local currency in my hand, my trembling feet sinking into the mattress, gazing wild-eyed around the room. And Trey and Easy-E would be with us, it would be the four of us, together forever; we would remain perpetually embarked on this expense account–fueled odyssey. Our home would be the business-class section of whatever airline we had ticketed, our closets the overhead compartments and our showers the hot towels dispensed by the lovely stewardesses of the Far East's flagship airlines. As I swayed wildly, my head inches from a glass-bead chandelier, I felt a flush of connectedness with the universe: with the molecules and atoms that comprised all things, with the particles and waves that comprised the atoms, with India, with the mystery of writing, with Trey and Easy-E and especially with Gal. The bungalow swirled around me, for the moment transformed into the vastness of space-time itself, and I managed to convince myself, for a millionth of a second, that I was on the verge of discovering something great.

At some point that evening, in a fit of generosity, while Trey went back to the business center so that he could call Manhattan as magazine editors were arriving in their offices, I bestowed upon Gal a tattered pile of rupees as fat as a waterlogged paperback novel. I wanted her to have them. I wanted everyone to have whatever they wanted.

I woke at eleven to Easy-E tugging my shoulder. I had told him to wake me at dawn so I could make my morning meditation sessions and then my scheduled massages. I vaguely recalled the night before, the rich sense of possibility I had felt, and though I was not sure why I had felt that so much was impending, I was still certain many wonderful opportunities were afoot. Gal lay sleeping beside me, her lovely tanned features resting in a shaft of marmalade-colored morning sun.

When creeping doubts began to surface about the reality of this sense of revelation, I squelched them, dismissing the suspicions as the return of my natural cynicism. Why couldn't this be a season of revelation and transformation? I thought as I slipped on my magenta shorts and tank top and slid into my sandals, stuffing my white robe into my backpack. Of the thousands who had come out here looking for something to believe in, why couldn't I be the one who found love?

After meditation, I went to see Ma Satya, a Danish woman with brown hair, round blue eyes, clear, pallorous cheeks, a soft nose and wide, slightly chapped lips. She looked like the sort of woman who had been beautiful once, before too much harsh Asian sun had given her the faint beginnings of wrinkles around her mouth and eyes. She was still pretty, but in a slightly tired way, as if her looks had already been used so many times for leverage and gain that they could no longer muster the energy to entice each new prospect.

She was to be my masseuse, taking me through a session of Healing Love, a popular course at the ashram. She asked me what I ate—raising her eyebrows in some surprise when I mentioned that I still ate red meat—and if I drank, smoked, took drugs. I answered her honestly, leaving out some of the specifics about frequency and intensity. I let her know there were certainly toxins in my body that, if possible, we should work on releasing. We were in a white stucco-walled cabana alongside a path of stones sunk into mossy soil. Birds flitted from dewy branch to branch, the thick, vined trees providing a delicious covering of shade from the morning sun. The room reminded me of a brothel room: the harsh fluorescent light, bottles of exotic lotions and oils arrayed on a silver tray, a box of tissues with one ready for the taking, an old radio with extended antenna and a small sink with a plastic drainage pipe that was next to the door. But instead of a mattress, there was a hardened padded massage board atop sturdy metal legs. Above the sink, where the mirror should have been, was a blown-up photo of a bearded Osho, his hooded gaze fixed upon me.

I took off my clothes and lay back on the magenta towel that Ma Satya had spread on the massage board. She slipped off her magenta robe, revealing a magenta tank top over a pair of loose-fitting magenta pantaloons. As she tied her hair into a ponytail, I could see the wild, dark hairs of her armpits. Popping the top of a bottle of saffron oil, she slicked her hands and her forearms in a manner that reminded me of a doctor scrubbing before surgery. She poured the bottle of oil so that a dollop fell to my chest, slithering down my abdomen.

I was naked, on my back, looking up at this Danish masseuse with glistening arms and a tired expression; this particular massage therapy was known as a real "kundalini releaser." I was at her mercy.

She smiled at me and shook her head. "What are you looking for?"

I couldn't answer that. I lay there and waited for her to begin. She told me her hands would be cold at first but that they would warm up. She ordered me to turn over and began kneading the oil into my neck, back, thighs, calves and feet; her hands did have a healing effect, a sureness in how they moved about my body. Ma Satya had been at this too long to be tentative.

She had been here at the ashram for five years, first as an eager devotee seeking the light, then as one of Osho's inner circle, now as healer and masseuse. Thousands of innocents had come and gone since she had begun here; they arrived sure they had stumbled onto the true path. Sometimes they stayed, sometimes they gave up and went home, sometimes they lost their minds out here, occasionally they died: overdoses, suicides, drug-related accidents. We were the worst ever, she had told me before she began, this year's crowd wanted everything without sacrificing anything. We did not understand that finding God and revelation, whether in the form of Osho or any other guru or swami, took effort, was not the result of some admixture of sex and drugs.

I didn't tell her I thought she was wrong, that I had found what I had been looking for and that it had been serendipitous: Gal had fallen into my lap.

She worked over my body thoroughly, with a soothing touch that lulled me even as her hands left me in a state of obvious excitement. Noticing this "tension in the sex centers," she spread more oil over my thighs, bending my legs forward at the knees so that they pressed against my penis. She began to work my legs from side to side and back and forth, so that I was rubbing against myself. She delicately continued this procedure, gently bringing me to orgasm before I had a chance to realize that I was essentially jerking myself off.

When I returned to the bungalow, I found Easy-E seated on the bed wearing a pair of black soccer shorts and a set of headphones, percussive hisses of raga music leaking from around his ears. Smoking another of his bangh cigarettes, he shook his head when he saw me. "You find God?"

I shrugged.

"He's not here, I think," Easy-E said, stopping the cassette player.

"In Pune?" I asked.

"India," Easy-E said, making a small, palms-up gesture to indicate the whole subcontinent. "We have a thousand gods, ten thousand—what's bigger than ten thousand?"

"Million."

Easy-E rolled his head in that circular motion that Indians answer every question with. "A million gods. But they aren't for you. Don't you have gods where you come from? Why do you come here and look for our gods?"

I couldn't answer that.

"You come here, take our medicine, drive from city to city—that's no way to find anything, I think." He was about to put the Walkman back on.

"Where's Gal?" I asked.

Easy-E did that circular motion again.

I noticed her olive backpack was not on the armchair where she had left it.

"Miss Gal and your friend, they have gone." Easy-E slipped on the Walkman. "I think."

"Where?"

He continued to bob his head. "Your friend, he told me to tell you: He found God."

Trey and Gal had cleared out, taking with them the wads of money I had been throwing around the night before. I checked my duffel bag and then sat down on the bed, holding my traveler's checks and passport in my hands. I believe I felt all those things that one is supposed to feel when you have been dumped, betrayed and used. But there was a commotion just then outside the French windows of the bungalow, and as I stood up to see what was going on, I saw a gardener with a hoe, pinning a cobra's head to the moist earth while another gardener came running along the patio with a machete. With one overhand swing, he hacked the snake's head clean off.

While I shook out a few brown shards of heroin on a sheet of tinfoil, I thought of pursuing Gal and Trey. Easy-E had told me they were taking the train, either to Goa or back to Bombay. But what would I do if I caught them, how could I convince Gal that she was mistaken? How could I hope to rebuild a friendship with Trey?

I did not know what to do. My wish was for the drugs to assuage the pain, to bluntly blot out the hurt. I had only known her a short while, I reasoned, how could this be so crushing? It did not make sense to abort everything, to give up my journey. Instead of embarking on a humiliating search for what had to be an unrequited love, I would pull myself together and continue my mission of discovery, redoubling my efforts, turning my back on this easier, softer way to spirituality to seek the real stentorian God, the chain-gang spirituality that is offered in the tougher, less tourist-friendly communes. My Summer of Love, plainly, was over.

Without Gal and Trey, my journey became an austere pilgrimage. I paid Easy-E and sent him back to Bombay, promising to look him up at the Mighty as soon as I returned to town. I traveled alone, unsure how to go, bumbling through airports and train stations, unable to make new friends and not bothering to look up those few I had. Drugs now seemed a meaningless diversion, a placebo prescribed for an incurable illness. Alone in an air-conditioned room, I balled up the tinfoil and flushed all the powder down the toilet. I was reading books of the teachings and writings of various yogis, swamis and gurus. As I wandered from Ganeshpuri, where I tried to calm myself in Siddha yoga's Peacock Chamber, to Varanasi, where the air smelled of burning human flesh, to Thammosat, where a boy guru named Swami Niket ordered me to undergo an extensive course of hydrotherapies and enemas, I felt an oppressing solitude as I became myself again, free from mind-altering chemicals and confronted by the grim reality of what had transpired. I viewed those days with Gal as an Eden—it seemed an era of such rich contentment that it became, in my mind's eye, the apotheosis of all that was good about life. I tried to conceive scenarios by which I could become that happy again: another woman, a plethora of women, great success as a writer, fabulous wealth. These all seemed to pale in comparison with the glory of the epoch just ended. It was as if every experience I conjured to replicate that fleeting time with Gal would be merely derivative, a sham of some lost romance.

This was, I know, insane. But in the seeking, studying and supplicating I was now attempting, I felt an emptiness that I imagined no god could fill. I began to wonder if the very neediness of my search would preclude ever finding any spirituality. As I jetted across the subcontinent, crisscrossing from Bombay to Bangalore, from Goa to Calcutta, in the hope that I would be able to forget, to become the person I was before all this had happened, I found that in my frenetic hunting I had become a late-twentieth-century, first-world, computer-toting ersatz yogi, abandoning the self in the search for God, trying to lose myself in my journey, yet feeling crushed by the bogusness of my mission. But if I was lost, so too were my fellow seekers.

"I came here looking for God," said Ian, a muscular, tattooed, gold-toothed, shirtless boy who swayed on a cliff over Baddam beach one brilliant dawn. "And I found nitrazepam methylmorphine."

The road from Bangalore to Puttaparthi cut through rough, arid terrain. The land was rocky and poor. Every few kilometers, the track leading to the city that has grown around Sai Baba's ashram was blocked by women who had hauled stones and cacti onto the road, demanding rupees from me before they would let me pass. The drive from Bangalore to Puttaparthi, Sai Baba's spiritual center, would have taken three hours without the harassment; the grinding poverty of the region that forced women to blockade the road in order to feed their families added another two hours to my trip. The southern Indian climate was brutally hot and, monsoon season notwithstanding, plagued by chronic water shortages. As I drove in the reliable white Ambassador, the craggy boulder-strewn hills and dramatic, gravity-defying granite formations kept stirring memories of another locale. Then it hit me: Antelope, Oregon, the town nearest Rajneeshpuram, Osho's controversial American ashram, had had a similar eerie barren feel. Coincidence, or perhaps gurus liked their remote retreats surrounded by miles of buttes and boulders that require back-breaking pilgrimages and discourage quick departures. The effect was of a world that was breaking apart, as though the earth itself were all shook up by the god-man down the road.

Sai Baba's incarnation as a deity supposedly occurred at Urvakonda on October 20, 1940. "Honor every religion, each is a

path to the one God," said Sai Baba. And that one god, for his estimated forty million disciples, was Sai Baba.

The arch over the entrance into Puttaparthi bore the white-
painted, cast-metal inscription DUTY IS GOD, WORK IS WORSHIP.

By sunrise, when I had parked and made my way through
the gates, the gaunt, gray- and white-robe-clad devotees were already up and active, some carrying bits of bread and small tins
of water, others hurriedly scribbling down Sai Baba's saying of
the day.

I sat through an orientation where the strict schedule was
perfunctorily laid down by Iyar, a bespectacled instructor who
reminded me of a harried bureaucrat in a totalitarian state. "You
should get up at four, make your meditation, your washing, ladies
in back, gents in front. First bell goes at five-ten, you may then sit
in the mandir and begin meditation. At five-twenty, everyone
chants 'om' twenty-one times and the room will be energized by
the swami's energy. Then we have two minutes of silence. Then
three ladies will sing supravada. Don't worry if you haven't seen
Swami yet, he is always hearing your prayers. Then all will sing
prayers. Then stop chanting at six-oh-five. Darshan line begins
then. Swami comes between six-thirty and seven . . ." Iyar out-
lined the entire day, by the minute, for each devotee. Several
times he mentioned that donations could be made in cash or in
money orders directly through the Bank of India. When one of
the new arrivals, a woman from Mauritius, questioned the quality
of her accommodation, Iyar snapped, "Even in a five-star hotel
where you pay two or three hundred dollars, you'll find something wrong. Be silent and listen."

I shivered. This was the real thing. This wasn't cult lite, this
was a cult. But I had come because I had heard that just a week
before, the prime minister himself had visited and, according to
those who witnessed the event, kissed the guru's feet. (But then
imagine what an American president would do to secure forty
million votes.)

The mandir, the meditation hall where Sai Baba communed with his disciples—there were about fifteen thousand on the compound at any given moment—was a massive, airplane-hangar-size shed of green and white corrugated plastic capacious enough for a reclusive swami's Spruce Goose. Devotees from all over the world shuffled in; a Canadian couple was leading a tour group of followers from Quebec, all of whom, apparently, were eager for a glimpse of the guru. A row of Japanese women knelt amid red flower petals, while a few tattooed English girls whom I recognized from another ashram sat in the back of a long row of devotees, furtively sneaking suspicious glances at yet another holy man's rituals. I knelt down along one of the pathways cleared through the throng by white-robed ushers who used whisk brooms to shoo us away from Sai Baba's intended route.

The hushed silence was broken by a wave of chanting, a collective murmuring that rose up from the eastern entrance of the mandir and then rippled through the crowd in mounting, multi-decible waves until the room was awash with an echoing, rhythmic throb. The guru appeared, clad in a new, vibrant orange robe. He walked on flower petals scattered before him by a phalanx of attractive European female devotees. With his giant, puffy, Jheri-Curled hairdo, light brown skin and endearing grin, Sai Baba at first came across as a slightly ridiculous figure; he resembled one of the more obscure members of the singing Jackson clan—Marlon or Tito, one of those siblings of Janet and Michael who makes the news only for legal problems. Yet Sai Baba demanded a level of adulation that surpassed even the *Thriller*-era Michael Jackson. No one dismissed Sai Baba. And as I gazed up at him, though we had been ordered to remain prone with our heads down, I saw that his grin possessed equal mixtures of mirth and malevolence, and his thick lips were pursed in the sullen, condescending smirk of a rich, pampered child. He looked as if he was amused by this spectacle and had not yet decided how to best put all of this energy to work for him.

During darshan, Sai Baba wandered through the massive auditorium followed by his white-robed retinue. He accepted missives and questions, allowing devotees to kiss his feet. He tossed out handfuls of candies—we were, after all, children of the one God. The flavors varied—during the morning darshan, I caught a Vicks orange-flavored throat lozenge.

After darshan, while most of Sai Baba's disciples stayed and meditated in the mandir, I wandered around the compound—we had been explicitly warned during orientation to minimize visits with the village and contact with the outside world. The ashram was sprawling, with statues and garish fountains everywhere and dormitory-style buildings that were terraced on a hill around a museum displaying a host of badly proportioned wax figurines rigidly posed against crudely painted papier-mâché backgrounds. Lord Krishna wielded a visibly wilting sword in a re-creation of a scene from the Bhagavad Gita. Moses stood atop a pile of what looked like bricks, clutching the stone-tablet Ten Commandments. The connective message: no matter your faith, or who your god, the living embodiment of all gods was just a few hundred meters away—in a house that resembled a drug kingpin's mansion. Sai Baba, by insisting that all religions are the same, presented himself as the one-size-fits-all prophet, messiah and avatar.

I returned to afternoon darshan determined to get a prime place in the mandir. If Sai Baba was the real deal, if he really knew the way, then he could tell me, or show me, or somehow communicate it to me.

While wandering the compound during the day, I had neglected to eat, finding the bowls of soggy rice and boiled yams offered at the communal dining rooms unappetizing. I was also dehydrated; the water in Puttaparthi was not potable, so I'd had only one Sprite to drink all day. Walking unsteadily, I secured a place near the central path of the mandir. As Sai Baba tossed candies and accepted missives, genuflection and foot kisses, he seemed to be making his way toward me—did I seem so needy, so obviously out of balance and desperate for spiritual guidance? Could he sense that I was ripe for initiation?

Then he paused before me, the Guru himself. The chanting had reached an ear-ringing pitch, the thousands of devotees belting out "Master, Master, Baba, Baba" in unison and rocking back and forth. Despite the shade of the mandir, it was swelteringly hot, and as I gazed up at the cherubic face of Sai Baba, I became dizzy as I tried to make out his beaming eyes, his knowing smile, his condescending tilt of the head. The air was filled with hundreds of pink petals thrown aloft by his female praetorian guard. He wore a body oil redolent of talcum and patchouli, or was that the devotee seated beside me? In the heat and the commotion, I had trouble telling my senses apart, differentiating taste from hearing, sight from smell, all the sensory perceptions were blending into one neurological mélange. I say this to explain what I saw: an aura. It was a shimmering yellow light, barely perceptible, like the glow I sometimes see around streetlamps when I am driving home after a long night and I am very tired. It flickered for an instant, I blinked and it was gone.

"What is the true way?" I asked Sai Baba.

He made that circular gesture with his head, as if he had not heard me over the chanting. Then he closed his eyes and, opening them, said, "There are many ways."

But in the tumultuous din of the mandir, I could not be sure I heard him correctly, and as his female flower-petal tossers were overwhelmed by a surge of robe-clad followers desperate to touch the Master, I wondered if I had misheard him. Perhaps he had said, "There aren't any ways."

I got out of there that night, the trusty Ambassador running the roadblocks all the way to Bangalore, and then out by plane back to Bombay.

Trey and Gal had left India together, intending to fly from Bombay to New York via London. When the British Airways flight landed in London to refuel, Gal and Trey stepped off the plane to the transit lounge to have a few drinks. Having run out of cigarettes, Gal excused herself and told Trey she wanted to buy a duty-free carton while here at Heathrow: she liked English cigarettes.

Trey says he never saw Gal again.

SAMSON

Samson and Shore Patrol crouched side by side in starter's stances at the vending machine outside RIP, a roach-infested bar off Roppongi Dori. Only a few of the dozen spectators standing in the twilight drizzle knew that the race, from the Pocari Sweat vending machine to the UCC coffee machine, was to decide the future of two Tokyo strip clubs.

Both men were athletic, and each was sure he could beat the other in a hundred-meter footrace. Anytime, any place, they had challenged each other for months whenever they met.

Their enmity had been born at two A.M. one Friday when they simultaneously stepped up to an attractive Swedish girl who had shown up at Ying Yang in a coral-blue cocktail dress, Balinese warrior tattoos on her fleshy upper arms and high white stilettos strapped to her bony feet. As she bobbed her head to sip her vodka rocks, Samson and Shore Patrol appeared before her.

"You looking for work?" their voices chorused, Samson's tenor complementing Shore Patrol's bass.

The girl sucked at her drink through the swizzle, swung her gaze from Samson to Shore Patrol and back to Samson, then shrugged.

"Work?" Samson asked.

"Dancing?" Shore Patrol queried.

The Swedish girl, whose stringy blond hair rose around her head like a shabby lion's mane, smiled at the two earnest would-be headhunters. "Try elsewhere, you losers."

And she walked away to join a Japanese businessman who awaited her in a corner booth.

Samson and Shore Patrol sized each other up for the first time.

Samson, twenty-seven, never told anyone his real name. He was, he told me, from somewhere in eastern Canada, perhaps Nova Scotia. When I met him, he tried to sell me a knockoff Breitling watch.

Shore Patrol, twenty-four, admitted to being from San Gabriel, California. He had been so nicknamed because one evening when an American serviceman at RIP had jokingly shouted out "Shore patrol," Shore Patrol had managed to clear the premises so quickly that he appeared to be out the door before the bottle he had dropped hit the barroom floor. An AWOL U.S. serviceman, he was known as Shore Patrol, or SP.

It was Shore Patrol's hurried bolt from RIP those months ago that had won him the reputation of possessing blazing speed. He had been a sprinter in high school, so he relished the rumors that had spread among the clientele at RIP.

Yet Samson, who had not witnessed Shore Patrol's run for the door, was skeptical. Samson had also been an athlete during his youth, a fleet-footed high school wide receiver playing Canadian-rules football. It irked him that someone else should be known as the fastest runner in the crowd. He had been sizing Shore Patrol up for some time and was convinced he had better wheels, and whenever talk of the barroom flight came up, Samson shook his head and told anyone who would listen, "That punk ain't fast."

I had been sent to Tokyo by *Vogue* to write about the most expensive hotel in the world. Before I reached that mountaintop hot-springs resort, I was sidetracked by the crowd of scumbags, lowlifes, cutthroats, thieves, dealers, pimps and hustlers who hung around RIP, a has-been dive that in its glory days had hosted the likes of Keanu Reeves, Sting and Seiko Matsuda but was now relegated to serving Asahi in cans to Samson and Shore Patrol. Randall, the frizzy-haired, tattooed, rugby-player-size Aussie who ran the place, along with his partner, a straight-haired, weedy Japanese actor named Haru, were desperately seeking a scheme that would enliven the bar and restore it to its former status. Various ideas came and went as to how to refurbish the joint. One evening I came in to find Randall busy behind the bar with arsenic-smelling bug spray, killing cockroaches and beaming because he had stumbled onto the idea that was going to turn RIP around.

"Piercing station," Randall said as baby roaches scurried across the bar toward me. "This whole piercing craze is about to hit Tokyo. The Japs will go crazy for it."

I shrugged and ordered my J&B and soda.

"We're out of Scotch," Randall told me, slapping at cockroaches with his bare hands. "How about a nose ring?"

But RIP was wallowing in perpetual decline, consigned to being a backwater of the Roppongi party scene that fewer and fewer of the party people deigned to drop in on anymore. As it devolved into a place where the trendy dared not tread, it evolved into the perfect hole-in-the-wall for those who did not want to be seen, who needed a darkened, quiet, secluded spot where they could conduct business with other similarly light-of-day-shy creatures. In Tokyo, with its paucity of spacious housing, deals are usually done in public places. Even as Randall and Haru scratched their heads trying to come up with a new theme that might woo back the smart set, they were inadvertently luring a new clientele that came precisely because the smart set was nowhere to be found. RIP's location down a seldom-traveled side street fifty meters from Roppongi Dori made it centrally located yet discreet. RIP became the venue of choice for shady dealers.

The decor was suitably frowsy, languishing in a state of disassembly because the themes Randall and Haru came up with required tearing down bits and pieces of the bar but were abandoned before any reconstruction took place. There were stretches of exposed steel beams and two-by-fours. Chicken-wire plaster braces showed through behind the racks of empty bottles. The dance floor had been stripped away, revealing that the bar had been constructed over a parking lot.

I too was in flux. My nascent marriage to a Dutch woman was showing signs of miscarrying. A contracted novel I had completed and sent to my publisher was about to be rejected. Needing a break, I had cobbled together a few queries and cajoled my editor at *Vogue* into assigning me this relatively easy story about the most expensive hotel in the world. I had also convinced *The Nation* to provide a few thousand dollars in the form of a research grant; I was to produce for them an article about the Japanese economy, then in a severe slump. But I had been in Tokyo for over two weeks and my research had ground to a halt; I had not been anywhere near the mountaintop retreat I was sent to write about.

Instead I had found among RIP's shadow dwellers kindred spirits. They were all hiding out from something, those of us over thirty from what we had become, those still in their twenties from their inevitable future. There was no mystique about the place, no hallowed past or gilded myths to toast; it was the absence of mystique, the total lack of any kind of decor, that spoke to me the first time I walked into the place.

There was another problem I had come to Tokyo to escape. In Los Angeles, during the writing of that doomed novel, I had taken to ingesting prolific amounts of narcotics. I didn't take these drugs—Vicodins, Percocets, Dilaudids, morphine sulfates, Talwins, Darvons, codeines, the occasional balloon or bindle of street heroin: basically, all the hairy-chested analgesic opiates—to help me write; I took these substances to make me feel better about how badly I was writing. I had convinced myself that what I needed was a quick trip back to Japan, where I had been relatively drug-free during the five years I had spent there in the late eighties and early nineties. What was required, I was sure, was a return to the site of former glories, to where I had written numerous magazine articles and come up with the material for my first and only book. My life in Los Angeles, with its failing marriage and dimly plotted writing projects, was without luster. In Tokyo, on the other hand, my life could regain lost sparkle. I would become the person I imagined I used to be: vital, charming, intuitive, a thorough journalist and artful writer. My drug addiction would magically fall away from me, like a tearaway jersey ripped from a streaking tailback.

But Tokyo had changed.

The Tokyo where I came of age, amid the splash and glitter of the Bubble economy, the dazzle of a gaudy, turbocharged boom that spit out six-figure salaries and fancy imported suits and allowed me for the first time in my life to feel like a grown-up, was gone. Those were years when high school–dropout hostesses, fresh off jumbo-jet steerage one-way from Vancouver, Los Angeles, London, Stockholm or Melbourne, boasted of saving a million yen a month, and scruffy, snotty punks like myself, smarmy in Italian suits and gelled hair, abounded, inhabiting the neon-lit streets and shrieky nightclubs and black-lit bars with such aplomb because we were sure, totally, that we were in the right place at the right time. The vibe had been rapacious, but with the sense of optimism that springs from believing there is enough to go around.

The city that I flew into that dark February of 1996 was a half-decade removed from the glory of the Bubble and mired in myriad political and financial scandals—the prime minister was teetering, the banking system was on the verge of collapse. The mood of the city was somber. I took as my economic barometer the condition and well-being of Tokyo's foreign hostesses. If during the glory days there had been an insatiable demand for more hostesses, more good-time girls to pour drinks and make small talk with expense-account-riding executives grown fat on Japan, Inc., there was now a plethora of unemployed Caucasian blondes and brunettes roaming the Roppongi and Ginza streets. Expense accounts had been slashed. It was no longer acceptable at Nomura, Dentsu or Mitsubishi to run up multithousand-dollar tabs, and the corporate warriors could no longer afford to spend millions of yen wooing these nocturnal flowers with lavish gifts and pecuniary displays of affection. Girls who used to make thousands of dollars a month and revel in diamond and gold perquisites were now unemployed.

But hostess bars, with their posh atmosphere, steady flow of drinks and beautiful women, had always helped businessmen close crucial deals. Times may have been tough, and businessmen less patient, but the need for a place to entertain clients and get a few cheap thrills ogling sexy, ostensibly available foreign women remained as real as ever. Just because business was down didn't mean that business had stopped.

And it was the patrons of RIP who fueled the upstart industry that was replacing hostess bars as the evening entertainment of choice for well-heeled Japanese executives.

Samson squatted beside a carbon-caked 250cc motorcycle, his blackened hands twisting and fiddling in an attempt to adjust the Suzuki's carburetor. He had arrived in Japan with just one skill—he was a whiz at repairing and restoring internal combustion engines. The small garage space he rented in Koto Ward was no larger than a walk-in closet allowing him to store three motorcycles if they stood handlebar to exhaust. During the day he unfurled a canopy over the sidewalk to stake out a few more precious feet of working space and set to tinkering with motorcycles, scooters, mopeds, even the odd lawn mower or hedge trimmer. Renowned in this neighborhood as the *kuroi te no gaijin* (foreigner with black hands), Samson quickly made a reputation for himself as reliable, dependable and, most important of all, trust-worthy. He also developed an extensive web of connections that allowed him to traffic in hard-to-trace stolen motorcycle parts, as well as illicit substances that he would transfer from the foreign community to the Japanese community and vice versa.

He stood up when he saw me, wiping his hands beneath a Husqvarna poster of a preposterously top-heavy Hispanic model leaning forward over a set of chrome handlebars. I had met Samson at RIP, where we were introduced by a mutual acquaintance who knew of my chemical predilections. After unsuccessfully trying to sell me a dodgy watch, Samson told me to come see him at his shop.

In the shadowy light beneath the canopy, framed by exhaust pipes and mufflers arrayed on the wall behind him, Samson appeared hauntingly thin, his narrow cheekbones and cleft chin giving him a drawn, hungry look. He had brown hair that he kept short and well groomed. By design, there was nothing exceptional about his appearance, save that he always seemed to be smirking around his two prominent buckteeth. He spoke in English. "So how do you know Motoko?"

"We used to work together," I told him.

He considered my answer, rolling his upper lip beneath his lower as he did so. He posed questions about why I was in Tokyo, about who I worked for.

We spoke of Bangkok, of pharmacies along Patpong, of bars we both knew. The conversation circled around but never quite settled on what I had come to see him about: heroin. I was impatient, my last few Darvon were staving off serious discomfort. But I had concluded that in order to successfully research and complete my assignments, I would need stronger narcotics.

My plan to wean myself from synthetic and nonsynthetic opioids in Tokyo had failed. I had sniffed what was supposed to be my last bindle of heroin on the plane to Tokyo. The dozen Percocets and bottle of Valium in my briefcase had been intended as a gradual detoxification kit. But the first morning in Tokyo, awake early because of the discomfiting combination of leg cramps and jet lag, I had wandered in the gray mist to see a sympathetic elderly doctor I knew who provided me with a few dozen candy-colored Darvons and some French tranquilizers called Cercine. That had been a few days ago. Now I was running out of pills.

A few minutes later, while Samson washed his hands with powdered soap over a tiny plastic basin, he said, facing the mirror, "So you're riding the horse?"

After he dried his hands, he removed a bindle of Japanese newsprint from behind the busty Hispanic woman and carefully unfolded it, revealing a mound of brownish powder. He had already pushed in the bike he had been repairing and shuttered his modest establishment. There was barely room for the two of us to stand without touching. He poured out a two-centimeter-long line of the powder on a shiny vinyl motorcycle seat. I inhaled the powder with a rolled-up thousand-yen note and handed the note to him.

As we stood face-to-face in the crowded little garage, we agreed that I would buy the remainder of the bindle for twenty thousand yen. Samson, relaxing after his day's work, handed me a deck of Polaroids.

"What do you think?" he asked.

The dark, shadowy photographs were of women, in bikinis or naked, with teased, stringy blond hair. Most of the girls were standing, but one or two were lying back on what appeared to be dining room tables, holding their feet with their hands to show their splayed genitals to the camera. I was reminded of the "Girl Next Door" sections of various adult magazines.

"Who are they?" I asked.

Samson explained they were strippers, twenty-four of them, and they were en route to Tokyo via Vancouver. He had arranged housing, feeding and transportation for these girls, who were to work in Bachelor Party, one of the new strip clubs opening around Tokyo. He had found them through a scout who worked in Ohio, Kentucky and West Virginia, hiring girls to dance in the Far East. The new Tokyo clubs were competing for exotic dancers. Samson, along with Shore Patrol and a few other foreign hustlers, had gone into business providing girls for the new Tokyo topless and bottomless clubs. He kept an eye open for out-of-work hostesses and foreign girls fresh to Japan, but the clubs were increasingly requiring the top-heavy, silicon- and collagen-enhanced beauties of the type on the Husqvarna poster. Those sorts, the archetypal lap-dance queens, were harder to come by in Tokyo. Each club needed about fifty girls. For the girl with stupendous cleavage and firm buttocks, the money was very, very good.

"There's a definite shortage," Samson told me, "of classy ladies."

When those girls whose Polaroids Samson had shown me arrived and were ensconced on Japanese executives' laps, Samson would net his biggest score ever. None of the local agents had delivered twenty-four girls. Bachelor Party, an upstart club in Shibuya, would instantly leap to the fore of Tokyo's new wave of erotic entertainment; Samson would then allow himself to leave Tokyo. He wanted to exit a winner, on the heels of a big score, a memorable move, one the patrons of RIP would be recounting to one another for months to come.

Like so many people I met in Tokyo that dark season, he wanted out.

That February the drizzle was persistent, an enveloping, ultra-fine mist that wilted everything it touched. My enthusiasm for the various articles I had been sent to complete had also dampened as I found I was unable to regain that old Tokyo magic in this sodden gray city. The streets that I had remembered as being full of hip movers and shakers were traversed by raincoat-clad and umbrella-wielding salarymen and office ladies. The bustle and energy I had hoped would reinvigorate me was nowhere to be found.

I had been at the Ministry of Finance most of the afternoon. That gray-brick, concrete and steel bunker that hunkered on a

Toranomon city block in central Tokyo was the grubby nexus of an elaborate and particularly egregious, even by Japanese standards, *jusen* (savings-and-loan) scandal that was rocking Japanese securities markets and consumer confidence. The usually smarmy ministry officials who, in prior meetings, had always communicated to me a breezy self-confidence regarding their stewardship of the world's second largest economy now seemed markedly downcast. The dingy corridors—Japanese ministries are always remarkably grimy—were crowded with slowly walking, shell-shocked bureaucrats who, for perhaps the first time in their lives, had no excuses.

"We simply did not know," one assistant minister said of the ministry's role in exacerbating the scandal by throwing more money at it. "We had hoped things would get better."

The mood of the ministry was like the bridge of the *Titanic* after striking the iceberg. As I was exiting through the lobby, I saw security officers in white caps and gloves seated before vast control panels with bright red and green blinking lights, staring straight ahead, arms at their sides, doing nothing. The ship, plainly, was sinking. And no one knew what to do.

Bachelor Party was swarming with salarymen. They sat in black upholstered chairs, beneath a ceiling of black velvet with heavenly constellations of five-pointed gold stars, sipping Scotch-and-waters, smoking Casters and Mild Sevens and staring at Sindii Starr, who was strutting on an elevated stage, clad in black-strapped stilettos and a gold ankle bracelet. She undulated to the front of the stage, blew a kiss to a gent in the back and then bent over backward so that her face was reflected in a mirror behind the stage and her bleached blond pubic hair was inches from a bespectacled, intoxicated Sanwa executive.

The crowded club smelled of sweat, smoke and Scotch. Girls in various states of undress were working every pit and booth in the joint, straddling salarymen, pressing their breasts into flushed, drunken faces, grinding their buttocks into stiffening trousers. Amid all this, liters of tequila and Scotch were disappearing down off-work gullets as fast as the bartenders could ring them up. The businessmen were throwing blue-and-white thousand-yen notes and brown-and-yellow ten-thousand-yen bills at the girls in frenzied efforts to get more of whatever they had to offer. Every once in a while a girl would shout and slap at a guy, then acquiesce to whatever he had requested when the appropriate bouquet of banknotes had been proffered. The girls drew the line at biting.

The Sindii Starrs, Dawns, Dixies and Renatas were all big tits and shaved genitalia, thorough wax jobs and lacquered makeup. These were professionals, the best the San Fernando Valley had to offer. And they were here, in Tokyo, and they were the only ones who appeared to be cashing in on a downward economic spiral.

The ambience was vastly different from that at a hostess bar. Hostess bars forced men to be patient. There were rules: you were greeted by the mama-san, you were shown to your table, you paid for the young lady's time, her drinks, maybe a preposterously overpriced snack, and if you were lucky, after a half-dozen visits, you kissed the young lady on the cheek. After three months and tens of thousands of dollars, you maybe got to sleep with the girl.

But here, at this new breed of Tokyo strip club, the only rule seemed to be take what you could when you could because who knew when the girl would move on to the next booth. The women were little more than human erotomatons to be fondled and probed by the drunken men. That small hostess-bar nicety of meeting and greeting and pretending to be interested in more than sex had been jettisoned. Here you were greeted by a tuxedo-clad Nigerian named Mr. Jackson who led you to a booth, took your drink order and asked you to pick out a girl. When she arrived, her top already open to artificially enhanced cleavage and her vibrator visible in a tiny leather purse, she asked immediately if you would like a friction dance.

"If hostess bars are a commercialization of the courtship

ritual," observed Rie Yamaguchi, hostess turned journalist, "then Tokyo's strip clubs are the instant ramenization of that ritual."

Samson led me through the club to a VIP lounge on the second floor where older versions of the first floor's salarymen sat in more generously padded chairs, attended to by slightly more attractive versions of the girls on the first floor. We were greeted by Mr. Amano, a youngish Japanese man with long, stringy black hair in an unkempt ponytail. He wore a silver-gray suit, white shirt and a diamond stud earring. Instead of a conventional necktie, there was an intricate black knotting of fabric at his collar that resembled crossed shards of lightning. Carrying a leather notebook and two cellular phones, he showed us to a booth in the middle of the room. A gentleman in a getup like an Old West saloon barkeep—apron, tuxedo shirt and bow tie—brought us iced oolong tea.

Amano's phones rang incessantly. No matter who was calling, his answers consisted entirely of profuse apologies.

Samson removed from the inside jacket pocket of his made-in-Seoul polyester suit the envelope containing the Polaroids he had shown me back at his shop.

Amano took the Polaroids and shuffled through them perfunctorily, wiping his brow with a damp cloth midway through and then setting them down to apologize to yet another caller. He pushed the power button on a gray plastic phone, telling Samson that these girls were fine.

Then a barrel-chested Nigerian whose muscle mass appeared to be straining against his starched white shirt and black jacket loomed above Amano's right shoulder. Amano, seeming to sense the Nigerian behind him, flipped through the Polaroids again, holding them a foot to his left so they were in the Nigerian's line of sight.

"Fine, fine," the Nigerian said, then, looking up at Samson, he added, "That is all we ask for: classy ladies."

He shook his head as if the shortage of suitable Caucasian

strippers in Tokyo were a genuine tragedy on par with corrupt prime ministers or collapsing savings and loans.

Everywhere I went with Samson, the primary topic of conversation was classy ladies, young ladies or attractive ladies. New clubs were opening at the rate of about one a week. There was Dior in Shibuya, there were six Seventh Heavens scattered around Tokyo, there was Body Heat, Contact, Bachelor Party, Stopless, two Maximuses in Yokohama, one J-Foxx and a One-Eyed Jack's. Every new club needed classy ladies, young ladies, attractive ladies. The male patrons of RIP were scheming various means of importing more of these needed females. For a few of the patrons, that meant flying in an old girlfriend or former flame. For others, elaborate subterfuge was involved, with visa regulations to circumvent, taxes to avoid and bargain airfares to track down. Clubs were paying a premium per girl, 50 percent of her first month's earnings to the "agent" who had introduced her. A skillful operator such as Samson stood to make at least $50,000 for the strippers whose images he was carrying around in his jacket pocket.

Predictably, Randall and Haru had come up with the idea of turning RIP into a strip club. Work had commenced on a small circular stage in the back, next to a DJ booth. Yet even as he jumped aboard the bandwagon, Randall lamented this new direction in Tokyo nightlife, putting words to my thoughts when he said, "I'm not crazy about this whole *gaijin* stripper craze. I liked hostesses. You see, a hostess comes to Japan innocent and then has her heart broken. A stripper doesn't have a heart to break."

There were dozens of teased-hair, leather-clad vixens looking right off the set of a RATT video who would drop into RIP to see Samson, Shore Patrol or any of the other foreign agents who had set them up at their clubs of employment. The girls came looking for a new joint, having heard about a better-paying gig, or they just wanted to talk to another Yank or Aussie or Canuck who would at least pretend to understand what they were going through. The clubs were owned by Japanese and managed by a combination of Nigerians and Japanese. (The Nigerians had risen to middle management in the Japanese adult-entertainment industry because of their surprising aptitude for the Japanese language and, perhaps more important, the fact that many of them were built like linebackers. It was cost-effective to have managers able to serve as bouncers.)

The girls glided in on their strappy stilettos and black leather jeans, snapping gum and smelling of hair spray. They would set down their satchels containing G-strings, lubricants, whatever erotic toys or gimmicks they employed in their acts, and then unload to whoever would listen about how Mr. This or That had mistreated them, victimized them or otherwise done them wrong. Inevitably, these malfeasances occurred in the financial realm. Though the girls made the majority of their income in tips, their housing and transportation were supposed to be paid by the clubs. Shacked up as they were in tiny, six-tatami-mat, *gokiburi* (cockroach)-infested apartments, many of the girls could not believe that the $700-a-month housing allowances were being legitimately spent.

We male patrons of RIP would gawk at the whinging females and shake our heads. We knew they were making tens of thousands of dollars a week. And it was our conclusion that they were spoiled rotten by their own good luck. They happened to have landed when Tokyo was uniquely poised to indulge the gluttony of turbocharged foreign strip clubs. Just four years ago, this proliferation of topless and bottomless clubs featuring *gaijin* women would have been unthinkable. There had always been a few foreigners who worked in the *mizu-shobai* (water trade), that catchall term for brothels, massage parlors and strip clubs. But these clubs had been confined to specific areas of the city and were staffed almost entirely by Japanese, Koreans, Filipinos or Thais.

The new generation of strip clubs was in the same sections of town the foreign hostess bars used to be, often in the very same venues. I was saddened whenever I visited a bar I used to know and found it shuttered or converted to a strip club.

Samson never stopped to wonder at these transformations. He had been in Tokyo for four years. He perceived the atmosphere of anxiety and desperation as one where a foreigner such as himself could prosper. The Japanese were repairing old motorbikes now rather than buying new ones. The Japanese were taking more illegal drugs than ever before. And the Japanese were hungry for a glimpse of foreign pussy. Samson inserted himself into these various markets and was gradually bankrolling a small fortune, more money than he could make back home, wherever that was.

No matter how many girls Samson, Shore Patrol or other agents found for the clubs, the clubs always needed more. Samson and Shore Patrol, as they sat at RIP's recently delaminated bar, answering pages and making calls on their mobile phones, had come to resemble the harried businessmen clients of the bars for which they were hiring. Samson and Shore Patrol had taken to renting vans for the evening and shuttling girls from one club to another, alleviating with such stopgap measures the appearance of a shortfall.

But both Samson and Shore Patrol knew there simply weren't enough girls in Tokyo to staff all the clubs that were opening. The foreign-stripper population in Tokyo had swelled to approximately four thousand, according to Hideo Yasunobu, a club owner in Shinjuku. "But we could easily employ double that."

The competition among the foreign agents for girls had become so intense that the guys were now poaching girls from one another, employing whatever means necessary to provide enough girls for their clubs. Occasionally, when an attractive girl showed up in RIP, fights would break out between agents over who would represent her and where she should work.

The two leading agents were Samson and Shore Patrol. Neither man succeeded because of natural charisma or charm; there were other men around who had much more. They had become the top earning agents because of diligence and hustle. They worked tirelessly, making the rounds of Roppongi nightspots to attempt to shake out one more woman who might be willing to take her clothes off for money. Samson would happily ride his motorcycle up to an Ogikubo *gaijin* house to check on a rumor of a potential stripper having taken up residence. Shore Patrol sometimes took the train out to Narita airport, waiting in the arrivals lounge to poach newcomer dancers booked into competing clubs.

I tried hard to make myself comfortable in this new Tokyo. I befriended Samson, I dated a foreign stripper, I visited the new nightclubs. But my plan to rediscover my happiness in Tokyo was not working. I was ingesting even more pills and powders than I had back in Los Angeles. The depression that had come on there had not dissipated here. Instead, with each rain-splattered day, I became more sure that the melancholia was a permanent attribute, some delicate imbalance of neurological chemicals that could only be home-remedied with opiates. Here in Tokyo, I should have been able to shake off whatever drabs had enveloped me back in Los Angeles. On the doorstep of Asia, continent where I had enjoyed so much of my twenties, I had imagined I would regain my lost enthusiasm for myself and for what I might become. But I found the opposite: with each night that I sat at the bar of RIP, with each evening that I made the rounds of topless Tokyo venues with Samson, I sunk further and further into myself.

To be fair, Tokyo was not an ideal city in which to reinvigorate oneself. The city was going through a paroxysm of self-doubt and self-pity. Newspapers, in between articles about an indigenous savings-and-loan scandal that dwarfed the American version of the late eighties, wearily reported continuing downsurges in consumer confidence and national sentiment. TOKYOITES CITE FUTURE AS NUMBER ONE SOURCE OF ANXIETY, the *Yomiuri Shimbun* helpfully informed us. A NATION OF PESSIMISTS, proclaimed the *Mainichi Shimbun*. In the wake of the Aum religious cult's gassing of the Tokyo subway system and the devastating Kobe earthquake, for the first time since the mass destruction of World War II, the Japanese people could imagine unseen metaphysical forces aligned against them. "It is as if we are being punished for our excesses of the past decade," a finance ministry official told me. This downturn, afflicting a generation of baby boomers who had come of age amid unrelenting prosperity and economic growth, created a sense of desperation and panic new to Tokyo. In the midst of corporate downsizing and diminishing wages, canceled bonuses and enforced early retirements, it no longer made sense to bide one's time patiently, waiting for the inevitable raises, promotions and perks. Who knew if there would be any position to be promoted into tomorrow? In this atmosphere of fear and insecurity, it behooved one to be rash, bold and predatory.

Why save money when the S&L in which you deposited might collapse tomorrow? Why sell your soul for the company when the company might not be there tomorrow? Why patiently romance and seduce a hostess when you barely had the money to make mortgage payments on a three-bedroom house way out in the suburbs on which the loan was now worth more than the house?

So drop into Bachelor Party, down a few shots of tequila, throw a wad of cash on the table and grab your pleasure in greedy handfuls.

In this world of bitter, drunken salarymen and their objects of lust, the foreign strippers, the modern-day flesh traders such as Samson and Shore Patrol had become unlikely power brokers. Both men were near the eye of the fiscal and sexual storm, purveyors of the flesh that precipitated hurricanes of interest and desire. The clubs were very big business, and owners were eager to placate Samson and Shore Patrol to ensure a steady supply of "classy ladies." They were granted entrée into unlikely spots. Samson was frequently wined and dined at preposterously expensive restaurants by a Japanese "businessman" named Mr. Gondo who ran several of Roppongi's strip clubs. Another "businessman" named Testsuo Yamada had invited Samson down to the very hotel I was supposed to be writing about. Samson had declined.

I hung around with Samson in the hopes that some of his ebullience and genuine good cheer would rub off on me. He seemed to me to be vitally alive. Whether he knew it or not, he was now at a business, nightlife and underworld hub that appeared to me to be an exciting and glamorous spot. Events and forces outside his control, those same events that perhaps could be blamed for Japan's monumental economic woes, had placed him in the position of being much sought after and, for the time being, integral.

It had been a long time since I had felt sought after, or at the center of anything. I made rounds with Samson, from RIP to 999 to Buzz to Ying Yang to the Breakfast Club to the various bars and nightclubs where he put in appearances and seemed to be doing the nightlife equivalent of a politician's pressing of the flesh. As he shook hands, kissed cheeks, pounded down shots, dispensed E's, collected debts, gathered photographs and basically ran his entire operation out of his cheap-suit-jacket pockets, I realized that there is perhaps nowhere further from the center of things than being adjacent to it.

Samson greeted all females as "babe" or "mama." All foreign men he called either "punk" or, for those he was particularly close to, "butt boy." With Japanese he was always rigorously polite, employing almost flowery honorifics when dealing with the club owners. He spoke to their Japanese underlings in simple, uninflected first-person Japanese, as if they were merely listening in on an interior monologue. The Nigerians he regarded with disdain, speaking to them in English and always employing the butt-boy pronoun. For some reason he singled me out, giving me the moniker "Buttley."

He was possessed of phenomenal energy, even when he was "riding the horse," capable of staying up all night and well into the morning, which was when most of the dancers and strippers might be tempted to change clubs. Samson could be embarrassingly persistent.

I once asked him how much money he had made.

"Can't tell you, Buttley," he said. "But let's just say after those two doz from the Midwest, it's *sayonara,* Mr. Gondo."

We sat around a steel table at Buzz while it cracked dawn outside, witnessing the narcotized dregs of a never-was rave party stumble around on a dance floor of black rubber on which spilled beer had pooled and dried into a sticky goo. Samson had seated himself between two heavy-chested, wavy-haired blondes, each about five foot three. Both were currently dancing at Maniac, a small club on the third floor of a Nogizaka building, across the street from the Department of Defense.

Samson had run into them at 999 and was intent on luring them to work at one of the clubs for which he recruited. An acne-faced Japanese DJ who had been accompanying them was dispatched by Samson to go buy drinks while he laid out the benefits of working at Bachelor Party.

I was seated across from the girls, who, bereft of makeup, appeared, beside their preposterously large bosoms, very plain. Next to me was Laney, my former high school classmate, who had introduced me to the guys at RIP. In his shearling jacket with his deep blue eyes and sturdy chin, he looked like a fighter pilot in a World War II–era cigarette advertisement.

During Samson's pitch, the girls kept sneaking looks at Laney. And Laney, as he sat there tapping his feet against the sticky floor and smoking his Japanese Marlboros, was clearly not interested. He had his pick of the sex-industry employees who traipsed in and out of RIP; this pair was unexceptional.

Noticing that they were taken with Laney, Samson rubbed his chin and leaned over to Laney to ask for help.

"Listen, butt boy, I'm gonna get rid of this DJ. They're not comfortable talking to me with someone from their club here," Samson told Laney. "You just chat these two up. Tell them what a swell guy I am."

"Why?" Laney asked.

"You're not doing anything." Samson said. "You're just sitting there. Help me out."

Laney shrugged, and Samson got up to look for the DJ.

When Laney slid over to chat with the girls, I was envious of the obvious glee he inspired in them. I could not imagine what it would be like to have women react to me like that.

"So you're thinking of working for Samson," Laney said in his raspy California accent.

One of the girls said, "Do you think it's a good idea?"

"He's a real asshole," Laney said, lighting a cigarette.

The girls giggled. I looked at Laney. He winked.

When Samson came back to the table, Laney got up and left, the girls both looking disappointed as he did so.

The rest of the night, Samson kept telling the girls they had to come to Bachelor Party. He guaranteed they would make $1,000 a night. They were making less than half that at Maniac.

Still, the girls resisted. I was amazed as I watched Samson buy them drink after drink, offer them cocaine, reiterate for the twelfth time why Bachelor Party was a good idea. Even in my state of opiated exhaustion, I could tell that Samson's war-of-attrition style of career counseling was not going to work.

When I departed at six A.M., Samson was still cajoling.

The next day I found out from Laney that Samson hadn't convinced the girls to switch.

But Shore Patrol had gone by their squalid six-mat apartment with flowers, champagne and a picnic basket, and they had agreed to go to work at Seventh Heaven.

"Don't mean nothing. I'm still faster than that punk," Samson assured me that night, patting the Polaroids he had taken to carrying around as a sort of good-luck talisman. "Air Canada Flight 707. Two dozen very classy ladies."

My own projects weren't faring much better than Samson's. The interviews I had scheduled, at various government ministries, newspapers, politicians' offices and banks were unfolding as a series of lifeless briefings during which the bureaucrat, reporter, politician or banker in question would drone for a while about his innocence regarding the scandal du jour, and I would dutifully scribble notes and attempt to ask coherent questions.

The Norinchukin, Japan's Central Agricultural bank, occupied an immense polished granite and plate-glass edifice, spanning a square block of downtown Tokyo. The view from the plush, immaculately kept upper offices was of the dusty gray Imperial Palace walls, the busy Akasaka section of Tokyo and the twin-spired city hall that loomed through the fog in the distance, shiny silver against gray clouds. This institution is the central bank for Japan's system of agricultural, forestry and fisheries cooperatives, founded as a quasi-government institution where staid farmers and thrifty fisherman could deposit their hard-earned savings for a rainy day. Spurred by the vast inflation of postwar Japanese real estate and capital markets, this bank then had total assets of ¥44.6 trillion (about $500 billion), making it one of the five largest banks in the world.

A handsome, well-spoken upper-level bureaucrat in a necktie with a silver tie pin and shot cuffs sat before a placid painting of a Japanese peasant girl, flower in her hair, who stared vacantly out at the twentieth-floor office. The bureaucrat explained with considerable anguish the plight of Japan's "farmers," who collectively threw the GNP of a small nation at the insatiable maw of Japan's real estate dragon in the late eighties, and now shook their heads with wonder at how they, backwoods rubes that they were, had been taken by the city slickers. "We had no input or decision making as to the type of loans the *jusen* were making." Kawai shook his head sadly. "We were shocked to discover the level of negligent lending that was going on."

Everyone was innocent. Everywhere I went, I heard the same story: "We didn't know."

After about a half hour, I noticed my assistant gently nudging me. I had nodded during the upper-level bureaucrat's briefing, pretending to look over a glossy brochure outlining the Central Agricultural bank's sinlessness in the current scandal.

"Do you need to lie down?" he asked.

In the past, I had been able to somehow piece together these briefings and meetings into a coherent story. I would listen to the men in suits until something they said stuck in my mind, some scene they described or meeting they recounted, a moment that crystallized the political or economic climate I was supposed to make sense of. But that ability to organize, arrange and structure data into a story had been lost. I felt constantly preoccupied, as if those gigabytes of brain necessary to do the subconscious work of making an article, of writing, were now unavailable. My mind was busy with drugs.

The days slipped by, a procession of gray, damp afternoons and cold, wet evenings. Automobile headlights were particularly beautiful in the persistent light rain, appearing as sets of silver moons, levitating through the Minato-ku streets. Even with Samson and the crowd at RIP and my loyal assistant, who kept on arranging interviews and meetings though I was proving worthless at conducting them, when I woke up on the tatami-mat floor of my assistant's apartment, the rain pattering against the thin wire-mesh windows, I had never felt so alone.

Then one morning I called my wife in Los Angeles. She did not say very much. She had bought a ticket back to Amsterdam. She was leaving me.

Samson had bivouacked the two dozen midwestern strippers at a weekly mansion in Gotanda, about five minutes from the train station up a steep cobblestone road. Their first morning in that sleepy suburb of Tokyo, they appeared a vanquishing army of buxom Amazons as they made their way down in groups of twos and threes to the narrow shopping street that ran from the station. They were blondes and brunettes, accustomed to travel and shacking up in less than luxurious accommodation. Most of the girls had their hair tied back in ponytails and their sleepy, jet-lagged faces unadorned by makeup. Clad in sweatshirts and sweatpants that failed to obscure prominent busts and ample, muscular haunches, they sought coffee, cigarettes, croissants, orange juice, cold cream and tampons. Samson had not counted on their being up this early; he had forgotten how jet lag afflicted new arrivals to the Far East, making it impossible to sleep until first light.

The salarymen, grandmothers and schoolchildren of Gotanda, heading out to the office, fruit stand and school, gawked at these exotic new arrivals who, in the morning rain, had no umbrellas and seemingly no idea where they were going. The foreign girls, whose profession was obvious perhaps only to the salarymen scurrying to buy newspapers and train tickets, had been given paltry per diems by Samson upon their arrival the night before. Yet even the simplest financial transaction, at the bakery, pharmacy or coffee shop, proved complex and laborious. The girls had not yet figured out Japanese currency, instead holding out palms full of cash and coins and allowing the shopkeepers to choose the appropriate denomination.

It seemed the narrow market street, usually quiet at this hour, was in the throes of a large-mammaried occupation. Because of their trade, the girls were impervious to inquiring or curious eyes; they procured supplies and sipped $5 cups of coffee with a sleepy insouciance that some of the locals mistook for arrogance.

If twenty-four strippers showed up simultaneously in your town or on your block, you would take notice. For the citizens of Gotanda, the sudden manifestation was cause for consternation, resulting in hushed conversations conducted while hanging out laundry and in discreet calls to the local *koban* (police box). News travels fast in Tokyo, and the arrival of two dozen women ideally suited to the demands of topless and bottomless dancing did not go unremarked among the salarymen on their way to work that morning. The pulchritudinous phalanx became a leading topic of discussion in various offices around Tokyo, and word was passed from ear to ear until a cellular phone in a certain AWOL sailor's shirt pocket jangled with the news that by now had been exaggerated into a torrent of American womanhood washing up on southern Tokyo.

"Dude," a gravelly-voiced partner of Shore Patrol announced. "Hundreds of prime American babes, out there in the 'burbs."

Shore Patrol hailed the first taxi he saw.

By the time Samson showed up at the Lion Mansion to prep and acclimate his quiver of classy ladies, Shore Patrol had come and gone and planted in the girls' minds the notion that Samson was underpaying them. Shore Patrol had told them that Tokyo clubs were desperate, willing to pay top dollar. Whatever Samson had promised them per night—fifty, a hundred thousand yen?— he could get them more. The prospect of providing for his clients at Seventh Heaven twenty-four fresh bodies and faces, none of whom had been seen on Tokyo laps before, was dizzying to Shore Patrol. He made lavish offers, disparaged the accommodations Samson had arranged and assured them the contracts they had signed were not legally binding.

"From my mouth to your ears," Shore Patrol told them before he left. "Help me help you."

Samson walked into cramped apartments that now housed tense, sleep-deprived women who had suddenly taken up the cry that their needs weren't being met. They had been flown halfway around the world by this bilker, and they were not about to let the fleecing continue. As Samson tried to calm them and make sense of this sudden swelling of dissatisfaction, it leaked out that Shore Patrol had inserted himself into the situation, planting the seeds of dissent. Several of the women, already taken with Shore Patrol's Rutger Hauer–like Arian features, so unlike Samson's vaguely rodentlike appearance, claimed that unless Samson met some untenable terms—shorter working hours, no payout to the club at the end of the night, no groping during lap dances, more spacious accommodations—then they would refuse to work at Bachelor Party. Despite Samson's protests that Shore Patrol did not intend to meet any of these obligations, the girls were now perilously close to open rebellion and subsequent termination of any relationship with Samson.

After dispensing wads of currency and assuring the girls that he would search for better housing, Samson ducked into a restroom, snorted a line of heroin and reemerged, having reassured himself that the situation was under control.

He hopped on his Suzuki and fired back up to RIP. It was time to settle things with Shore Patrol.

Shore Patrol was sipping an orange juice and playing cribbage with Laney, who leaned over the bar to peg four holes. Randall and Haru were spray-painting different colors onto the wallboard at the back of the bar, testing various color schemes for the strip club they now envisioned. There were about a dozen patrons in the bar, a few reading newspapers, a few sipping drinks or canned coffee. A Japanese kid in a blue vinyl jacket nodded on a stool next to the out-of-service pay phone. A salaryman who had apparently stumbled into the wrong joint hurried to finish the beer he had paid for. Two frizzy-haired blondes in black leather jeans showed up and quickly locked themselves into the restroom for a few minutes.

The bar smelled like the usual combination of cigarette smoke and bug spray.

"Hey, butt boy," Samson said, striding over to Shore Patrol who was holding all fives in his hand and was reluctant to set it down. He turned and nodded.

"Those are my girls, okay, punk?" Samson said. "Step off."

Shore Patrol nodded again and winked at Laney, who studied his cards. "Your girls?" Shore Patrol shook his head. "I didn't see any brands on them."

"Listen, butt boy. You and I both know what's right is right. This is my thing. These aren't some out-of-work hostesses walking around on Roppongi. I brought these girls over. On a plane."

Shore Patrol stood up to face him. "Hey, all I did was go down to see them, tell them what was what. If you're a little slow on the draw, then that's not my fault."

Samson squinted. "Who's slow?"

"You," Shore Patrol said. "You're slow. Maybe it's all that crap you take, the drugs, ruining your body, fucking with your mind. You're slow."

"One thing I'm not is slow." Samson waved an index finger. "I'm fast. Fastest guy in here."

"Bullshit," Laney chimed in. "SP's the fastest guy here."

"You ain't fast." Shore Patrol pointed at Samson. "You ain't nothing."

Samson, in a rage over Shore Patrol's poaching his girls and boasting of his putative speed, shouted out, "That's it. We race. Once and for all. We race."

"Now?" Shore Patrol asked. "When?"

Samson had already begun taking off his cheap suit jacket. "Now. Right now."

Shore Patrol held up his hands. "I'm in boots."

"So am I."

"It's raining outside," Shore Patrol told him, making no move to take off his leather bomber jacket.

"I'm the fastest guy in here," Samson said. "I'll beat you in shoes, barefoot, sneakers, boots. Rain. Snow. On fucking ice, you punk. I am faster than you."

"Fuck you," Shore Patrol told him, standing to peel off his jacket. "I'll race you for the girls."

By now Randall, Haru and several other regulars had gathered around to listen. Samson, reluctant to show his fear, slowly nodded, as if he was trying to convince himself he really wanted to go along with Shore Patrol's idea. "Then if I win you give me twenty girls. You give me twenty girls to bring to Bachelor Party. My choice."

Shore Patrol shrugged. "Then we race."

It was over before it really began. As both runners crouched in the stark white light of the Pocari Sweat vending machine—Samson's gray rayon shirt showing dark spots where he had sweated through the material and Shore Patrol's black cabled sweater beading with water—the crowd stood at the entrance, cocktails and cans of coffee in their hands, cigarettes sending up narrow ribbons of smoke in the chilly twilight air. Laney and I stood at the finish line, the front of the coffee vending machine, outside the front door of an old-fashioned Japanese-style restaurant with a sliding *shoji* door. The street was slanted slightly downhill, the wet pavement giving way in one spot to a thickly painted white crosswalk and a subsequent meter of white stripes before resuming its slick blackness for the rest of the track. They would run into and out of the cone of one streetlight.

Randall, who held his arm up, gazed for some reason at his watch, as if the race were being timed. The winner was first across the line. The winner would get the girls. The winner would make a fortune.

Randall held the runners in their crouch for an awkwardly long time. Several cars were forced to detour around the growing crowd that had now stopped to watch the footrace. A car honked. Someone sneezed.

"Go!"

Samson slipped on the wet pavement. He never caught up.

Bachelor Party, running out of girls, shut its doors three weeks later.

I am lying in a natural hot-spring bath, a damp towel splayed over my head, staring up at petals of snow swirling down from a black-gray sky. It is after midnight. My legs are aching. I have taken my last three Darvons; tomorrow I will be out of drugs.

The hot water splashes into my *ofuro* (bath) through a two-inch-thick bamboo pipe that tilts at a forty-five-degree angle on a wooden swivel when water hits its carved, sharpened mouth. I am trying to relax in my own personal hot spring, an ovoid stone pool set in a Kamakura-style rock garden just outside my $1,000-a-night suite of the Goro Kaidan Hotel atop a five-thousand-foot mountain in central Japan. My feeling, as I gaze down the hillside at the strung lights of a funicular line, the twin headlights of mountain road traffic and the scattered yellow lights of other lodges and hotels, is that from here it is all downhill.

I will leave Japan the next day, for a drug-treatment center in Newberg, Oregon.

I hear that Samson is in Shanghai, where there is a burgeoning market for foreign strippers.

THE CIRCUIT

I lean the motorcycle on its kickstand, the weight of the 150cc Honda settling onto the spring-loaded metal with a slow groan. It is midday on a coastal macadam road on a small island some-where in the Gulf of Siam. The sun is bright, and I am sweating through a Singha tank top, the black dye from the shirt running down my cutoff army pants and mingling with the rivulets of blood that now stream from my calf.

I have been in a motorcycle wreck. A mile back, on an elbow of dirt road, the rocks and sand seemed to open up beneath the front tire of my Honda and sent me sprawling. For a moment I was suspended in air, surprised to be viewing my handlebars from above, and then I was skidding along the hard dirt, ripping up my calf and mingling a streak of dirt, dust and pebbles with the blood that immediately bubbled up around the strips of dis-lodged flesh. I remembered the motorcycle wheel, the clutch still engaged, spinning inches from my ear, an evil buzzing sound like a surgeon's saw cutting through rib cage.

I had been on heroin when I crashed, having sniffed a small dose of whitish powder, plentiful and cheap here in Thailand. I now do not recall how I righted the motorcycle and climbed on for the mile ride to the cluster of bungalows beside the road. I only remember resting the motorcycle on its stand and sitting in the shade, shooing flies away from my wound, while a Thai waiter set down an orange soda in front of me. The air smelled like a combination of chicken shit, dust and body odor, an earthy smell that implies by its rancidness the infectious agents borne aloft on the hot breeze.

Gingerly rising from the bamboo stool, I stumble over a stone divide and make my way to the nearly deserted beach, where a few Frenchwomen are sunbathing and reading waterlogged two-month-old copies of *Paris Match*. As I collapse in the sand, I realize I have lost my sunglasses at the scene of the accident. Even through closed eyes, I can see an outline of the hot ball of sun. I turn over onto my side, my bloody calf pushing painfully into the sand, and begin to shiver. I have been out here for years, traveling and partying throughout the Far East. Now I feel this has all gone wrong. The drugs. This trip. Now this accident.

"Karl?" a woman's voice asks. I open my eyes. Dina stands above me, her face backlit by the sun. She wears a tie-dyed bikini top, a black sarong and her men's Rolex Daytona. "You've got the shakes, eh?"

Her voice is a soothing, warm reminder of a good place, a home—someone's home—far away. Someplace I have never been. Then she sees my leg.

"Bloody hell, what have you done to yourself?"

My eyes adjust to the light and I can make out her small mouth, her pert nose, her almost Chinese eyes.

"Motorcycle accident."

"Get up. Let's scrub that out. It's gonna turn septic on you."

I keep my eyes closed. I am still shivering. "Jesus, Dina, I'm so fucking scared."

She doesn't say anything for a moment, and I can hear the waves breaking and what sounds like wind shimmying through palm fronds and the thwacking sound of someone chopping pineapple on a wooden plank.

"Your fears," she says, "they're like a person you keep seeing over and over again. They follow you around until you find a way not to be afraid anymore. Now let's get you cleaned up."

Kathmandu, 1997

I was stuck in Kathmandu. Waiting for my story to arrive. And hoping that it would before I found myself standing drunk in one of Tamil's loosely regulated pharmacies, telling the stubbled, turbaned pharmacist that I would like sixty of those blue ten-milligram Valiums, sixty of those Roussel Darvons and, oh, how about a hundred of those big, thick white morphine-sulphate tablets?

This was my first story in Asia since I had stopped drinking and drugging, my first sober foray back into the fleshpots that had been the site of so many of my most crippling debauches. I had sworn off the sauce and mood-altering substances and was facing life for the first time unfiltered. I was making a clean start here at the roof of the world; in Nepalese smog and on Kathmandu turf, this was my new beginning. I had long ago lost the ability to regulate my intake of intoxicants. If I slipped again, up here in the Himalayas, it would be a long, long way down. After six weeks in rehab and a year spent putting my life back together—restoring my family's trust, rebuilding my marriage, re-learning how to write—I was, in a sense, making a comeback.

I was in Kathmandu writing a story for *Condé Nast Traveler*. But the story that had begun in Tokyo and gathered momentum in Bangkok was now gasping here in Nepal. I was covering a crowd of kids who lived the circuit. They wandered, as I had done for years, between Asian boomtowns and beaches.

And though the names and faces change from season to season, somehow the cast never really seems to change: wiry boys with protruding rib cages and shaved heads and tattoos, and girls with tan, skinny legs and flat stomachs and belly-button rings and, on the French ones at least, a quiff of armpit hair. But the last time I had seen the crew of trendy American and British travelers who personified this sort of cutting-edge Comme des Garçons and Gucci-clad new Asian hand, they were lying in their Koh Sahmet hammocks smoking joints or sitting at a cyber café, eating Bavarian cream doughnuts and accessing their Hotmail accounts. I had tired of their Ecstasy-driven, ravey island decadence and, fearing for my always tenuous sobriety, headed back to Bangkok, making sure I arranged with this stoned gang of digital-audio-tape-toting vagabonds to rendezvous here in Kathmandu. I had been here a week, and my fellow travelers were nowhere to be seen. I now wondered who or what they had been e-mailing, because I had been sending them e-mails repeatedly for the last five days without response.

Visible through thick billows of Kathmandu smog, between snowcapped Himalayan gorges, the orange sun cast dim rays that barely broke through the haze. Dotting the foothills around Kathmandu were sprawling villages made up of mud huts and handkerchief-size vegetable farms. Occasionally, when the wind from the hills blew the smog back up the valleys away from the city, one caught a whiff of manure and nightsoil, earthy smells of the family farms surrounding the city. The odor struck me as obscenely organic in its bouquet, as if nature herself had let out some great, sphincter-relaxing fart.

Wiping the dust from my eyes, I stepped into the crowded Tamil street, hailing a *tempo* that would take me to Turihil, the gated military parade ground where, in the afternoon, some local college students played soccer with some European expatriates and a dozen other Westerners who, like me, were stranded in Kathmandu for one reason or another.

In almost every city in the world, there are easy-to-access pickup soccer games. I travel with cleats in damp, rainy Europe and turf shoes in dry, dusty Asia. Unlike other travelers, who worry about hotel fitness-club hours, tennis-court reservations, and golf-course tee times, I need nothing more for my sport than a swath of grass—or dirt, or pavement, or mud—a ball and a half dozen or more players. I have played in pickup games around the world: Bangkok's Lumphini Park, Amsterdam's Vondelpark, Berlin's Reichstag lawn, Barcelona's Ramblas, Tokyo's Yoyogi Park, Hong Kong's Victoria Park and Paris's Bois-de-Bologne. I have come to view soccer not only as a way to get to know locals, make friends and stay fit but also as a vehicle for discovering a culture and its people. A day spent playing football with Moroccans, Chinese or Italians will tell you more about national character than any number of guidebooks, language courses or sight-seeing excursions. Beware, though: you will fall prey to ethnic stereotypes that are based on how frequently an Arab player passes the ball or how a Mexican plays defense. You will judge a German's character by how he reacts after allowing a goal, and a Japanese man's emotional maturity by his post-goal-scoring celebration. You will quickly realize the fellow American you befriended last night at the bar is actually a selfish, thoughtless ball hog who would rather lose the ball on the dribble than pass it. And you discover that the quiet, balding Greek whom you dismissed as a sociopath is actually a kind soul, one who would sacrifice an easy, ingenuous shot to attempt an ingenious crossing pass.

The game reveals character and intellect and provides a brief glimpse into one's soul. If you are frightened—of this new strange city, of returning home, of never returning home, of slipping back into drug addiction—then it will show on the pitch, will be made apparent by how awkwardly you handle a ball. But if you are at peace, resting up from the last journey and readying for the next, then the game will be the pleasant diversion it was meant to be. Your exhausting, relentless running, sidestepping and backpedaling will be spontaneously choreographed steps subsumed in some massive ten- or twenty-man dance in which you feel integral. Playing with Nepalese and Thais, Egyptians and Germans, if the game is good and the players are generous and you are at your best, you come to believe you are part of some *spiritus mundi* of manly good feeling that transcends borders, ethnic groups, religions and GNPs. You play the game. They play the game. You belong.

I sat on the pitch near a white-painted wooden fence, slipping on a pair of Diadora turf shoes while nearby a dozen or so Nepalese and Englishmen kicked around soccer balls, jumped up and down in place and swung their arms in wild forward and backward gyres. After I stretched, bending so that my nose touched my knee, I took a moment and bowed my head. I often prayed before I took the pitch, especially on an unfamiliar field. I didn't know who I was praying to, or why, but I asked that I be allowed to play honestly and to play simply and within myself. That I be patient and let the game come to me. Then we played.

The game enabled me to forget that I was stuck in Kathmandu, that I was waiting for some THC-saturated ex-stockbrokers and washed-out nightclub owners and failed models who were a week overdue, and that the article I had been sent to write was showing signs of miscarrying.

But there were greater issues I played to escape: it is hard work staying sober in a strange town, especially when you have nothing to do but wait for a gang of well-heeled wastrels to blow in from whatever stretch of Asian sand they have laid up on. I fumed as I imagined the clique of Brits and Americans whom I had foolishly let out of my sight, sprawled in some sumptuous bungalow on some pristine Southeast Asian beach while I waited in smoggy, dusty Tamil. The game took me away from my petty worries and my needing a drink, from the temptations of a little legal or illegal sedation to help get through the listless waiting in a town full of inebriated expats.

I could even forget that I was in Kathmandu; instead I was transported to Soccer Land, a magical country whose boundaries are two goals and whatever one is using as touchlines but whose domain is infinitely vast and encompassing. I had no thoughts outside the game, no wants, no desires. The earthly realm fell away. The surrounding scenery of blooming poplars and sagging bodhi trees, the sacred cows that wandered alongside the pitch, the motorcycles and *bajajs* that rattled past on the narrow road, even the foul smog that we breathed receded into distant, barely perceptible blips on some ignored radar screen. My wants and desires were forgotten. The lures of liquor and drugs, the cravings of the flesh, all vanished.

But after forty-five minutes, I felt my concentration begin to break; I stumbled and gasped, taking deep breaths, losing my easy stride. My errant passes went to the other team; my attempts to carry the ball were hopeless. It was like being in one of those dreams where you flee an unknowable evil, yet no matter how hard you try, you find that your legs and feet cannot generate any speed. At the same time, I noticed a player I had not seen earlier in the game, when we were dividing up our sides. A swarthy man of medium build, he must have come in after the game started. I could not tell his age or his nationality. Because he was tirelessly in motion, it was hard to catch a clear glimpse of his face, but he had a ruddy complexion and deep-set black eyes obscured by a shadowy, protruding forehead. He wore a black acrylic jersey, colors of a soccer club whose name was written in an alphabet whose characters I did not recognize. His most noticeable trait was the almost metallic sheen of his hair. It was not the mottled gray hair of an aging man; it was as if this fellow had had his hair surgically replaced by thick silver filaments.

There was something disconcertingly familiar about the metallic-haired player, like the grown-up version of someone I had known in the first grade or, more perplexingly, like a character from a dimly recalled dream, one of those vestigial phosphene images that stays with you for a few moments, burned into your eyelids, before you're fully awake.

He played with ruthless efficiency, a fluid, consistent, creative athlete who made all those around him seem to play better. And he was a physical defender who humiliated me several times, inflicting pain: he slide-tackled me, stripping the ball from me cleanly without committing a foul. On those few occasions when I dared challenge him, he would rake the ball from my feet with such strength that I felt a shiv of pain run up my leg. The other players did not pay particular attention to him. It was obvious to me, however, that he had transformed the character of the game from a friendly afternoon match to a steely macho test of wills. Even the scarlet globe of sun had vanished behind thick black clouds of smog, making the sky darken and the late-afternoon city seem more somber. The air now tasted acrid, and each breath of internal combustion was unspeakably rancid.

I played until this new fellow tackled me near my own goal, pulling the ball back and scoring with a neatly heeled shot while I lay crumpled on the pitch, my nose pressed down into a clod of dried horse manure. As I lay there, all my anxieties and fears returned. What if those hip, swinging travelers never showed up in Nepal? What if I wound up waiting here for months, running up an expense tab that would alienate me from Condé Nast forever? And, more important, what if in the boredom and dissolution of Kathmandu nights I decided I could have just one drink, just a few ten-milligram Valiums? I tried to shake off that thought as I brushed the manure from my nose.

The game ended. As I slipped off my turf shoes and peeled away a layer of sweaty socks, I looked around for the metallic-haired player, but he had already gone; he must have jumped the white-painted fence immediately after the game and hailed one of the little white Daewoo taxis. I asked some of the other players who he was, what country he came from, but they shook their heads; they had not noticed him.

Bangkok, 1997

The Bangkok game was different. This regular game of embassy employees and long-term expats took place in Lumphini Park three times a week. Most of the players involved, particularly the half-dozen Thais, had serious skills. I looked forward to the Lumphini game whenever I was in Bangkok. Although I was one of the worst players on the pitch, it was always exhilarating to be part of some first-class soccer.

As I climbed from the taxi on Rama IV, I felt the damp air waft over me and the immediate beginnings of sweat beads along my eyebrows and upper lip. My cleats were slung by their laces over my shoulder. The night before, when I'd arrived from Kathmandu, a hint of breeze had blown up from the Gulf, but by day the heat settled over the city like a collective bad memory. Everywhere I went in Asia, I was choked by exhaust, forever wiping soot from my eyes. I had left Kathmandu upon receipt of a telegram, of all things, from my gang of wandering, trendy Asian travelers, who had finally made it back to Bangkok and were planning a short stay. They were capriciously peripatetic, these international ravers, but I had also begun to think of them as a bunch of smug, self-centered Ecstasy-swallowing morons.

I had arranged to meet two of the fellows, Englishmen named Trev and Derrek, at the McDonald's near the Robinson's department store at the southwest corner of the park. Trev had been modeling in Tokyo—and Milan and New York—while Derrek was a DJ who seemed to be involved with the rock group Oasis in some capacity. As they had kept me waiting in Kathmandu for over a week, I was surprised to discover they were here early, seated at a plastic table near the door, drinking Diet Cokes and picking at an order of french fries. Both boys were fair-haired, with cleft chins and high cheekbones. That Trev was a model and Derrek was not must have been the result of some arbitrary selection process a long time ago in London. They were equally handsome, and in very similar ways, feminine eyes and noses, soft pink mouths, manly, jutting chins and slender builds. Wearing expensive-looking tracksuits, Adidas running shoes and the bored expressions of spoiled lads who almost always get their own way with whatever they apply themselves to, they merely shrugged when I greeted them. They slipped on their Oakley shades and shuffled to their feet.

Despite considerable pregame whining that the match would not be up to the high standards they were used to back in London, and despite their boasting about who would score more goals, Trev and Derrek turned out to be below-average players, plainly not up to the Lumphini level of play. And part of the fun of this particular game was that I participated in their humiliation.

Unlike most English players, who are dependable and intelligent if unflashy ball handlers, Trev and Derrek were lousy footballers. I have so often struggled in athletic endeavor and known the feeling of being derided for my on-the-field mistakes that I never thought I would be one of those who vociferously berate other players. Yet I could not help myself. There was something compelling about watching Trev and Derrek come up short on the athletic field, about observing boys who simply were not up to the level of competition and whose every attempt to rectify their inadequacies only compounded their failure.

"Pass the fucking ball!" I shouted at them. "Try passing the fucking ball to your own team!"

I knew a couple of the other players. There were the Nigerians Akemi and Godfrey; Dane, a wire-service reporter and veteran of Stanford 1-A soccer; and Paolo, a wonderful Italian midfielder. I had played with the Nigerians in Tokyo, at a pitch next to a hospital atop Hiroo Gardens. Paolo and Dane I knew from this game.

"Don't these guys suck?" I shook my head and said to Paolo during a lull in the action. He looked at me strangely, as if he didn't understand what I'd said.

"Everybody sometimes sucks," he said in his Neapolitan accent, and made a run across the bald patch of earth that was the middle of the penalty area. During the next break, he grabbed my shirt when I was telling Trev to get his ass back onside: "Hey, you are talking too much. Just play."

It was then that I realized I had neglected to pray before the game, neglected to meditate and ask God or Shiva or Buddha or my higher power or whoever to help me enjoy this game, to help me play honestly and authentically within myself, to allow me to be the best player I could be. And that was when I noticed the same metallic-haired player who had totally knocked me off my game back in Kathmandu. I was not terribly surprised—hundreds of people fly between Bangkok and Kathmandu every day—but still, I found his presence disquieting. As soon as I saw him at the far end of the pitch, limbering up and running in place, I lost my concentration.

He stood silhouetted next to the coconut tree that served as a post for the western goal. Clad in the same black jersey, shorts and socks he had worn back in Kathmandu, he appeared to be staring at me, his mouth turned down in a slight smirk. Or was I imagining the smirk? Was he just another player of pickup games, a fellow traveler? Was he as surprised to see me as I was to see him? Had he even noticed me?

But from the moment he entered the game, I was consumed by self-doubt. Not just about soccer but about my whole life. Thoughts of the story I had been sent to write returned: I was running out of time and overbudget. There was still so much more I wanted to put into the story: the whole decadent culture of these rich kids, the gritty jadedness, the hipper-than-thou vibe. And then the little details: the backgammon hustling, the way the girls were pretty and young and blond and tattooed in all the right places, the silver Indian bracelets they were all wearing, the camouflage shirts the boys preferred. But I wanted to get something else across—that out here, miles from home in exotic Asian lands, nothing counted. The girls and boys could do as they wanted, and because it all happened so far from home, it was somehow off the record. Anything went, because no one from home was bearing witness.

But if that reasoning made sense, then why shouldn't I dabble in some artificial mood enhancing myself? Here I was in Bangkok, home to some of the best pills and powders and most liberal pharmacies in the world. Why couldn't I partake of the lax morality that pervaded the circuit? No one was bearing witness. My wife was thousands of miles away. My family was in Los Angeles. None of this counted. So what if I had put together twelve sober months, had stayed off drugs for three hundred and sixty-five long days? What I did out here on the circuit could stay out here. No one back home would ever know.

By then I had fallen totally out of the game. The metallic-haired stranger was dominating, as usual, gracefully passing to Trev and Derrek, building up a triangular attack that made those two fey Englishmen seem like brilliant players. My perfunctory attempts to break up this new, efficient attack were falling short. And when I received the ball, I second-guessed myself instead of doing what came naturally. I was overthinking and then panicking. I was playing in fear.

The player with the metallic hair and black jersey came trotting by me several times. Each time I noticed his smirk had grown wider, as if he had realized some fundamental weakness about my game and my character. It was as if he saw through to some essential defect deep within me, could determine my vulnerabilities and knew how to exploit them, on the pitch and in real life. Here on this Bangkok soccer field, while traffic whirred by fifty meters away on busy Rama IV Road, while we played between coconut-tree goalposts, I felt that I had been unmasked as a fraud. I was a bad soccer player. I was a bad writer. I was a drug addict. I had traveled to escape those shortcomings, those flaws, and for a time, out here in Asia, I had been able to fend off knowledge of them.

After all, why do we travel? We travel, in part, to remake ourselves, to reinvent new, better versions of the defective personalities we have become back home. Out here, on the circuit, we can pretend we are anything we like.

"You're nothing," I thought I heard the metallic-haired player whisper under his breath at he ran past me, "nothing at all."

John Travolta and Uma Thurman were twisting away up there on the projection television. The soundtrack was muted and Jimi Hendrix's "Machine Gun" was turned way up, so the two stars improvised to the lefty's caterwauling guitar. The bar, a wood-paneled tavern across from Privilege on the illustriously grubby

Kao San Road, was crowded with eager-to-get-fucked-up, man-it's-awesome-being-in-Bangkok tourists who hadn't flown thousands of miles on crowded, discount Air Pakistan flights to watch a bootleg video of *Pulp Fiction*. The vibe in a Khao San Road bar on Friday night is just about the same as it is any other night of the week. It's all about getting as much as you can as soon as you can and then hoping you don't throw up and then doing it all over again every day for the whole two weeks of your holiday before you're due back in Hamburg or Newcastle.

The gang of swell punks I had been hanging with was here for only one reason: they were supposed to meet a German DJ, Manfred, who had a box of DAT tapes that Derrek needed to DJ a rave at Baddam beach in Goa next week. But Manfred had not shown up, and the old Thai lady at his guest house said that she had last seen him two weeks ago.

Trev and Derrek had ducked into this bar to stew over the missing DAT tapes of London acetate pressings that would enable Derrek to get over as the DJ he claimed to be. Clad in Versace camouflage shirts, Oakley sunglasses, white Pepe jeans and green glow-in-the-dark necklaces, they sullenly drank Mekong-and-Cokes and cursed Manfred for being unreliable. He had assured them at the Breakfast Club back in Tokyo that he would be here, and now where the fuck was he?

As I listened to Trev and Derrek hatch plans and formulate strategy, dicuss possible sources for substitute DATs, other raves where the music had been slamming, other venues on the circuit where the vibes had been trippy, I realized that I had already grown tired of them and the rest of the gang of glamorous expats I had been following. It wasn't that Trev and Derrek were boring; I simply wasn't interested anymore. Their concerns seemed trivial. Some DJ, another rave, a great beach, the flash new spot: none of it seemed to matter. Despite my earnest attempts to rejoin their world, a world I had once known, I was an interloper now, a journalist sent from the outside to steal a little of their energy, fun and good times. I was five years older than Trev and Derrek; the circuit was their scene now. It was time to say good-bye to my own decadent past. It was time to leave Thailand, to leave Asia and return home to my family and friends, to where I felt safe.

But I was here tonight for Dina, to see her one last time before I got away. She had those Balinese tattoos running up her fleshy, fuzzy arms—you had to resist reaching out to touch the flesh of her upper arms, to bend over and take a sniff of the crease opposite her elbow. Her nose was now pierced, and her left ear jangled with an array of silver bangles and gold baubles that she fingered as she sipped Mekong and Coke. In her right ear was a newer, even gaudier diamond stud as big around as a raisin. In her mid-twenties, poshly accented and cooly intelligent, she lent the evening and this crowd of travelers what class they had. Compared to Dina, Trev and Derrek were parvenus—name-droppers and social climbers. Their good looks and connections to swinging London had gained them only toeholds on the sort of life that Dina had come from and took for granted. She had not left her country to find a better or more thrilling life out here on the circuit. Instead she possessed the charm and allure of having turned her back on precisely the lifestyle everybody else was seeking; decadent, narcotized freedom was her birthright. Trev and Derrek and the others treated her with appropriate deference. As for the rest of us, she had drifted in and out of our lives. She and I had enjoyed varying levels of intimacy, and even when we parted badly, as we sometimes did, I always sought her out again because she had a way of seeing through to the heart of things, of telling me the truth. And she was beautiful.

I told her I was leaving. I was done with my trip. I had enough for my story. I was worried that if I stayed in Bangkok, in Asia, I would use drugs again. I told her about the metallic-haired soccer player who was following me. I wanted to go home.

I reached down to my calf and and felt the scar from the motorcycle accident. It had long ago healed and was now just a rough patch of skin. Did she remember that time on the beach, years ago, the season I first met her, when she had found me laid up in the sand after the motorcycle wreck?

She nodded. "Are you still frightened?"

I was.

New York, 1997

It is a brisk autumn afternoon; the oak trees around the Columbia University campus have turned a feverish red; leaves litter the trodden pathways linking venerable old buildings. I am going to school again, on a journalism fellowship. I play soccer with the Columbia Business School team. Today we are practicing on campus, on the narrow lawns before the imposing gray Butler Library. I jog across the pitch, gasping for breath, running to take a crossing pass from a Dutch teammate.

The metallic-haired player is nowhere in sight.

SPEED DEMONS

Jacky talks about killing him, slitting his throat from three till nine and hanging him upside down so the blood drains out of him the way it ran from the baby pigs they used to slaughter in her village before a funeral feast. He deserves it, really, she says, for his freeloading, for his hanging around, for how he just stands there, spindly-legged and narrow-chested and pimple-faced with his big yearning eyes, begging for another hit.

She has run out of methamphetamine, what the Thais call *yaba* (mad medicine), and she has become irritable and potentially violent. Jacky's cheeks are sunken, her skin pockmarked and her hair an unruly explosion of varying strands of red and brown. She is tall and skinny, and her arms and legs extend out from her narrow torso with its slightly protuberant belly like the appendages of a spider shortchanged on legs.

Sitting on the blue vinyl flooring of her Bangkok hut, Jacky leans her bare back against the plank wall, her dragon tattoos glistening with sweat as she trims her fingernails with a straight razor. It has been two days—no, three—without sleep, sitting in this hut and smoking the little pink speed tablets from sheets of tinfoil stripped from Krong Tip cigarette packets. Now, as the flushes of artificial energy recede and the realization surfaces that there's no more money anywhere in her hut, Jacky is crashing hard, and she hates everyone and everything. Especially Bing. She hates that sponging little punk for all the tablets he smoked a few hours ago—tablets she could be smoking right now. Back then she had a dozen tablets packed into a plastic soda straw, stuffed down her black underwire bra. The hut was alive with the chatter of half a dozen speed addicts, all pulling apart their Krong Tip packs and sucking in meth smoke through metal pipes. Now that the pills are gone, the fun is gone. And Bing, of course, he's long gone.

This slum doesn't have a name. The five thousand residents call it Ban Chua Gan, which translates roughly as Do-It-Yourself Happy Homes. The expanse of jerry-built wood-frame huts with corrugated steel roofs sprawls in a murky bog in Bangkok's Sukhumvit district, in the shadow of forty-story office buildings and glass-plated corporate towers. The inhabitants migrated here about a decade ago from villages all around Thailand. Jacky came from Nakhon Nayok, a province near Bangkok's Don Muang airport, seeking financial redemption in the Asian economic miracle. And for a while in the mid-nineties, conditions in this slum actually improved. Some of the huts had plumbing installed. Even the shabbiest shanties were wired for electricity. The main alleyways were paved. That was when Thailand's development and construction boom required the labor of every able-bodied person. There were shopping malls to be built, housing estates to be constructed, highways to be paved.

Around the same time, mad medicine began making its way into the Do-It-Yourself Happy Homes. It had originally been the drug of choice for long-haul truck and bus drivers, but during the go-go nineties, it evolved into the workingman's and -woman's preferred intoxicant, gradually becoming more popular among Thailand's underclass than heroin and eventually replacing that opiate as the leading drug produced in the notorious Golden Triangle—the world's most prolific opium-producing region—where Myanmar (Burma), Thailand and Laos come together. While methamphetamines had previously been sold in either powdered or crystalline form, new labs in Burma, northern Thailand and China commodified the business by pressing little tablets of the substance that now retail for about fifty baht ($1.20) each. At first only bar girls like Jacky smoked it. Then some of the younger guys who hung out with the girls tried it. Soon a few of the housewives began smoking, and finally some of the dads would take a hit or two when they were out of corn whiskey. Now it has reached the point that on weekend nights, it's hard to find anyone in the slum who isn't smoking the mad medicine.

When the *yaba* runs out after much of the slum's population has been up for two days bingeing, many of the inhabitants feel a bit like Jacky, cooped up in her squalid little hut, her mouth turned down into a scowl and her eyes squinted and empty and mean. She looks as if she wants something. And if she thinks you have what she wants, look out. She slices at her cuticles with the straight razor. And curses Bing.

But then Bing comes around the corner between two shanties and down the narrow dirt path to Jacky's hut. He stands looking lost and confused, as usual. Jacky pretends he's not there. She sighs, looking at her nails, and stage-whispers to me that she hates him.

Bing, his long black hair half tied into a ponytail, stands next to a cinder-block wall rubbing his eyes. Above his head, a thick trail of red army ants runs between a crack in the wall and a smashed piece of pineapple. He reaches into his pocket and pulls out a tissue in which he has wrapped four *doa* (bodies, slang for speed tablets). Jacky stops doing her nails, smiles and invites Bing back into her hut, asking sweetly, "Oh, Bing, where have you been?"

This mad medicine is called *shabu* in Japan and Indonesia, *batu* in the Philippines and *bingdu* in China. While it has taken scientists years to figure out the clinical pharmacology and neurological impact of Ecstasy and other designer drugs, methamphetamines are blunt pharmaceutical instruments. The drug encourages the brain to flood the synapses with the neurotransmitter dopamine—the substance your body uses to reward itself when you, say, complete a difficult assignment at the office or finish a vigorous workout. And when the brain is awash in dopamine, the whole cardiovascular system goes into sympathetic overdrive, increasing your heart rate, pulse and even your respiration. You become, after that first hit of speed, gloriously, brilliantly, vigorously awake. Your horizon of aspiration expands outward, just as in your mind's eye your capacity for taking effective action toward your new, optimistic goals has also grown exponentially. Then, eventually, maybe in an hour, maybe in a day, maybe in a year, you run out of speed. And you crash.

In country after country throughout Asia, meth use skyrocketed during the nineties. And with the crash of the region's high-flying economies, the drug's use has surged again. The base of the drug—ephedrine—was actually first synthesized in Asia: a team of Japanese scientists derived it from the Chinese mao herb in 1892. Unlike Ecstasy, which requires sophisticated chemical and pharmaceutical knowledge to manufacture, or heroin, whose base product, the poppy plant, is a vulnerable crop, ephedrine can be refined fairly easily into meth. This makes meth labs an attractive family business for industrious Asians, who set them up in converted bathrooms, farmhouses or even on the family hearth.

There is something familiar to me about Jacky and her little hut and her desperate yearning for more speed and even for the exhilaration and intoxication she feels when she's on the pipe. Because I've been there. Not in this exact room or with these people. But I've been on speed.

During the early nineties, I went through a period when I was smoking *shabu* with a group of friends in Tokyo. I inhaled the smoke from smoothed-out tinfoil sheets folded in two, holding a lighter beneath the foil so that the shards of *shabu* liquified, turning to a thick, pungent, milky vapor. The smoke tasted like a mixture of turpentine and model glue; to this day I can't smell paint thinner without thinking of smoking speed.

The drug was euphorically powerful, convincing us that we were capable of anything. And in many ways we were. We were all young, promising, on the verge of exciting careers in glamorous fields. There was Trey, an American magazine writer, like me, in his twenties; Hiroko, a Japanese woman in her thirties who worked for a Tokyo women's magazine; Delphine, an aspiring French model; and Miki, an A&R man for a Japanese record label. When we would sit down together in my Nishi Azabu apartment to smoke the drug, our talk turned to grandiose plans and surefire schemes. I spoke of articles I would write. Delphine talked about landing a job doing a Dior lingerie catalog. Miki raved about a promising noise band he had just signed. Sometimes the dealer, a lanky fellow named Haru, would hang around and smoke with us, and we would be convinced that his future was just as bright as all of ours. There was no limit to what we could do, especially if we put our speed-driven minds to work.

It's always that way in the beginning: all promise and potential fun. The drug is like a companion telling you that you're good enough, handsome enough and smart enough, banishing all the little insecurities to your subconscious, liberating you from self-doubts yet making you feel totally and completely alive.

I don't know that it helped me write better; I don't believe meth really helps you in any way at all. But in those months, it became arguably the most important activity in my life. Certainly it was the most fun. And I looked forward to Haru's coming over with another $150 baggy—the drug resembling a little oily lump of glass. Then we would smoke, at first only on weekends. But soon I began to do it whenever I had a free weekday evening. At first only with my friends. Then sometimes I smoked alone. Then mostly alone.

The teens and twenty-somethings in Ban Chua Gan also like to smoke *yaba*, but they look down on Jacky and Bing and their flagrant, raging addictions. Sure, the cool guys in the neighborhood, guys like Big, with a shaved head, gaunt face and sneering upper lip, drop into Jacky's once in a while to score some drugs. Or they'll buy a couple of tablets from Bing's mother, who deals. But they tell you they're different from Bing and the hard-core users. "For one thing," Big alibis, "Bing hasn't left the slum neighborhood in a year. He doesn't work. He doesn't do anything but smoke." (Bing just shrugs when I ask if it's true that he hasn't left in a year. "I'm too skinny to leave," he explains. "Everyone will know I'm doing *yaba*.") Big has a job as a pump jockey at a Star gas station. And he has a girlfriend, and he has his motorcycle, a Honda GSR 125. This weekend, like most weekends, he'll be racing his bike with the other guys from the neighborhood, down at Bangkok's superslum Klong Toey. That's why tonight, a few days before the race, he is working on his bike, removing a few links of the engine chain to lower the gear ratio and give the bike a little more pop off the line. He kneels down with a lighted candle next to him, his hands greasy and black as he works to reattach the chain to the gear sprockets. Around him a few teenage boys and girls are gathered, smoking cigarettes, some squatting on the balls of their feet, their intent faces peering down at scattered engine parts. The sound is the clatter of adolescent boys. Whether the vehicle in question is a '65 Mustang or a '99 Honda GSR motorcycle, whether it's in Bakersfield or Bangkok, the posturing of the too cool motorhead trying to goose a few more horsepower out of his engine while at the same time look cool in front of a crowd of slightly younger female spectators is identical.

The slang for smoking speed in Thai is *keng rot,* literally "racing," the same words used to describe the weekend motorcycle rallying. The bikers' lives revolve around these two forms of *keng rot.* They look forward all week to racing their bikes against gangs from other neighborhoods. And while they profess to have nothing but disgust for the slum's hard-core addicts, by four A.M. that night on a mattress laid on the floor next to his beloved Honda, Big and his friends are smoking *yaba,* and there suddenly seems very little difference between his crowd and Jacky's. "Smoking once in a while, on weekends, that really won't do any harm," Big explains, exhaling a plume of white smoke. "It's just like having a drink." But it's Thursday, I point out. Big shrugs, waving away the illogic of his statement, the drug's powerful reach pulling him away from the need to make sense. He says whatever he wants now, and he resents being questioned. "What do you want from me? I'm just trying to have fun."

In Jacky's hut, Bing and a few bar girls are seated with their legs folded under them, taking hits from the sheets of tinfoil. As Jacky applies a thick layer of foundation makeup to her face and dabs on retouching cream and then a coating of powder, she talks about how tonight she has to find a foreign customer so she can get the money to visit her children out in Nakhon Nayok. Her two daughters and son live with her uncle. Jacky sees them once a month, and she tells me about how she likes to bring them new clothes and cook for them. When she speaks of her kids, her almond-shaped eyes widen. "I used to dream of opening a small shop, like a gift shop or a 7-Eleven. Then I could take care of my children and make money. I used to dream about it all the time, and I even believed it was possible, that it was just barely out of reach."

Jacky was a motorbike messenger, shuttling packages back and forth throughout Bangkok's busy Chitlom district until she was laid off after the 1997 devaluation of the baht. "Now I don't think about the gift shop anymore. Smoking *yaba* pushes thoughts about my children to the back of my mind. It's good for that. Smoking means you don't have to think about the hard times." Bing nods, agreeing: "When I smoke, it makes everything seem a little better. I mean, look at this place—how can I stop?"

Bing's mother, Yee, slips off her sandals as she steps into the hut, clutching her fourteen-month-old baby. She sits down next to her son, and while the baby scrambles to crawl from her lap, she begins pulling the paper backing from a piece of tinfoil, readying it for a smoke. Her hands are a whir of finger-flashing activity—assembling and disassembling a lighter, unclogging the pipe, unwrapping the tablets, straightening the foil, lighting the speed and then taking the hit. She exhales finally, blowing smoke just above her baby's face. Bing asks his mother for a hit. She shakes her head. She doesn't give discounts or freebies, not even to her own son.

I ask Yee if she ever tells Bing he should stop smoking *yaba*. "I tell him he shouldn't do so much, that it's bad for him. But he doesn't listen."

Perhaps she lacks credibility, since she smokes herself?

"I don't smoke that much," she insists.

"She's right," Bing agrees. "Since she doesn't smoke that much, I should listen to her."

"And he's only fifteen years old," Yee adds.

Bing reminds her he's seventeen.

"I don't know where the years go," Yee says, taking another hit.

For the countries on the front lines of the meth war, trying to address the crisis with tougher enforcement has had virtually no effect on the numbers of users or addicts. Asia has some of the toughest drug laws in the world. In Thailand, China, Taiwan and Indonesia, even a low-level drug-trafficking or dealing conviction can mean a death sentence. Yet *yaba* is openly sold in Thailand's slums and proffered in Jakarta's nightclubs, and China's meth production continues to boom. Even Japan, renowned for its strict antidrug policies, has had little success in stemming speed abuse. Most likely, these countries and societies will have to write off vast portions of their populations as drug casualties, like the American victims of the eighties crack epidemic.

Asia's medical and psychiatric infrastructure is already over-whelmed by the number of meth abusers crashing and seeking help. But in most of the region, counseling facilities are scarce, and recovery is viewed as a matter of willpower and discipline rather than a slow and tenuous spiritual and psychological re-building process. Drug-treatment centers are usually run like a cross between boot camp and prison. Beds are scarce as addicts seek the meager resources available. In China, for example, the nearly 750 state-run rehab centers are filled to capacity; in Thailand the few recovery centers suffer from a chronic shortage of staff and beds. While the most powerful tools for fighting addiction in the West—twelve-step programs derived from Alcoholics Anonymous—are available in Asia, they are not widely disseminated and used.

What started out as a diversion for me and my Tokyo crowd degenerated in a few months into the same chronic drug use as Jacky and her crowd's. I began my days smoking alone. In the evening I'd take Valium or Halcion or Cercine or any of a number of sedatives to help me calm down. When I stopped smoking for a few days, just to see if I could, a profound depression would overcome me. Nothing seemed worthwhile. Nothing seemed fun. Every book was torturously slow. Every song was criminally banal. Every movie crawled. The sparkle and shine had been sucked out of life so completely that my world became a fluorescent-lighted, decolorized, saltpetered version of the planet I had known before. And my own prospects? Absolutely dismal. I would sit in that one-bedroom Nishi Azabu apartment and consider the sorry career I had embarked upon, these losers I associated with compounding the very long odds that I would ever amount to anything.

These feelings, about the world and my life, seemed absolutely real. I could not tell for a moment that this was a neurological reaction brought on by the withdrawal of the meth-amphetamine. My brain had stopped producing dopamine in normal amounts because it had come to rely upon the speed kicking in and running the show. Researchers now report that as much as 50 percent of the dopamine-producing cells in the brain can be damaged after prolonged exposure to relatively low levels of methamphetamine. In other words, the depression is a purely chemical state. Yet it feels for all the world like the result of empirical, clinical observation. And then, very logically, you realize there is one solution, the only way to feel better: more speed.

I kept at that cycle for a few years and started taking drugs other than methamphetamine until I hit my own personal bottom. I spent those six weeks in a drug-treatment center working out a plan for living that didn't require copious amounts of methamphetamines or tranquilizers. I left rehab five years ago. I haven't had another hit of *shabu*—or taken any drugs—since then. But I am lucky. Of the crowd who used to gather in my Tokyo apartment, I am the only one who has emerged clean and sober. Trey, my fellow magazine writer, never really tried to quit and now lives back at home with his aging parents. He is nearly forty, still takes speed—or Ritalin or cocaine or whichever uppers he can get his hands on—and hasn't had a job in years. Delphine gave up modeling after a few years and soon was accepting money to escort wealthy businessmen around Tokyo. She finally ended up working as a prostitute. Hiroko did stop taking drugs. But she has been in and out of psychiatric hospitals and currently believes drastic plastic surgery is the solution to her problems. Miki has been arrested in Japan and the U.S. on drug charges and is now out on parole and living in Tokyo. And Haru, the dealer, I hear he's dead.

Despite all I know about the drug, despite what I have seen, I am still tempted. Its pull is tangible and real, almost like a gravitational force compelling me to use it again—to feel just once more the rush and excitement and the sense, even if it's illusory, that life does add up, that there is meaning and form to the passing of my days. Part of me still wants it.

At two A.M. on a Saturday, Big and his fellow bikers from Do-It-Yourself Happy Homes are preparing for a night of bike racing by smoking more *yaba* and, as if to get their 125cc bikes in a parallel state of high-octane agitation, squirting STP performance goo from little plastic packets into their gas tanks. The bikes are tuned up, and the mufflers are loosened so that the engines revving at full throttle sound like a chain saw cutting bone: splintering, ear-shattering screeches that reverberate up and down the Sukhumvit streets. The bikers ride in a pack, cutting through alleys, running lights, skirting lines of stalled traffic, slipping past one another as they cut through the city smog. This is their night, the night they look forward to all week during mornings at school or dull afternoons pumping gas. And as they ride massed together, you can almost feel the surge of pride oozing out of them, intimidating other drivers to veer out of their way.

On Na Ranong Avenue, next to the Klong Toey slum, they meet up with bikers from other slums. They have been holding these rallies for a decade, some of the kids first coming on the backs of their older brothers' bikes. *Keng rot* is a ritual by now, as ingrained in Thai culture as the speed they smoke to get up for the night of racing. The street is effectively closed off to non-motorcyclists and pedestrians. The bikers idle along the side of the road and then take off in twos and threes, popping wheelies, standing on their seats; the tricks are really third-rate motorcycle stunts, the kind you might see in a local Memorial Day parade in the United States. But souped up and fitted with performance struts and tires, these bikes accelerate at a terrifying rate, and that blastoff from the line makes for an unstable and dangerous ride if you're on the back of one of them. It is the internal-combustion equivalent of *yaba:* fast, fun, treacherous. And likely to result, eventually, in a fatal spill. But if you're young and Thai and loaded on mad medicine, you feel immortal, and it doesn't occur to you that this night of racing will ever really have to end.

There are still moments when even hard-core addicts like Jacky can recapture the shiny, bright exuberance of the first few times they tried speed. Tonight, as Jacky dances at Angel's bar with a

Belgian who might take her back to his hotel room, she's thinking that she'll soon have enough money to visit her children, and it doesn't seem so bad. Life seems almost manageable. A few more customers, and maybe one will really fall for her and pay to move her to a better neighborhood, to rent a place where even her children could live. Maybe she could open that convenience store after all.

By the next afternoon, however, all the promise of the previous evening has escaped from the neighborhood like so much exhaled smoke. Jacky's customer lost interest and found another girl. Even the bike racing fell apart after the cops broke up the first few rallying points. And now, on a hazy, rainy Sunday, Jacky and a few of the girls are back in her hut. They're smoking, almost desperately uploading as much speed as possible to ward off the drab day and this squalid place.

Jacky pauses as she adjusts the flame on a lighter. "Why don't you smoke?" she asks me.

She tells me it would make her more comfortable if I would join her. I'm standing in the doorway to Jacky's hut. About me are flea-infested dogs and puddles of stagnant water several inches deep with garbage, and all around is the stench of smoldering trash. The horror of this daily existence is tangible. I don't like being in this place. And I know a hit of the mad medicine is the easiest way to make it all seem bearable. Taking a hit, I know, is a surefire way to feel good. Right now. And I want it.

But I walk away. And while I hope Jacky and Bing and Big can one day do the same, I doubt they ever will. They have so little to walk toward.

Acknowledgments

Over the years, I've been lucky enough to work with many magazine editors who gave me space and time when I needed it. Thanks especially to Walter Isaacson, Jim Kelly, Norman Pearlstine, Adi Ignatius, Don George, Klara Glowczewska, Victor Navasky and Katrina vanden Heuvel. Gratitude also goes out to Gail Ross, Howard Yoon, Bruce Tracy, Ptolemy Tompkins, Steven Martin, Christopher Seymour and Jason Tedjasukmana.

I wouldn't have been able to live this life—much less write about it—without Josh, Foumiko, Silke, Esmee and Lola.